Loca.

£2

MUD LANE
A FICTIONAL MEMOIR

STEPHEN R. DRAGE

ISBN: 146629180X
ISBN-13: 9781466291805
Library of Congress Control Number: 2011916261

CreateSpace, North Charleston, SC

DISCLAIMER
This book is a work of fiction. Any resemblance the characters have to real
people is purely coincidental.
www.mudlane.net

DEDICATION

To Jerry, John, Kaylee, Caitlyn and Emma,
that they may know of a world before iPods.

WARNING

This book is not intended as an instruction manual for skydiving,
tunneling, archery, driving, ghost hunting or handling explosives.

CONTENTS

Acknowledgments vii

INTRODUCTION ix

1. Friday 27th October. 1
   OSCAR FALLS IN THE STREAM

2. ROGER PILCHARD'S PROBLEM 17

3. Saturday 28th October. 33
   SEARCH FOR THE CANVAS SHEET.

4. AN UNWILLING PASSENGER. 49

5. A VISIT TO GRANNY. 61

6. Sunday 29th October. 81
   DISTRESSING NEWS FROM MRS. SNOBBIT

7. THE HOBBINS / CRIPPIN ENTERTAINMENT HOUR. . 97

8. RYAN GOES SKYDIVING. 109

9. Monday 30th October 123
   A DAY OF TORTURE

10. THE OTHER GRANDPARENT. 139

11. Tuesday 31st October 151
    NEW WHEELS.

12. Wednesday 1st November.. 165
    BENITO THE TRAITOR

13. AN ARCHERY LESSON. 185

14. Thursday 2nd November 197
    DAD AND I TRY SPACEFLIGHT

15. Friday 3rd November. 215
    SQUEAKY JOINS THE GANG

16. Saturday 4th November 233
    WILHELM'S PARADE

17. Sunday 5th November 255
    LOST AND FOUND

ACKNOWLEDGMENTS

To my whole family who have given me with so much laughter over the years.

To my editor, Ann K. Fisher for her genius and wisdom.

And finally, infinite and eternal thanks to my wife and soul mate, Anita. Without her patience, encouragement and faith this book would not have been possible.

INTRODUCTION

Remember, Remember the fifth of November,
Gunpowder Treason and Plot.
We see no reason, why Gunpowder treason,
Should ever be forgot.

(Traditional English Rhyme.)

Henry VIII was famous for two things, having more wives than any other English monarch, and forming the Church of England.

The first of these two, his obsession for changing his wife every few years, obviously created problems for him since England, like the rest of the Christian world at the time answered to Rome, and divorce was not legal within the Catholic Church.

Henry's solution to this problem was his second great deed of notoriety, forming his own religion. The Anglican Church allowed man to put asunder what God had joined and allowed Henry's eye to continue wandering.

Following this decree, English subjects were required to abandon their Catholic views and convert to the new Church of England, swearing an oath to King Henry as their supreme religious leader and forsaking their old religion. Those who did not went to prison. Catholic property was confiscated, monasteries were burned and all went well for the new religious order, but this separated England from the power of Rome, and the rift that was created continues to this day.

During the reign of Elizabeth I, things didn't improve for the Catholics. New laws introduced the death penalty for anyone who did not join the Church of England, and Catholics left the country, converted or were driven underground to practice their beliefs in secret.

Following Elizabeth's death in 1603, James I of Scotland came to the throne. Based on his past history, Catholics were optimistic that he would be more tolerant towards them, but he was not, and they continued to be oppressed in horrendous ways.

A small group of Catholic conspirators responded to this disappointment by hatching a plot to kill King James, his son and most of the English government. A few days before the opening of Parliament on Nov 5th 1605, thirty-six barrels of gunpowder were smuggled into the cellars under the House of Lords in Westminster palace, the plan being to explode them during the governmental session. This is known as 'The Gunpowder plot.'

Allegedly, an anonymous letter reached the King informing him of this plot and in the early hours of Nov 4th the King's men raided the cellars beneath parliament and apprehended one of the conspirators. His name was Guido Fawkes or 'Guy' Fawkes, and within a few days he had been 'encouraged' to disclose all the details of the conspiracy. The rest of his friends were then rounded up, tortured and executed.

This event continues to be celebrated today all over England and is called Guy Fawkes Night or Bonfire Night. During this festivity, an effigy of Guy Fawkes is made and then burned on a large bonfire while fireworks are set off and the spectators make merry. Usually it is the children of the village that construct the Guy and take it round the community chanting 'A penny for the Guy.' The funds that are collected are used to purchase fireworks.

Sounds simple doesn't it?

CHAPTER 1

FRIDAY 27TH OCTOBER
OSCAR FALLS IN THE STREAM

Nestled in the heart of the English countryside, the weathered stone cottage at 23 Mud Lane had stood defiantly against the ravages of time. It was about four hundred years old, but because of its lack of upkeep and the destructive effects of my brother's wayward behavior over the last decade, it appeared much older.

I entered through the front door and passed under the three-foot thick archway constructed of stone, mud and straw and representing the pinnacle of building technology at the time of the home's creation. In the familiarity of the dimly illuminated hall, I walked past a stack of firewood and a collection of mud-covered boots. On the whitewashed wall, competing for three coat hooks, a mountain of threadbare outer garments waited to protect our family whenever we ventured outside to brave the horrendous English weather. The kitchen door swung open, its oil hungry hinges heralding my approach to those within.

The kitchen claimed almost half of the ground floor. It was the main all-purpose, cooking, eating and meeting room, and therefore the most frequently occupied. In the center stood a scarred and stained oblong oak table that would serve almost any purpose from cooking to carpentry, ironing to gun cleaning, dining to chainsaw repair. It was also the courtroom where my father would sit as judge and jury to pass sentence on my brother for his various transgressions.

"Hello Boy" said my mother, glancing over her shoulder and waving a worn out tooth brush, then promptly returned to her task at the sink.

My name is Steve. My mother knew this well being the one who actually chose the name, but despite this she insisted on calling both my brother and me "Boy." Mum had evolved this effective habit of addressing both her offspring with such a simple and anonymous title so that she could scream at us in the heat of battle without having to pause to remember the name of the child she was yelling at.

The kitchen sink in which she was vigorously scrubbing was strategically located next to a window that overlooked the lane, so that as Mum worked she would not miss the latest developments as village life unfolded. No matter what task engaged her, one eye was always directed toward the lane. This one eye now got a good look as Benito and Oscar walked past. Even at this hour, with the sun now below the horizon and the only illumination outside provided by light from Mrs. Snaggins's front window, Mum could see Benito and Oscar accompanied by their lengthening shadows as they walked past.

"Isn't that the new kid from down the lane," she asked.

"Yes," I mumbled. Fortunately the darkness made it difficult for my mother to see his condition in detail.

"Why is he walking like that?" Mum asked with a mother's keen insight for when something is amiss.

"He fell in the stream," I said. "It was lucky me and Benito were there to help him out."

I looked around, unable to meet my mother's suspicious gaze. Something was different – there was an odd smell in the room, a mixture of fresh paint, petrol and something else, a sweet and sickly aroma hanging thickly in the air.

"What happened to the walls?" I asked.

"Do you like them?" replied Mum, not answering my question.

The walls in the kitchen had for the entirety of my recollection been painted white. My father would renew this vanilla covering every couple of years or sooner if it became necessary because of an unexpected kitchen fire or badly orchestrated chimney-cleaning operation. But early last week Mum decided that the kitchen needed something to brighten it up a little. She did this with some architectural feature of the house every three months, which kept my father quite busy and quite miserable.

After a few moments of thought it had been settled. White was too sterile, too harsh. The kitchen needed a softer color, one that would add warmth and a cozy informality. A fresh coat of paint would breathe new life into those boring walls, and Mum had asked Dad repeatedly to find an appropriate color so that she might perform the task without involving him in the work.

Looking around I saw that the walls were now a gentle shade of pink. Earlier that day as I left for the long and torturous walk to school the room had been white, so I knew that Mum had obviously rushed to complete this project before we returned home.

"Why pink?" I inquired.

"I didn't have much choice, boy," she answered, without further explanation.

"I don't like it very much," I told her.

"Too bad," she replied with finality.

Mum was now turning from the sink carefully carrying a rusted flat tin, its faded exterior proclaimed that it had once contained Scottish shortbread. The smell of petrol became stronger, overpowering the other mixture of exotic scents in the kitchen.

"Where did Dad go?" she asked, placing the tin on the kitchen table.

"Don't know" I told her. "Are we going to eat?"

The appearance of the rusty tin and its spirituous aroma suggested that this probably wasn't anything to do with supper. In the bottom of the tin, laying in about half an inch of petrol, my father's cleaning fluid of choice, a collection of old dissembled carburetor pieces retained their grip on the grime that dulled their surface.

This procedure was not an uncommon occurrence in our household. At least once a month, there would be a catastrophe involving the mechanical failure of some aging contraption that Dad depended on, and the kitchen was always selected as a suitable work area. Here Dad had plenty of light and access to running water for flushing eyes, soothing burns or washing bloody wounds received from the misuse of tools. Additionally, there was usually an available supply of slave labor to assist him, in the event that heavy lifting was involved.

It took no detective skill to locate the cause of this latest calamity. On the kitchen table were a collection of mechanical pieces that had been laid out in a specific formation to approximate the exploded view diagram in the dirty, dog-eared repair manual. This allowed me to estimate that if it could ever be re-assembled it would constitute about three-quarters of a nonworking lawn mower. Dad changed lawnmowers even more often than he changed employment. He said this was because having two boys in the house meant that you never knew what unexpected surprise lay hidden in the grass, waiting to be discovered by the rapidly moving blades of a lawnmower. My brother argued that if Dad were to cut the grass more often instead of waiting for it to reach the altitude of farmer Potter's corn field, the hidden and dangerous objects might be more easily seen. It is true that I had once left a bike chain in the grass that demolished one lawnmower. My brother Pete had also inflicted considerable damage on another with an adjustable wrench, and even Mum had been known to forget to clear up after a gardening session, which enlightened us to the fact that lawn mowers are not particularly fond of garden rakes either!

My father entered the kitchen carrying a few inches of black rubber hose about the diameter of a pencil. He sat down on a wooden chair and focused intently on one of the freshly cleaned carburetor parts.

"Now," he paused, scrutinizing the components in his hands, "this should be just the thing to..." he said thoughtfully and optimistically. The remainder of the sentence was replaced by a face indicating something of a struggle. His cheeks were pulled back to display a row of bared teeth through partly open lips. This was an expression he reserved for anything that required any degree of effort, and since he went out of the way to make life difficult for himself, he had frequent opportunity to use it.

He was trying to fit the rubber tube, which was clearly too small, over a protrusion on one of the aluminum parts. Despite Dad's repeated efforts, it was reluctant to remain in place. Eventually though, his struggle paid off and the pipe remained attached, just long enough for him to begin admiring his achievement. It looked like a very professional job for about three seconds, and then slid off with a faint pop.

"Aaaaaaaaa," groaned an irritated father.

Once again he took up the battle of the rubber pipe, and as his enthusiasm gave way to impatience, he struggled more intently. He now tried a variation on his previous technique, holding the metal part in his left hand and trying to attach the hose from underneath using his right hand. Just about the time when his contorted expression had tested the elastic limits of his face, the pipe slipped off again. What made things worse was that his left hand now unsupported, crashed down on the side of the old shortbread tin causing the petrol to spill all over the table, and add another layer of discoloration to the repair manual.

"Damn the thing!" he bellowed, slamming his other hand down onto the table, and catching the prongs of a dinner fork, causing it to somersault into the air.

Again this was fairly typical. My father could go from calm and collected to an angry outburst and back again in about three seconds. He would then seek to explain away his behavior as being that of a rational man pushed to the brink of insanity by all those around him. He stood up quickly and walked over to the window, keeping his back to us as he suppressed the urge to scream at someone, and then rhythmically expelled the first half syllable of at least four swear words before regaining his composure. Next, he whirled around attempting to solicit sympathy and said,

"Well, you have all this stuff on the table that's in the way." This was delivered in a hurt and offended tone that was intended to make everyone else feel both responsible and guilty for impeding the progress of his repair procedures.

The "stuff" my Dad was referring to in this particular case were the plates, cups and silverware that we would hopefully soon be using, and by all rights had more of a claim to the kitchen table than the broken lawnmower.

Regardless of this fact my mother sprung to his assistance and began gathering up the knives and forks. That was the way she was, ever supportive of whatever task he was involved in.

"I mean, it's impossible to get anything done round here with all this," he said in an unreasonable tone as he waved his hand in a sweeping motion over the kitchen table. He then took an old wooden crate that used to contain apples, but which was now lined with oily newspaper, and began to load it with the collection of lawnmower parts. My mother abandoned the meal preparation to temporarily assist. When it was full, Dad picked it up and carried it out of the kitchen.

"I'll do this later," he snorted as he exited through the kitchen door, mumbling just loud enough for us to hear "when no one's around to interfere."

My mother was always moving. She moved with beautifully choreographed ease, as she performed her ceaseless toil between the cooking, washing up, cleaning, laundry, bed making and general support duties to the males of the house. She was as useful with a chainsaw as she was with a needle and thread, and a more perfect companion to my father you could not find.

Just as Mum was a whirlwind of dynamic energy, Dad was the still point in a turning wheel. By this I don't mean that he was idle or in any way lazy, quite the opposite in fact, a harder working and dedicated man you would be hard pressed to find. My father had held jobs and done work that would kill most mortals, and although he endeavored to be a "jack of all trades" so far he had mastered none.

His current "employment" involved a special arrangement he had with Farmer Potter, and occupied three days of his work week. It consisted of taking Potter's tractor and trailer to a nearby wood to clear an area of old woodland by cutting down trees and hauling them away. For this he would be paid. The trees would be brought home and cut up using the saw bench outside the rat barn, where my brother or I would have to bag the resultant wood into flour sacks that Dad had borrowed from the

farm building next door. This would then be sold to the village resid⸺
for firewood.

Dad had a similar arrangement with Farmer Giles last summer, but it was not entirely successful and I was astounded to find that he had chosen to repeat a potentially hazardous experience.

"Never again!" I remember him shouting the day he returned from the woods, limping, soaking wet, with the burns on his legs visible through the singed holes in his trousers and angry red welts on his face arms and neck. As he sat down and consumed more tea and cigarettes than I had ever seen him do before, the disastrous story began to unfold. Apparently Dad had been swinging an axe to remove a particularly stubborn tree and in so doing dislodged a hornet's nest. The hornets has viewed the destruction of their place of residence in a very unfavorable manner and attacked him with a determination and resolve seldom seen in woodland creatures. Luckily Dad had been able to seek refuge by jumping into the pungent choking smoke of the fire where he had been burning some brushwood. After proving his superiority over the winged aggressors by tolerating the flames and smoke longer than they could, he sprinted a short distance to a nearby lake and jumped in to extinguish his burning clothes. Despite his well planned strategy he received multiple hornet stings. He had also twisted his ankle as he exited the lake.

The remaining two days of Dad's work week was assigned to ongoing home repairs and assisting local craftsmen and artisans, which occupied him with new ideas and allowed him to add new skills to his already extensive repertoire.

Considering the sporadic nature of Dad's employment he always managed to stay busy, working all day, often from before I awoke until after I returned home in the evening. He would then perform a series of fix-it jobs and home repairs, often necessary because of my brother's inconsiderate horseplay or carelessness. Then and only then would Dad assume his well deserved position as the head of the household, and prepare himself to be waited on by others. The one area of Dad's doctrine of family life in which he would accept no compromise was in his rules concerning the respective roles that the rest of the family should play. These roles would involve wife and children scurrying around making things comfortable for him as he issued instructions disguised as casual suggestion.

The kitchen door opened with it extended characteristic squeak and Pete walked in, the cheerful bounce to his step contrasting my fathers exhausted shuffle, but his hands, dirty with oil stains strongly indicated the genetic bond shared with our father. Pete was my brother, older by two years and I considered him a mechanical genius. He could make anything from anything with anything. He was never happier than when he had tools in his hands and he was obsessed with motorcycles. He sniffed the air and vocalized his deduction.

"Smells like petrol in here," he said.

We explained about the rubber pipe, and how Dad was in a delicate mood and should be approached with extreme caution. Pete's eyes lit up. If there was one thing he liked more than playing with engines it was antagonizing people. He was always quick to take a contrary point of view about almost anything and many people judged Pete to be deliberately awkward. In hearing this news about Dad's mood, Pete's interest perked up as he envisioned an entertaining target. Fortunately, my mother saw this spark of interest in Pete and forbade him from having any conversation with our father. While this act prevented him from direct involvement in an altercation with Dad, it unfortunately meant that he now had to find another outlet for his mischief.

"Oscar Gurney's Mum is mad at you," he said to me. A twinkle of satisfaction escaped from his eye as he winked at me.

"Why?" I asked, although I suspected that it might have something to do with Benito.

Benito Rolonzio, Oscar Gurney and I, had walked home from school that Friday evening, and with the prospect of a school free weekend ahead of us, we were all in good spirits. It was not at all uncommon for Benito and I to walk home across the fields, instead of using the shorter and cleaner paved road. The sound surfaces, while meeting with parental approval, lacked the excitement and adventure of the countryside. This was a new experience for Oscar. He had recently arrived in the village with his brother Willis and had taken up residence in the small thatched cottage next to the Maudly-Creechom's mansion. The humble four roomed abode stood in stark contrast to the towering limestone walls of Maudly-Creechom manor, with its pristine flower beds, well tended orchards and neatly edged lawns.

The Gurney's new residence was only a stone's throw from Benito Rolonzio's house, and in the coming months I felt that this distance would be tested frequently by Benito in the obvious literal manner. I also felt sure that the Gurneys would soon begin to regret their decision to live in such close proximity to the recalcitrant and bellicose Benito.

Benito Rolonzio was my oldest friend. We lived in houses separated only by old Mrs. Snaggins's gray slate roofed dwelling and an ancient, crumbling farm building, which not unlike Mrs. Snaggins, had become weaker and more unsteady with age. Benito seemed to have an endless collection of brothers and sisters of varying size and disposition. His parents had moved to England from Italy, soon after my own parents arrived in the village, and Benito, along with five of his eldest siblings had spent his early years in that exotic foreign land. He would often regale us with tales of a childhood spent in an unbearably hot and desolate wasteland, where nothing would grow and everyone had to stay indoors because it was so oppressively hot, but even this I thought must be preferable to the miserable British weather. I found it easy to communicate with Benito but I seldom heard the other Rolonzio family members speaking English, particularly when they were engaged in a family argument, which was most of the time. Benito was mischievous and frequently strayed into disobedience and trouble, usually derailing me to join him in his fiendish schemes. In fact, if it were not for my friendship with Benito, I'm certain that I would have enjoyed an undeniably spotless reputation within the village. As it was, I found myself often branded as guilty by association since I was regularly led astray by Benito's devious ways.

Oscar and I walked in single file along the stream's bank with Benito leading and acting as a guide. In several places the persistent effects of time had transformed old and leaning trees into fallen natural bridges across the overgrown waterway. These could be used with some difficulty as a daring method to cross, but the right location was critical, as these lands were full of illusion and false impressions. Being a newcomer, Oscar was unfamiliar with the terrain surrounding Great Biddington and our shortcuts and secret camps were unknown to him. It therefore seemed that this was an ideal opportunity to show him some of the more obscure routes for navigating our private rural areas.

We were now scouring the overgrown bank of the stream in search of a risk free and safe crossing place. Benito and I made a special effort to know all such places along the twisting waterway, for one never knew exactly when it might become necessary to escape wild animals or a rival gang.

A barely imperceptible upward slope in the field ahead had years ago caused the stream to change course and almost double back on itself. The stream's bank had become eroded by the rushing waters and had long ago caused a tree to break its roots free from the disappearing soil and fall toward the opposite bank. Benito paused and looked across the winding stream, his eyes coming to rest on this natural bridge over the cold flowing rapids.

"This is the place," said Benito.

Oscar looked at me and drew his head back slightly. A frown suggested a mixture of misunderstanding and disbelief. Clearly he was not used to the fun and thrills of country life.

"Here?" he said.

"Of course," I said.

"It looks a bit dangerous," protested Oscar.

"It's not," was Benito's curt response.

"Are you sure there is nowhere better?" he inquired, with just a hint of fear in his voice.

I shook my head. "No, unless you want to walk about another three miles to the bridge."

"And don't forget, we would have to walk through that field with the bulls in it!" said Benito, his tone revealing a hint of fear.

Oscar whirled around to look at Benito, but Benito was much too good at this to allow his expression to reveal his intent. By the time Oscar's concerned gaze fell on Benito, my long time colleague was already pretending to study the upper branches of a willow tree as it swayed ever so slightly in the breeze. Benito removed a long strand of grass from his mouth, squinted and said, "Is that swallow building a nest?"

Instead of looking toward the alleged nest, Oscar, beginning to show signs of panic, looked back to the stream.

Benito was a master at this sort of thing. The bit about the bulls was a nice touch. It was getting late and Oscar was obviously having doubts about attempting this crossing. The dangers of an encounter with wild and vicious bovines convinced Oscar of the lack of an alternative route, but his eyes were now filled with confusion and panic.

"I don't think it's safe," he said as he grabbed a handful of leaves from an overhanging bush and tentatively put his right foot on the fallen log. With hesitation, he rocked his weight back and forth between the foot on terra firma and the toe of the foot exploring the tree limb that extended across the rushing waters beneath. Realizing his unwillingness to proceed, and afraid that if he did not, we would be stuck here all night, I moved in behind him to cut off his retreat.

"Hurry up, it'll be getting dark soon," I said. My normally friendly and helpful manner was now losing out to impatience.

"I don't know" Oscar mumbled. "This branch doesn't seem very strong."

"It's fine," I said. I recalled some historical anecdote about the hidden strength of wood, but Oscar was not impressed. I suspected that we had reached an impasse, but Benito was not going to let this happen.

"You chicken!" he shouted with a sneer. "I don't even know why we let you come with us!" To emphasize the point he attempted to emulate an exaggerated clucking sound.

This did the trick. Not wishing to be branded as a coward, or lose his newfound friends, Oscar edged forward on the branch, a slight creaking noise suggesting danger and I felt sure that he would change his mind.

Oscar began to look very nervous indeed. His breath was found in short shallow gasps and his hand shakily reached out for support. He was crouched low for what he believed was stability, but when the branch began to let out a slow creaking noise, he started to edge backwards, his eyes filled with uncertainty.

That was when Benito yelled, "Jump – quick it's breaking!"

Benito's orders were barked with all the authority of an angry drill sergeant. Oscar panicked and unleashed the coiled up nervous energy in his hunched body, launching himself into the air.

Despite the fact that the thin branch from which he commenced his flight lacked sufficient strength for an effective take-off, we were initially impressed with both his altitude and trajectory. About a third of the way into the jump however, good fortune prevailed as he began to lose his balance – his arms started to flail wildly and his back arched. He had now officially lost control of the jump and nothing could prevent the inevitable.

Oscar realized this too, but was consoled by the fact that although he would not make it to the other bank, he would at least be able to land on some firm ground that to him almost looked like sand!

Squeaky Norrington, originally discovered "The quicksand," during a particularly disastrous fishing trip. Benito and I didn't witness the discovery, but upon hearing Squeaky's tale of woe, we insisted that he show us where this place was. Two or three days later when Squeaky's nerve had returned he led us to the fearful spot, and standing high on the bank he pointed it out with a trembling finger. Despite Benito's repeated attempts, Squeaky could not be persuaded to climb down and demonstrate the dangerous and messy nature of this area at close quarters, so Benito confirmed its existence by throwing a large rock into the center of the slimy terrain. He approved of the results and committed the location to memory. His reasons were now quite apparent.

Upon contact with the sinister soil, Oscar's relief swiftly changed to terror. His mouth opened and he let forth a mighty yell as his feet disappeared into the extremely well disguised sticky slime. The yell continued along with his descent into the filthy grime, a downward journey that finally arrested just before the sludge reached his knees, but that was good enough for Benito.

Not wanting to miss any of the show, we ran round the tight bend in the stream to a hidden place only a few feet away, where almost two years ago, Benito and I had spent an exhausting summer afternoon industriously engaged in a dam building project. Eventually the farmer down stream, distraught at the sight of thirsty cattle and poorly irrigated soil had destroyed our construction project, but there remained a series of stepping-stones that varied in both size and stability. We quickly crossed in relative safety, and Benito giggled with joy at having been finally treated to a longed for re-enactment of Squeaky Norrington's near brush with slimy death.

We hurried to assist Oscar up the bank, but for some strange reason he refused our help. As we watched him scramble up the muddy terrain, his anger was getting the better of him, and as is not unusual in these cases, it affected his climbing judgment. Oscar's feet, still slippery with Squeaky's quicksand, failed to grip the steep incline and after a few rapid steps with his feet skidding in place and his arms waving wildly in the air, his feet slipped out from under him and he fell forward with his face in the mud.

Oscar now gripped some greenery with both hands to prevent him from receding further down the bank as Benito threw his head back and roared with laughter. The tufts of grass that Oscar was clutching for support, slowly detached themselves from the soft earth and an unhappy Oscar slid back down the slope on his stomach.

The front of his short trousers, which had previously escaped the "quicksand" were now soiled with mud, as was his shirt, arms and the left side of his face. Benito's hysteria reached a crescendo and he fell on the ground clutching his belly, begging Oscar to end the comedy that this adventure had become.

In due course a soggy and sorrowful Oscar was retrieved and we began a long walk home. Oscar was angry and said nothing; he just glared at us from time to time with a clenched jaw, red face and bulging angry eyes. I shared in his silence not because I could sympathize with his dismay, but because I was not ready to further antagonize this new boy until I had been given an opportunity to assess his fighting skills.

Benito did not care. He would occasionally make a laughing sound in the back of his throat, as the squishing noise made by Oscar's shoes reminded him of the plunge to peril that would live fondly in his memory for many years to come.

About half way back to the strip of houses along Mud Lane where we lived, Benito said a strange thing.

"We should make a Guy this year."

We were taught in school that many years ago, a group of radical Catholics attempted to build a giant bomb and hide it in the cellar under the parliament building in London. When all the politicians were assembled inside, the radicals planned to do the obvious, but a loyal night watchman thwarted this dastardly scheme, and the man with the match, whose name was Guy Fawkes, was captured. He suffered a dreadful fate, involving months of torment, and then when the fiendish imagination of his captors was exhausted, he was condemned to death by burning. Not since Joan of Arc had such a fiery demise captured the attention of so many. Ever since then subjects loyal to the Crown have celebrated this close call, by making an effigy of Guy Fawkes and burning it on a large bonfire for all to enjoy. This occurred every year on November 5th and was called Bonfire night or Firework night, as there are also a large number of fireworks discharged as part of the celebration.

Billy Tadcome said that this was a symbolic warning to the working class not to challenge the power of the wealthy, but at such a tender age we did not fully comprehend his political philosophy, and blamed alcohol for his peculiar viewpoint.

Guys were usually constructed out of old clothing, fixed together in any way possible and stuffed with straw or old rags to fill them out into the shape of a man. The head was made from anything round, and the whole dummy was dressed up to resemble an old time political dissident. I had built them in the past but usually my efforts did not include hands or feet, just cuffs, sown up with the help of my mother to stop Guy's entrails from falling out through the trouser legs.

Benito was Catholic, and by rights should not have anything to do with this since it was his ancestors who masterminded this subversive event. Furthermore, it seemed out of character for Benito to suggest something that entailed hard work and effort.

"That sounds like a lot of hard work and effort," I said.

"No," he replied. "It's a good idea, because then we can raise money for fireworks."

It was customary to drag the completed mannequin to each residence in the community on a begging mission, repeatedly chanting "a penny for the guy." Upon hearing this familiar cry the person dwelling therein, would come to the door and give us money as compensation for all our hard work. In actual fact we planned to get a lot more than a penny from each homeowner, and put the collection to good use buying fireworks; danger and explosions being an important part of our lives.

"Do you have any Guy stuff?" I asked.

"No," replied Benito, identifying the first obstacle to the plan. We would need a good supply of old clothes and stuffing materials. The head would also be a problem. The previous year we made it from an old pillow-case stuffed with leaves which resulted in a very anemic looking villain, and burned much too quickly causing the incendiary spectacle to resemble the headless horseman more than the desired wicked conspirator.

Nothing further was said of the plan, and we walked on in silence, each engaged in mental exercises that would solve our various Guy making problems, and it was almost dark when we returned to civilization.

CHAPTER 2

ROGER PILCHARD'S PROBLEM

After being ejected from the kitchen, Pete and I walked out of the house and along a concrete path until we got to the freestanding structure which currently served as Dad's tobacco factory. This multipurpose building's use changed every so often as Dad adopted a new interest that required additional space. We called the building El Paso.

This unlikely name was coined one day while we were watching an old western on television. The film was called "The Guns of El Paso," or "Duel at El Paso" or something like that, and in it was a scene depicting a stagecoach stopping at a small dilapidated, way station in the desert. It had been attacked by Indians who had done a good job partially dismantling it with horses and ropes, and then finished it off by setting light to everything that would burn. Someone, probably Pete, remarked that it resembled our stone barn, and from that day forth we always called the place El Paso.

At the far end of this structure was a small room that Pete had claimed as his workshop. It was here that the motorcycle lived.

A few weeks earlier, Dad had purchased another car to replace his previous van. The van had suffered from failing health for some time and as a safeguard against the vehicle's imminent demise, my father had purchased a motorcycle from a local auction house. Dad was proud of the haggling skills he had employed to obtain such a low price for the bike, but in reality, the seven pounds and ten shillings probably accurately reflected the vehicle's age and the severe problems with its lighting system and exhaust pipe. After purchasing the replacement car, the motorbike, was no longer necessary in our vehicular arsenal, and knowing of his son's love of motorbikes Dad passed it down the family line to Pete, who was thrilled to be the recipient. Although hardly big enough to hold up the bike and certainly too young to ride legally on the road, Pete had grand plans to ride in the surrounding countryside, chasing sheep and generally getting covered in mud.

"Come and look at this," he said excitedly.

Opening the black wooden door Pete reached inside and turned on the light. A bare light bulb on the end of a frayed brown electrical cord lit up the dirt floor and stone walls of the interior. The room was small, quite narrow but deep. When Mum, Dad, and baby Pete moved into this humble abode, this room used to be the toilet, which explained the unusual dimensions. I feel so very blessed that I do not remember the experience of using this primitive outhouse, but I am aware of the discomfort associated with its use. Every few weeks, as part of a reprimand for some misdeed or other, Dad would remind us how lucky we were to have things so easy and comfortable. Part of this lecture would inevitably include recollections of having to use the "lavatory up the garden."

If this story were being told on a day when my father was enjoying fair mood and good fortune, the trip may be made during a warm spring day. In this version it would be possible for the subject to pass away the time while seated with an old squirrel gun, shooting through a knothole in the door at the local wildlife as it attempted to ravage the vegetable patch. But more often the account would be rendered in a manner more reflective of his mood.

He would start by describing the journey, which might be made at any time of night, in either rain or snow. This trip alone was almost bad enough to dissuade one from going, unless it was a matter of life or death. Once there, the oil lamp that was taken along for illumination provided the only heat in the room and cleanup would be made possible by old newspapers and magazines. However it was important to go through the magazines first and remove the glossy pages, as the slick and shiny sections of Mum's monthly copy of *Better Housekeeping* were more part of the problem than the solution.

But much had changed since then, and now the room looked very different. The toilet bowl was long gone and had been cemented over. Copies of Motorcycle Mechanics had replaced the old newspapers and cookery magazines and Pete's new bike, soiled with recently dried mud, leaned against one of the walls. On the opposite wall, large nails had been driven into the gaps between the stonework, as a storage system for Pete's tools – a large hammer, an adjustable wrench, a long bent screwdriver and a hacksaw. These four items alone were normally sufficient for most of his repair jobs.

The motorcycle only had a small engine but to us it was as big as any of the pictures of racing machines, ripped from magazines, which now adorned the wall of Pete's garage.

The problems the bike suffered from with its lighting system were no longer an issue as the lights had been removed and thrown into the corner. The problem of the exhaust system was dealt with in a similar manner. The mudguards, license plates, leg shields, speedometer, windscreen and carrier had all been dismantled and lay in a pile at the far end of the room. The tangled heap of red rusty metal and tarnished chrome now existed where once there had been pristine white porcelain.

This was Pete's basic procedure to convert the bike from roadworthiness to Pete-worthiness. Anything that contributed to unnecessary weight or safety was quickly and permanently removed.

He motioned me to move out of the way and as I stood up I felt a sharp pain just above my belt and to the left of my spine as one of the tool hangers ripped a large hole in my shirt and a smaller hole in my back. I let out a yelp but it was of no concern to Pete; he was absorbed with pushing the bike out of the old latrine.

He threw his leg over the seat and leaned the bike over. He reached down under the petrol tank and fiddled with something, then glancing down, he located the kick-starter and eased it onto the compression stroke.

"Dad's going to be really angry if you start....." The rest of my sentence was lost in the noise. Pete had raised himself up and came down with all his weight on the kick-start as the bike roared to life.

It was dark now, and as Pete revved the engine, a deafening noise accompanied orange and blue flames popping from the end of what used to be the exhaust pipe, but now thanks to an encounter with Pete's hacksaw, it was nothing more than twelve inches of steel tube.

I gave my brother a thumb up sign, intended to signal that I thought the tone of the engine was greatly improved by his exhaust pipe modification.

He, in turn, motioned for me to climb on the back, and he struggled to hold up the vehicle as I clambered on. Despite the fact that he was hardly a teenager, Pete's riding skills were admirable. I couldn't reach the rear footrests, and held my legs out at an angle to prevent them becoming entangled in unforgiving metallic machinery. I wrapped my arms around his waist and hung on.

Putting the bike in gear we took off so quickly that I almost slid off the back. I tried not to grip Pete as hard as the terror that I now experienced had gripped me, for I knew that if Pete sensed my fear he would just go even faster, if that were possible. We headed up Mud Lane toward Squeaky Norrington's house, and I know that we both secretly hoped that Squeaky was outside so that we could show off.

At the end of Mud Lane, at the point where the paving stopped and the rough dirt began, Pete leaned the bike over and we made a tight turn, retracing our journey back to the house. The main difference on this portion of the trip was that Pete rode even faster, helped by the downhill slope of the lane and the following wind. We were back outside the shed long before any of the neighbors had time to investigate the cause of the infernal racket that had just disturbed their relaxation and interrupted their evening meal.

The entire ride had lasted less than a minute but it left me feeling thrilled and elated. My heart was pounding and I was trembling with delight. We blasted through the night on our noisy fire-breathing death trap with the wind in our faces and the trees and houses rushing by in a blur. It made me feel invincible, daring, and proud to have a brother who must surely be the envy of the Mud Lane residents.

Upon our return, I was told to jump off so that Pete could perform his "Victory lap." I watched as he roared up the gravel driveway, past rat barn, made a right hand corner at the weed patch that had once been Dads tobacco plantation, a tight left around the apple tree that supported our tree house, up the slight grass incline and back onto the driveway. Pete always liked to finish the day in this manner. He claimed that it was necessary for the health of the engine.

Pete turned the petrol off and re-stabled his mount, while I ran excitedly toward the house.

"Don't tell Dad." Pete yelled after me. Pete had been forbidden, on countless occasions to ride the bike on the road.

As it turned out I didn't need to tell Dad anything, he had already heard. As I was running from the shed toward the house, my very irate father was running from the house toward the shed.

"Were you riding that thing on the road" he yelled past me, at Pete who was walking down the path trying his best to exude innocence.

"Err, just for a little way," replied Pete as he tried to avoid saying "yes."

"How many times have I told you not to ride that bike on the road?" Dad screamed. It was a good question but neither of us knew the answer, having lost count within the first two days of Pete's motorcycle ownership.

"Not many, why?" came the questionable guess from Pete. This answer did little to calm Dad's escalating blood pressure.

"Stay off the road with the bike," Dad shouted. That should have been the end of it, but having taken the trouble to annoy my father Pete wanted to get as much entertainment out of it as he could.

"It wasn't far," pleaded Pete.

"You don't have a license," said Dad.

"There was nobody else on the road," came the counter argument.

"What if there was?" queried my father, but I sensed that the way to win this was not with conjecture. Pete's next comment proved me right. "There wasn't," he said.

"That bike doesn't have an exhaust, and has just woken up every kid in the lane who might be trying to get to sleep." Persisted Dad.

I tried to calculate how many kids might be trying to sleep this early, and came up with zero. I was foolish enough to point this out.

"Well, that doesn't matter," said Dad. "People are probably trying to relax watching television or eating their supper." The television thing was probably the only real complaint. Some problem with the bike's electrical system caused it to create crackling white lines of interference on any television that got within its sphere of influence. I had personally seen many of Mike Mercury's speeches disrupted in this manner while watching Fireball XL5 during the children's hour.

"People don't want to hear that racket," Dad continued yelling, his voice now making as much noise as the motorbike had.

"So if I put the exhaust back on, can I ride it on the road?" asked Pete. Dad ignored the question and asked one of his own.

"What about a crash helmet?" Safety now became his main concern, as he pointed out the dangers of an unexpected accident. I sort of liked this part because it made me feel like there was some reason for his irate behavior, but it didn't last long, and soon he moved on to the real issue of concern, that of tarnishing the supposedly spotless reputation of the family name.

"What if someone had seen you and called the police?" Dad was beginning to calm down a little and trying to reason with Pete. I thought I would help by reassuring my father that detection by the law was unlikely.

"Dad," I said, "I don't think anyone could have recognized us because we had no lights."

The recklessness of this un-illuminated joy ride was instantly forgotten when Dad discovered that I was also involved in Pete's death-defying stunt.

Dad's fury increased again in order to deliver a full-length commentary on the importance of adequate illumination on a fast moving vehicle.

The reprimand continued all the way back down the path and into the house and was just about over as we sat down at the dinner table.

"Did you see some idiot just go past the house on a motorbike?" Mum asked, as she carried serving dishes to the table. Dad just rolled his eyes.

We were silent for a few peaceful seconds and then it started again.

"It's time you got your hair cut." said Dad to Pete.

Now the new conflict was to be over the length of my brother's hair. This was one of Dad's favorites.

The fashion for most of my father's life had been for men to wear their hair short. He had also enjoyed his time in the service of his country where men were encouraged to crop their hair even shorter. Even now his thinning locks continued to be trimmed in the short back and sides style that was popularized by his generation. Dad would not entertain any alternate view on the matter. Like so many of Dad's other opinions, Pete chose not to share this one.

I think the Beatles were to blame. Most children our age wanted to be in a pop group, and if that were not possible, we at least wanted to look as if we were. Pete was a very good example of this. He compensated for his total lack of musical ability by refusing to cut his hair. This had now become so much of an obsession with my brother that he feared the barber more than the dentist whom it was rumored had learned his trade from a very reputable carpenter.

The dentist was I think over one hundred years old and his name was Mr. Hatcher. Pete called him Hatcher the Butcher, and he was positively medieval in his methodology. Dental excavations and extractions were routinely performed without the aid of anesthetic, and his lack of accuracy with the drill was understandable for a man of his age. On our last excursion, Pete, reacting to the drill bit penetrating his tongue, had lashed out, overturning the small steel tray containing Hatcher the Butcher's instruments of torture, broken the overhead light and landed a punch in Hatcher's one good eye.

Dad continued in the throes of expounding his disgust, shame and humiliation at being associated with Pete and his hair. He likened Pete's appearance to that of a girl and threatened him with violence if he did not significantly reduce the length of the shaggy mane. This scene was repeated every month or so, and each time it would last two or three days leading up to the inevitable. This was day one.

Eventually Dad ran out of breath and we all sat down to eat, the meal being made especially appetizing by the strong smell of petrol in the room. Pete later confessed to me that during the entirety of my father's lecture he was dying to inquire about the condition of the lawnmower.

Halfway through my slab of gravy soaked Shepherd's pie, it became my turn to receive a parental scolding, when I was called upon to explain the rip in my school shirt. To find that Pete's motorcycle was once more at the root of the problem was a good thing because Dad had by now exhausted himself on this subject, and I escaped relatively unscathed. After supper Dad picked up the evening newspaper and his pipe and retired to watch one of the two television stations. Mum was left alone to wash up and generally made the house look spotless before joining him.

The living room, which we also referred to as the "other" room, was a more comfortable area than the kitchen. It was a cozy room with a soft carpet, and covering the small white-framed windows were heavy curtains to keep out the darkness and the cold. It was not usually occupied during the day, except by the cat, because there were no television programs to watch. This was something the cat didn't seem to care about. Additionally Dad resented anyone sitting in his chair while he was at work. This was something else the cat didn't seem to care about.

A heavy black beam adorned with polished brass spanned the rough stonework surrounding an open fireplace, which blazed throughout most of the year. This not only provided heat, but also bathed the small room in a beautiful amber glow.

The walls were decorated with a collection of china plates, mostly inherited from Granny, and pictures of sailing ships in all sizes, types and weather conditions, allowing my father to mentally stroll at will, back into his past.

One half of the room contained the couch, television set and Dad's chair, while the other half was furnished with an oval table and wheel-backed chairs that we reserved for the rare act of formal dining. We would eat here only on special occasions like Christmas or birthday parties or if we had visitors who by pre-arrangement were expecting to be fed. A formal meal would be in stark contrast to our "normal food."

A window overlooked the back garden. It framed a small apple tree perfectly, and in the morning summer sunshine, the lush green grass, contrasted with the warm brown bark of the tree that produced small apples, with a delicate sweetness. Sadly, England's summer season was somewhat on the short side. Most of the time if you scraped the frost off the window, and strained your eyes to see through the fog, you could just make out, beneath overcast skies, the bare branches of a tree, ravished by the winter cold, and wet with rain. Two other windows provided equally desolate views and fully covered the activity in the lane.

Entering this inner sanctum, Dad stepped into a well-planned relaxation zone, which over the years had been fine-tuned to his requirements. Being the king of our humble castle he had created a total environment in support of himself, and in the center of it was his throne.

The throne in this case was an old armchair, a large polished leather affair with significant wear showing on the arms. It was brown and smelled strongly of pipe tobacco and old socks but it was by far the most comfortable chair in the room. Over the years it had sagged in just the right places and formed itself to be a perfect receptacle for a tired body. The softest and most cloud-like cushion partnered it, and together they seemed to call out for you to come and sleep.

It was the closest chair to the fireplace, positioned so that Dad's feet could be placed within inches of the flames. Many a cold winter night, my father could be found toasting his socks while the rest of us, shivering, gazed on from a respectful distance.

This customized seating was also important because it pointed directly at the TV set. Anyone else partaking in this form of entertainment had to sit or lay on the floor for a good view, or occupy the couch with the neck twisted awkwardly in discomfort.

Dad was the only person allowed to sit in the chair. This rule was not written down anywhere, but it was well understood by all who entered, that is all except the cat, who would insist on sitting there, regardless of how many times she was told not to. Obviously she didn't understand English, and didn't care to learn. When Dad was not in the room, Pete and I would fight for the right to occupy this privileged location, but when its rightful owner eventually appeared, whoever was currently sitting there, moved. It was that simple.

Once, Pete had laid claim to the chair when Dad came in carrying his newspaper and pipe. Pete, who was always anxious to test people and their limits, especially my father's, pretended not to notice. Instead of springing up and taking a less coveted seat, he just sat there reading a comic book as my father crossed the room, stood by the chair and said,

"Don't you move boy, I can sit anywhere." But he didn't sit anywhere – he just continued to stand there glaring at Pete. His piercing gaze increased in intensity until my poor brother could stand it no longer. Within moments the staring contest was over, my father reigned victorious, and my brother was forced to move to the end of the couch.

As an additional and final attraction the chair had its own furniture in the form of a side table and lamp. The table contained a clock, Dad's pipe and tobacco and an ashtray that Mrs. Snaggins had brought back from Great Yarmouth as a holiday gift. The existence of this table was only important when one considered that no one else in the room enjoyed this level of luxury. Take for example the clock. Following the traditional supper-time arguments and a lecture from my father about how easy kids have it these days, the family would typically gather around the small black and white television set. The clock, located conveniently on Dad's table, would eventually creep round to eight signaling the commencement of another important family tradition.

"Would anyone like a cup of tea?" Dad would ask considerately. This was not meant to suggest in any way that he was going to get up and make a pot of tea. Anyone who knew him would realize that this was nothing more than a coded reminder to my Mum that Dad was ready for his tea now!

Mum would dart from the room and head for the kitchen to put the kettle on, then seek out additional duties to occupy her while it boiled. Meanwhile, Dad would carefully proceed to pack his pipe.

"Are either of you boys cold?" he asked, idly thumbing a carefully measured load of ready rub flake tobacco into the cherry wood bowl of his pipe. This was another piece of father's cryptic code and Pete, who was sitting next to me on the couch, was kind enough to alert me to that in the form of swift sideways kick.

"Why me?" I asked.

"You're closer," Pete said as if that explained it. Sensing the weakness in his argument he quickly added, "...Anyway, my leg hurts." He rubbed his knee for effect. This was an obvious lie, since he had just used the alleged defective limb to attack me!

I slowly trudged out to the hall. Fortunately there were two logs left. They represented the remainder of a once mighty stack of firewood. I picked them up. If we needed any more, some unfortunate individual would have to suit up in boots and coat, since nightfall brought with it an unpleasant drop in temperature, and make a trek outside. At the very edge of the frontier, next to rat barn, the unfortunate conscript would gather up another armful of logs and bring them back to the staging area in the hall. I could hear the howling of gale force winds outside and felt that I was indeed fortunate that I got the last two logs.

I re joined the group and placed the logs on the orange glow of the dying embers.

"Dad," I whined in a deliberately annoying tone, "next time we need wood, can Pete go for a change?" I was pleading now, hoping to appeal to Dad's sense of justice. Without looking up from his tobacco preparation he agreed to my heartfelt request, and I settled back down on the couch savoring the image of Pete, lumbering through the darkness with flashlight in hand, leaning into the frigid wind. With any luck it might even be raining by then.

Dad examined the thin trails of gray smoke drifting upwards from the pipe bowl, and placed the pipe in his mouth just as Mum returned carrying a tray, containing tea for four. She proceeded to prepare each cup before handing it out. Dad, of course, got his first and placed it conveniently on his private table. And here is where the real advantage of a personal side table became apparent.

While our father could casually reach over at any time to drink his tea, the rest us had no handy location on which to place the fortifying brew. Instead we had to select one of three inconvenient options. Either place the cup on the floor risking that it be inadvertently kicked over by

Pete, or even another family member, keep it on the dining room table and have to walk over there to drink it or balance the cup on our knees and sacrifice comfort.

"I think I'll put the television on for your mother," commanded Dad. This time it was Pete's turn to get up. We sat with necks twisted and cups balanced on our knees, as we waited several minutes for the television set to warm up and reveal the luminous magic. As we readied ourselves to watch whatever Dad wanted to watch, there was the sound of a knock at the door.

The usual reaction to a knock at the door was panic. More often than not, it would mean that Pete or I were in trouble; hopefully this time it would be Pete. My mind raced as I went through a mental checklist of all the things I might have done that would result in a parental visitation. Within moments I knew exactly who it was.

In a rare display of activity, Dad got up to answer the door, and I knew with absolute certainty that he would find Oscar's mother standing there, red-faced and angry. She would be holding her son, probably by the ear and he would look as if he had been crying. From the chest down Oscar would be varying shades of brown, and the filth would now be beginning to dry to the point where it could be chipped off a piece at a time. Any second we would all hear her raised voice, as she demanded an explanation from my father for her son's condition. At that point I would be called, and brought to stand before the unwelcome visitors while Oscar would extend towards me a finger of accusation. This gave me only precious seconds to invent an alibi.

"Hello, Rodger," I heard with relief.

The two men walked back into the living room with Dad leading.

"Mind your head, Rodger," he warned.

"Ouch," said Rodger, rubbing the top of his ginger head.

On his way through the hall Rodger looked through the open kitchen door and waved to Mum adding, "Your kitchen walls look nice."

The ceilings in the living room were similar to the rest of the house, low and plastered white supported by giant rough-hewn wooden beams painted black. If we received a visitor unaccustomed to the pitfalls of our abode, they soon discovered, often very painfully, the need to periodically duck as they walked around, especially in doorways. Rodger Pilchard never quite seemed to remember this.

Rodger was our neighbor from just up the hill, and I thought he was the most peculiar individual in Mud Lane. He was a tall lanky Londoner with bushy red hair, and a job as a traveling salesman. Like my father, he always seemed to be engaged in some new and interesting venture. Perhaps that's why he and Dad were such good friends. Sometimes the temporary fads that fascinated them would coincide, crossing like ships in the night; ironically one of these shared hobbies was sailing. Another time they became simultaneous mountain climbers.

There were two children in the house of Pilchard. Brian and Ryan.

Brian, the eldest, tall and thin, would likely grow up with his father's proportions. Ryan, on the other hand was small for his age. He was two years my junior, and like his big brother, had inherited his father's red hair. Pilchard had passed down his eccentricity to both children, and their games and pastimes were always just a little out of sync with the rest of the village. I liked their adventurous spirit and imaginative nature, admiring how they were always able to fashion weapons from everyday household items. They were not strictly part of our gang, but this did not offend them, as they usually preferred their own company and unconventional diversions. I respected their neutrality, because in our neighborhood you did not last long without protection. Despite this, I would have liked them in our gang, since their ingenious thought process and knowledge of ancient weaponry would have added useful skills to our group.

Mr. Pilchard had an optimistic nature, seldom found in Great Biddington. A perfect example of this was "Pilchard day." This occurred each year on the third Sunday in June, and on this day it was the sworn duty of Rodger's wife and children to buy presents for the head of the household. The problem was that the Pilchard children, being remarkably similar to their Dad, would make gifts rather than actually buy them. Last year, Brian's offering was a shoebox filled with interesting looking rocks that he had found. Ryan had taken great trouble in creating an odd looking device from a piece of broken broom handle, some yellow string and a bubble gum box.

Rodger was invited to remove his jacket and take the second most desirable seat in our living room. Dad also offered him a cup of tea, and at the same time, by implication, invited Mum to go back in the kitchen and make it. Mum rushed out, anxious to return before any of the really good gossip started.

We listened as the two men in the room exchanged pleasantries by discussing the weather, a subject on which my father felt he was something of an expert, and the state of the English road system, which was Rodger's forte. There was silence for a moment while Rodger leaned closer to the fire and rubbed his hands together.

"Did you hear some idiot on a motorcycle go up the lane earlier?" Roger asked casually. The muscles in Dad's neck tensed and he looked embarrassed.

"He must have been going about sixty miles an hour!"

Dad looked over at Pete, who was basking in pride at this recognition, and beaming brighter than his missing headlight would have, even when it operated correctly. Rodger caught this non-verbal exchange and understood.

"Oh," he said simply.

Then Rodger attempted damage recovery by reverting to small talk. He wanted to know if we knew how Mrs. Snobbit's leg was.

There was silence again, this time broken by my mother's return.

"I've put the kettle on," she said, and then inquired, "How are you, Rodger?"

In the conversation that followed we discovered that Rodger was quite well, much better in fact than Mrs. Snobbit's leg, which we learned from Mum was not so good. As the discussion progressed Rodger gradually made us aware of his problem.

He began to explain that he was planning a trip with the family to Scotland. On hearing this, Dad raised his eyebrows in anticipation as he realized the reason for Rodger's visit. Dad immediately began to offer an estimate of the temperatures, wind speeds, precipitation and fog warnings for Scotland and the north of England for this time of year. Rodger explained that this was not why he was here and continued with his story. He was planning to visit the Isle of Sky.

For a second time Dad's interest was piqued, and he reached for the collection of maps that he always kept at hand, so that they could plan the route together, but Rodger already knew what route he would be taking. No, Rodger's problem was more severe than the weather forecast and more desperate than a need for directions.

Rodger's car was an Austin 1100. It was very small, and accommodating all his baggage would be a problem. Additionally, he had a small boat, which he was planning to transport upside down on the roof rack of the car. He had to get his wife, two children and a cat named Bartholomew inside the car, while the tent and sleeping bags would consume all the available space in the tiny car boot.

Where would he put the luggage?

Upon hearing of this dilemma Dad sat silently puffing on his pipe deep in thought while his eyes tried to look at each of his eyebrows in turn. Eventually he came up with what he considered a brilliant solution. Instead of putting the boat on the roof rack upside down, it was to be placed right side up. The tent, sleeping bags, camping equipment, and the luggage could be placed inside the boat and the whole thing could be covered with a waterproof canvas sheet. Pete, always helpful, added that he could even put Bartholomew up there as well.

"Tomorrow morning," Dad announced, like the great problem solver that he was "we," he said, looking directly at me, "will find my canvas sheet for you."

CHAPTER 3

SATURDAY 28TH OCTOBER
SEARCH FOR THE
CANVAS SHEET

"Aaaaaaaaagh....get out of here!" Dad's voice penetrated my peaceful slumbers.

I opened one eye and rolled over to see beams of sunlight streaming through the window that overlooked the vegetable garden and the back wall of the so-called greenhouse, which was a ramshackle structure manufactured from old window frames. Dad was crouching in the middle of his cabbage plantation, on what looked like freshly turned soil. He was hunched low like a gunfighter, knees bent, feet apart, eyes wide with anger, teeth bared and fists clenched. He yelled again and looked mean enough to shoot someone, in the event that his efforts to scare them to death proved unsuccessful.

Now he had my interest. I sat up in bed and leaned toward the window for a better view. I shouted at Pete to wake up, for I was certain that he would not want to miss this thrilling escapade. As I blinked the sleep away, I saw the object of Dad's very genuine hostility. Once again Morris was trespassing. He stood about ten feet from Dad, staring menacingly and poised to spring into combat if necessary.

Morris was an insane brown boxer dog and considered by most to be the plague of Mud Lane. He would frequently escape from his owners and run wild through any available garden in pursuit of his hobby, which always involved lots of digging. He would romp into the yard of any unfortunate homeowner without a closed gate, and momentarily pause while he surveyed the landscape to locate the spot that would cause the most distress to the garden and gardener. With practiced eye, he would achieve this quickly and in a heartbeat he would bound off to the desired spot to commence his excavations. What made matters worse, was that Morris was owned by Mr. and Mrs. Maudly-Creechom. People in the lane thought slightly less of the Maudly-Creechoms than they did of Morris, so this was very much a case that added injury to insult.

For what seemed like an eternity, Dad and the dog faced each other unflinching. Then, in a moment of derangement, without taking his eyes off the lunatic hound, Dad reached down and wrapped his hand around the first thing he found, which was an uprooted cabbage, and hurled it at Morris. The dog did not move. Obviously, more drastic measures were needed. Still yelling obscenities, Dad jumped up and down a few times, grabbed another unearthed vegetable and swinging it wildly in the air over his head, he lunged toward Morris.

Pete joined me at the window just in time to see the boxer dog, with tail firmly between its rear legs, bolting off down the driveway as Dad gave chase with a makeshift rhubarb sword.

Our house had two bedrooms upstairs. Mum and Dad occupied the one at the top of the stairs, and Pete and I shared the other one. The space allocation was deliberate. Mum and Dad's room offered a strategic location from which to apprehend Pete when he tried to run away in the middle of the night, something he was fond of doing.

The bedroom floor was comprised of wooden planks of varying width that created an elongated patchwork appearance. The gaps between the boards were wide enough so that if you dropped any small plastic toy it was very likely you would never see it again. Almost every step caused a creak or a groan somewhere in the room and the uneven texture of this surface made every piece of furniture rock slightly whenever it was touched.

For about four feet up the walls, the loose wall plaster was held in place by ivy patterned wallpaper climbing up a brown wooden trellis.

On Pete's side of the room the walls were covered with pictures of motorcycles and race cars, and over his bed was a page torn from a magazine depicting the latest teen singing sensation. My side of the room was decorated with pictures of rockets and astronauts. We spent many happy hours in this room talking and playing together, but most of our time was dedicated to refining our fighting skills in preparation for an unexpected Rolonzio attack.

Try as I did to return to the land of slumber, Mum came up to remind us that we had been volunteered to assist our father in finding the canvas sheet for Rodger Pilchard. We dressed and made toward the wooden staircase that twisted into a tight winding descent requiring some considerable skill to navigate. There was no handrail and such inconsistency in tread dimensions that it was all but impossible to climb them in the dark. I liked to think of this as our burglar alarm.

Of course burglary was not really a serious consideration for us. The antiquated construction techniques used in this dwelling were such that you could probably easily break into the house with a blunt stick, but any potential burglar would not even have to go to that much trouble because we seldom locked the door. That was one of the advantages of living in a village where the crime rate was, apart from a few rare occasions, practically nonexistent, and since we were generally involved in these few rare occasions, and not as the victims, our sense of security remained intact. The possibility of any unauthorized personnel entering a residential dwelling was also minimized because of the protocols of village life. The spread of information by word of mouth would travel so fast that it had been known to reach the last person in Great Biddington before the first person had finished speaking. If any stranger entered one of the local houses, within about five minutes, not only would everyone in the village know about it, but they would also have a complete description of the perpetrator including clothing, make and model of car and possibly name and address.

But the hazardous design of the stairs afforded me a sense of even more security. In the unlikely event that during our absence, some uninvited guest did decide to pay an unannounced visit, the intruder would certainly meet with very limited success. We would upon our return surely find the wrongdoer immobile in a heap at the bottom of the stairs. If he was ever to regain consciousness, he would no doubt find himself the victim of several broken bones and perhaps even worse depending on the severity of his unexpected and rapid descent.

Below the stairs was a cupboard. For some reason that was never made clear, Dad decided that Mum did not need it, so it was sealed up with wood and painted over.

Just prior to this, Dad was cleaning out one of the areas around our estate where he would store old junk, and had need to dispose of one or two hundred old jam jars. He thought that a good place to dump them would be in this unused cupboard, and so it was done.

As if boarding up an old dark hole was not suspicious enough, we soon discovered an additional unexpected element to this deed. At night, when the house was quiet and the moon was full, and the wind blew from the north, if you strained your ears, you could just hear the faint ghostly rattle of the jam jars, crying out in the darkness. We never understood how the breeze penetrated the dark and supposedly sealed corner of the house, but the evidence that it had was clear.

Downstairs, Mum was quietly humming an up-tempo song as she busied herself positioning the morning fare on the table. Dad came in. The chase with Morris had left him breathless, but had not taken the fight out of him. Pete took full advantage of this emotionally charged situation to further agitate Dad by asking what he did after he caught the dog. Dad was embarrassed to admit that once again the crazy pooch had evaded him, but saved some of his pride by declaring that the next time he saw the uninvited beast he would, without hesitation, shoot it. To make a point he loaded his old shotgun, and stood it in the hall underneath the coat rack next to the front door.

Mum was leaning over the stove making some final adjustments to our breakfast. The stove was a large gray box with a drop down front trap door that was probably an antique at the time when the electricity that it depended on was first discovered. It had been installed by a neighbor, and required the user to throw three separate switches around the house before it would work properly. A switch on the wall kept resetting with a popping noise, and so had to be manually held in place with one hand while the frying pan was stirred with the other.

We ate a hearty breakfast of bacon, eggs and fried bread, and Dad rolled another cigarette as he disappeared off to the bathroom to complete his morning ritual. The bathroom was accessed through the hallway, and had been a pantry when my parents first moved to the house. It was converted to a bathroom when Dad purchased a well used white enamel toilet bowl and bathtub from Bollington's auction room in order to exploit the more desirable aspects of indoor plumbing. The bathroom ensemble had seen a lot during its long service in a now demolished hotel room where it had resided until being acquired by Dad. An option to purchase six more just like it was ignored by my father, a decision I am sure he always regretted. It came complete with overhead cistern and an ornamental pull chain to start the floodwaters. Prior to this fabulous renovation, bath time would be a ritual performed on Friday nights, in an old galvanized tin tub in front of the fire.

He soon emerged, energized and ready for the day. He had his cough, another cigarette and glanced at the newspaper headlines before declaring that we would now venture forth to the barn in search of the old ground sheet.

Our house stood on the southeast corner of an ample property. When Mum and Dad first moved in, it was overgrown with trees, thick hedges and all manner of rare plants and shrubs that would scratch, sting, or otherwise assault the inexperienced explorer. Over the years they had been able to reclaim about a quarter of it but the rest remained untamed wilderness. Dad sometimes referred to this area as "the orchard," because we believed that somewhere within the unreachable interior were several fruit trees. On the south side of this elongated land parcel, a dangerously unsafe stone wall bordered and leaned out over the footpath beside the road waiting to ambush an unsuspecting traveler with lethal effectiveness.

To the west, following the road were a string of farm cottages including the Ricketson place, and beyond that the Pilchards and the

Norringtons. The great unknown wilderness ran behind their property and ended at the top of the hill close to Mrs. Snobbit's stone cottage.

To the north, bordering a field, low wooden fencing surrendered more of itself to the encroaching hedge with each passing year. This arrangement suited my father very well, as he was constantly recycling the fence timber to feed his various carpentry projects. Beyond the fence was a meadow gently sloping down to the stream at the far end. In the springtime lambs could be seen playfully springing around, and in winter the expanse of bright white snow was a joy to behold. It was one of the better views in the lane, which angered the Ricketsons, Pilchards and Norringtons since their view of it was blocked by the overgrown trees and bushes of the great unknown wilderness.

To the south over a low stone wall, cement capped and moss covered, was a farm building, desperately in need of demolition. Like Mr. and Mrs. Snaggins, who lived on the other side of the barn, we nervously awaited the day when it would collapse under its own weight, but unlike our neighbor we offered up a silent prayer each night that when the building finally fell, it would do so on Mrs. Snaggins's house, not ours.

Besides the house, there were two other permanent structures on the property, both of them were situated on the border between the garden and the uncharted wilderness beyond. One was the stone building that formed part of the lane wall and ran almost to the Ricketson house. This was El Paso. The other building was the dreaded Rat barn.

El Paso was composed of three sections. At one end was Pete's motorcycle toilet and at the other end were the remains of a crumbling stone shed that leaned out over Mud Lane in a manner that proved so threatening to passing traffic that the county council made us demolish it. This was accomplished with a farm tractor borrowed from Snaggins, and a length of chain. The roof came off easily and went on to become a chicken barn for Benito's dad, and the stone was stacked up behind Rat barn to become part of one of my father's future construction projects.

The center portion of the line of buildings was still used. There was not much room inside, it being filled with what Dad described as "his current project," and what Mum referred to as "Dad's clutter." Once upon a time, Dad kept the car in there, but the car gave up any chance of occupation after a wooden floor was installed over the dirt to aid in building a boat. Sadly, he ran out of wood halfway through the boat building project, which forced him to cannibalize the floor to complete part of the hull. Following the removal, unsuccessful maiden voyage and rapid sale of the boat, the building was left with a floor half covered in wooden boards, and half covered in dirt.

Like the windows, part of the roof, and many of the other components in this building, the floor was scrounged. In fact, this floor represented possibly Dad's greatest scrounging achievement owing to the size and complexity of the scrounged article.

In this case the ancient wooden floor was retrieved from the wreckage of a meeting hall that burned down in a nearby village. The few remaining good parts had been gathered up and brought home in sections in the back of Dad's vehicle, which at the time was a large van that had in it's previous incarnation been used to deliver pork pies. All that was required in order for the scrounged floor to be reconstructed to cover the uneven earth of El Paso was a few nails and half a bag of cement that Dad was able to scrounge from a building site opposite the pub.

Scrounging was one of my father's favorite hobbies, the only one that had continuity, as all of his other fads and flights of fancy came and went. Scrounging was like a religion to my father, and in support of it, he could deliver a lengthy dissertation on the efficiency of nature and how things are recycled indefinitely. His goal was to never throw anything away, and never have to buy anything. On the path to attaining his dream he would collect everything that he thought might at some point in the future be useful. He was living proof that one man's junk is another man's garbage. Above all, he was proud of his ability to scrounge and never missed an opportunity to boast about his skill.

If you were to compliment Dad on the nice job he did building a fence, instead of a modest nod of recognition, you would get, in far too much detail an explanation of the entire process, and it would always end in, "...and, every bit of wood was scrounged!"

If you were to inquire about the origin of the old window frame he was struggling to unload from the roof of the car, on its way to becoming the rear wall of a greenhouse, he would turn, straighten up with pride as if about to salute his country, and then you would be told, "I scrounged that from the rubbish tip on the Whimpton Road!"

By and large his scrounging efforts were highly successful, but sometimes they did not yield the desired success. These failures were hushed up and we all, with the exception of Pete, knew better than to mention them. A good example would be the garden seat.

Dad returned from Bollington's auction one day with two cast iron ornamental garden seat ends; all that was needed were four planks of wood to complete the seating and back rest surfaces. It was amazing to us that he had no suitable wood in his extensive collection, but good luck prevailed when Dad was able to scrounge wood of perfect size and strength from the local rubbish tip. The planks had the insignia of the national railway company stamped on them and had been treated with Creosote, but Dad was able to mask both of these design distractions with a good thick coat of glossy green paint. The project was completed and the garden seat was placed under the apple tree facing the fields behind the house.

Creosote is a sticky tar-like substance that is used to preserve wood. My father was a great fan of the stuff, and used it liberally to protect the rotting walls of rat barn. The one problem is that it never really seemed to dry. In winter it was fine, and as Dad proved, could be easily covered by paint, but in summer the black sticky substance would liquefy and ooze out of the wood breaking up the painted surface and creating a filth hazard for anyone who strayed within its proximity. Mrs. Leecham was the first to discover this black messy booby trap and despite her friendship with mother, had never really forgiven Dad for the destruction of her "church" dress. Dad explained his failure to the rest of us by claiming that the seat was for "ornamental purposes only," and was never intended for normal use. Much to Dad's consternation, Pete immediately christened it as "The seat that no one dare sit on," a name that was quickly adopted by all except Dad.

Dad thought that the canvas sheet was in Rat barn – a large, wooden construction that was set back on the very edge of the civilized portion of our land. We walked up the gravel path that led from the front door to the garden gate, depressed by the thought of entering this terrible place. As we approached the end of the path next to Dad's workshop, he stopped and gazed at the well, obviously deep in thought. This bothered me because the last time I saw this look, Dad was planning a well cleaning project.

Ever since plumbing had been introduced to Mud Lane, the well had been used as Dad's private little rubbish tip, but one day driven by boredom and the need to punish me for some imaginary crime, he decided that we would clean it out and return it to its original condition and purpose. Pete, of course vanished quickly and mysteriously, leaving me to be lowered into the dark abyss on the end of a rope. Dad sat on the grass in the sunlight and smoked cigarettes while I dug my way through the layers of abandoned junk like an archeologist excavating his way through time. As I began tracing the past by probing older and older layers of the forsaken scrap, I soon found that the upper layers were not only the easiest to clear, but also the freshest in my memory. After two hours, I found the handlebars from my first bicycle, at three hours I was retrieving items I remember from the time when I was just starting school, four hours and I had some old window frame unearthed that I could just barely locate on the fuzzy edges of my memory. Each time I had to remove the lifeline from my waist to send up an antique oil drum or part of a car engine I crouched alone in the damp and silent darkness, trembling and praying for the frightful ordeal to end. It was a dreadful day and I seriously considered that if Dad was planning a repeat episode I would run away from home.

"Now," he paused, with a finger in the air, "upon reflection I think the sheet is in El Paso."

Relief flooded over me. This was a double bonus. I had escaped the dark terror of both the well and rat barn.

Pete and I were overjoyed by this redirection. El Paso had electricity. It was also relatively clean and tidy which made locating things far easier than digging through the filthy black hell of rat barn. During the time since my family first began to occupy this location, El Paso had been a garage, workshop, rabbit factory, boat building chamber, and now, of course, a tobacco mill.

The latch to one of the two full height doors was lifted, and we knew to jump backwards quickly as the door swung outwards. The staggering smell of tobacco betrayed the buildings current utilization as a drying location for Dad's harvest.

My father was very fond of cigarettes; he seemed to delight in the pleasure of lighting one up and inhaling deeply, lost in the moment – the coughing, shortness of breath and addictive cravings momentarily forgotten. His interest in the subject extended not only to rolling his own cigarettes, but also to collecting pipes and, lately, growing his own tobacco. For some time now he had been trying to grow tobacco plants in the back garden between the greenhouse and the old apple tree, an area formally reserved for green beans. We all objected to the change because our love of green beans far exceeded our desire to smoke Dad's homegrown weed. At the end of the summer he had picked the leaves and they were hung in the center of El Paso to dry. This plan, however, did not result in the plants gaining the desired flexible leather-like quality of a good tobacco leaf. The damp English weather had proved entirely unsuitable for seasoning the inflammable crop, and some of the thin brown vegetation had already started to develop small white spots of mold. We were all waiting anxiously to see if Dad would throw these away or try and smoke them out of determination and desperation. Whether my father realized it or not, it was obvious that an alternative drying method would be needed if this project was to succeed.

We turned on the light and saw bunches of the brown leaves hanging from the roof. Pete said it looked like a cave full of bats. Dad took a moment to rub a sample of one of the leaves lightly between his thumb and forefinger, emulating an expert on the subject, and then with a satisfied nod, he moved on.

"Your tobacco looks a bit moldy, Dad." said Pete, deciding that if he had to spend the morning working at this unpleasant task he was going to make the most of it.

"It's not moldy," Dad retorted, refusing to admit failure and ignoring the obvious.

"Is it supposed to go rotten then?" Pete persisted.

"It's not rotten, it's just maturing nicely." To prove his point Dad began trying to unsuccessfully remove some of the white growth with his thumbnail.

"I bet you end up having to throw it all away," said Pete in a final statement.

"No I won't," Dad protested. His jaw was clenched now, and by the way Pete rolled his eyes I sensed they both knew that today's debate over tobacco maturity was over.

The hanging leaves occupied the center portion of the room and so the only available storage was the ramshackle shelving and the floor below it. We began our circumnavigation, passing a shelf containing pieces of a car exhaust system, a pair of roller skates with missing wheels, and a broken telescope. Beside the shelf, hanging on the wall was a rusty bicycle frame and under that was a sewing machine. The sewing machine probably didn't work, or my Mum would no doubt be using it, but the sight of it prompted Dad to point out an empty apple crate in the corner under the leaky fire hose, and instruct Pete to start a Bollington's box. Pete reluctantly complied, and the roller skates were placed into the container.

"Keep those on top for a fly catcher!" Dad said with authority.

Over half of Dad's possessions either came from Bollington's auction house or would eventually end up there. Dad's marketing approach for this junk had improved over the years and he now had an infallible presentation system. The box would be listed as "miscellaneous sundries." This gave no clue to the contents and allowed it to be filled with useless broken rubbish. On top of the heap would be placed something of value, which was intended to capture the attention of a potential bargain hunter and imply that there were more goodies underneath. Dad called this item a "fly catcher."

An expert in auction room group psychology, Dad explained that there was always one person in the crowd who, after spying the "fly catcher" would not be able to pass over this mystery collection. Ironically, that person in the crowd was usually Dad.

Throwing a length of iron chain in the crate, Dad urged us to continue on past a World war II German infantry coat hanging over a rusty tin bath full of lime green paint cans. When we reached the coiled ropes, backpack and mountain climbing equipment, we felt sure we were very close to finding the sheet. Instead we found only a partial set of three worn out dining room chairs that Dad never finished refurbishing.

"Do you have anything here we can use to build a Guy?" I asked. It was a reasonable question given the array of items before us. Pete agreed.

"Like what?" Dad asked, looking for a more specific request.

"Like old clothes and something to stuff it with." I felt that the explanation was unnecessary – Dad knew very well what a Guy was.

"I'm more interested in finding the sheet for Rodger Pilchard at the moment." He said with finality.

We continued on past some more worthless broken items and Dad pointed to a black rubber mask hanging on the wall.

"You can have that gas mask if you like," he offered chuckling. The gas mask had been brought home in a box with four others, one day when Dad returned from the ex-government shop, another one of his favorite haunts. I didn't really see the need for them, the war had been over for more than twenty years, the Rolonzios seldom attacked with poison gas, and I didn't think the masks would protect against the toxic effects of wood smoke if Dad ever decided to jump into another fire during a hornet evasion exercise.

After searching the back corner where the tent and camping supplies were stored, and finding no trace of the groundsheet, we gave up and stepped back out onto the gravel driveway, defeated. The search of El Paso had proved fruitless.

"Have we finished now?" asked Pete.

Dad didn't reply, he just picked up the Bollingtons box and put it in the boot of the car.

"I think we've finished," I said hopefully.

"I'll go and tell Mr. Pilchard that we can't find it then," volunteered Pete.

"No, we've not finished," said Dad, retrieving a length of vacuum cleaner hose from an old cardboard box near the door, and picking up a dusty jam jar half full of oil he said, "Son, get your motorbike out."

Pete knew that this was not what it seemed.

"I don't think I have any petrol," Pete said, praying that his objection would end this fruitless search.

"Well get the bike out anyway and let's see," responded Dad, wise to Pete's numerous tricks.

So this is what it had come to. There was to be no escape. We had no choice but to endure the torture of searching the rat barn.

Surprisingly enough the barn stood unsupported, although we all knew it would not take much effort to reduce it to firewood. In the front there was an overhang that provided protection from foul weather. It also supported a child's swing with a broken seat, long since abandoned in search of more exciting diversions. A pile of logs higher than Dad lined one side of the open area and on the other side, a saw bench waiting to receive them stood on a thick carpet of yellow sawdust. Beside this was a rain barrel full to the brim with cold English rain that was constantly replenished from a dilapidated guttering system.

Pete leaned his motorbike against the saw bench and Dad, opening the filling cap to the petrol tank, poured some extra oil into the two-stroke petrol mix.

"Shake that up a bit," he instructed Pete and my brother straddled the bike and shook it from side to side. Next, Dad uncoiled the unusually long vacuum cleaner hose. It was actually two hoses taped together end to end to provide the necessary length.

I heard the sound of running feet on gravel and turned to see Brian and Ryan Pilchard approaching, breathless and excited. Both the boys had catapults in their hands. As they reached us, Brian anxiously asked, "Mrs. Snobbit said you're going into rat barn — is it true?"

"Yes," came my depressing answer.

"Great," said Ryan, and ran over to climb a nearby ash tree in order to obtain a good viewing position.

Brian climbed onto Dad's saw bench and removed his catapult.

"Get down from there," instructed my father, "that's dangerous."

Brian clambered down from the steel workbench mumbling that it was not as dangerous as staying on the ground.

Dad stuffed several inches of the flexible hose underneath the gap beneath the barn door and the ground and spread the rest out in the direction of the saw bench and Pete's bike.

"Are you going into rat barn?" asked Benito who had appeared carrying Crumb Carrington's brother's air rifle.

"Yes," I replied. "Who told you?"

"Mrs. Snaggins," he replied.

Even without the benefit of gossip spreaders like the postman and paperboy, word had obviously spread quickly up and down the lane. I could already see Squeaky Norrington running down the hill towards us.

Benito attempted to take up a sniper's position on the saw bench, and again my father issued strong words of discouragement.

Everyone was now at a safe distance with Ryan up the tree, Brian crouched on the broken swing seat and Benito on the pile of logs next to the saw bench. Dad continued his work, attaching the other end of the hose to Pete's bike by pushing it firmly over what remained of the exhaust pipe.

"Start her up, boy," he instructed, and Pete kick-started the bike into life. It was less noisy than usual, but it was still able to drown out nearby conversation. After a few moments, Dad, who had been staring at the barn door near the hose entry point, switched his stare to Pete and made a twisting motion with his right hand. Pete understood and revved the motorcycle.

Benito and Brian stood ready with their weapons loaded as the first few wisps of smoke emerged from beneath the barn door. The fumes were heady and thick and colored blue from the additional oil in the fuel. As the barn filled up, the escaping smoke that leaked out was noticeably more concentrated. It thickened even more as the first rat appeared. It was a big one too, dark brown and fat. It came out from the gap under the door and ran directly toward Brian on the swing. Brian panicked, frozen in fear by the approaching creature. Benito however, was not being threatened by the oversized rodent and was able to squeeze of a shot with the air gun. He missed the rat, the shot coming dangerously close to Brian. Ryan's catapult shot came next. It also missed the intended target but connected with his brother's left arm, Brian's cry of concern, already in progress from the air gun's near miss, was now converted into a cry of pain as the small pebble fired by Ryan hit him above the elbow.

Squeaky arrived, excited and breathless. He was unnerved by the battle that was already underway and maintained a safe distance on the outer periphery of the action.

One more rat escaped into the Ricketson's back garden while everyone was reloading, and then two more came out side by side and evaded the attackers to take up refuge in the tobacco plantation opposite.

The smoke continued to billow from beneath the wooden door for the next several minutes, during which time we saw three more rats, all of which avoided harm and disappeared into the uncharted wilderness.

In due course Dad decided that the operation was a success and Pete turned the bike off while Dad and I opened the two large double barn doors to allow the fumes to clear. The assembled rat posse, disappointed with the morning's poor shooting efforts, left in a sad procession.

CHAPTER 4

AN UNWILLING PASSENGER

By the time we returned, the air in the rat barn had cleared quite well revealing piles of useless junk. Dad appeared to have made it his mission in life to fill up the barn gradually, starting from the back, using every bit of pointless debris, refuse and litter he could find. He was doing an excellent job and I predicted that his work would be complete within two or three years. The useful high quality articles that we saw in El Paso were nowhere to be found here. On top of the woodworm filled shelving system had been placed racks of jam jars and paint cans, brown iron chains and bald tires. On the dirt floor were collections of worthless wares that I don't think even Bollingtons would want.

We stepped inside, and began moving stuff around in the hope that the elusive canvas would be revealed. Clouds of dust filled the air mixing with the remains of engine fumes and we immediately began to cough, but at Dad's urging, we pressed on. Beneath one precariously built shelf, balanced on two bricks was a cracked enamel kitchen sink, which deprived someone of saying that this place had everything except one. Lying in the basin of the sink was a wire framed steel rat-trap that looked as if it could have found useful employment here.

A pair of bullhorns, one of which had the tip removed in the fashion of a primitive musical instrument sat on the shelf above the sink, and called to Pete in a voice only he could hear. After examining this article for a few seconds, Pete suggested that I try and play it. Rising to the challenge, I took a deep breath, placed it to my lips and immediately removed it to spit out the oil that the mouthpiece had been lying in and which now covered my mouth. Pete, of course, knowing about the oil beforehand, thought this a hilarious joke and began to laugh.

"You boys stop messing around now, and help," Dad ordered.

"What do you want us to do?" asked Pete.

"Look for the canvas sheet," said Dad losing his patience.

"What does it look like?" asked Pete.

"You know what it looks like," replied Dad.

"What if Mum threw it away?" Pete suggested.

"She didn't," defended Dad.

"How do you know?" Persisted Pete.

"She didn't," repeated Dad in a louder voice than I felt was necessary.

"Remember she threw your favorite hat away?" Said Pete in a parting shot, designed to evoke unpleasant recollections from Dad.

I had seen Pete sport with my father in this manner for hours, and there was no way I could predict how long it would go on. The answer came from my father.

"Stop wasting time. No more questions. Find the sheet."

Dad pointed into the gloom toward the back, at the highest pile. "We need to start there."

Pete rolled his eyes at me as we formed a human chain with Dad at the front, dismantling the heap piece by dirty piece. He would hand the removed items to Pete and Pete would hand them to me. My job was to throw each piece onto a relatively clear part of the floor. A broken table lamp, old paint cans, and ancient kitchen cabinet supporting half a bag of cement that had now solidified into uselessness. On and on we toiled.

About one third of the way down we took momentary relief from the torture, and went outside into the fresh air to recuperate. Dad rested on the edge of the sawbench and Pete and I fought over the right to sit on the swing. Dad was quietly staring into the one of the back corners of the barn at a cream colored steel box with a flat silver lid. It was about the size of a small stove and originally had four small wheels, now there were only two. Dad walked over and began to struggle with it. First he tried to wheel it outside, but the missing wheels made this impossible. Next he tried to rock it from side to side and gradually "walk" it out but one corner dug into the dirt and he fell over. He then walked off grumbling, leaving my brother and I to speculate on its purpose.

After a minute, we heard Dad returning, his measured tread accompanied by a rapid squeaking noise, and he appeared from behind a bushy tree pushing a sack barrow. Like many of Dad's possessions, it had been constructed from recycled materials. In this case the component parts were a heavily modified broken office chair and a set of wheels whose origin was hard to discern. He wheeled this contraption over the dirt floor toward the metal box. As he toiled, Dad explained that the device was a very rare antique. The top could be removed to expose a rack on which wet clothes could be hung. Then some kind of heating system in the base would dry the clothes. I asked what he was going to do with it and Dad said that it did not work and he would probably discard it next time he went to the Tip.

The Tip was short for rubbish tip, and was a common area on the outskirts of the village where the local inhabitants dumped all the stuff that they no longer needed or were unable to sell. I think we could have put the entire contents of this barn in the Tip and no one would have taken any of it.

Despite this, Dad had still been able to use the Tip as a source of materials to fill up multiple Bollington boxes over the years. Dad's ambition was to find something at the Tip, totally free and sell it at Bollingtons for good money. Unfortunately his acquired items usually made this trip in the reverse order, being purchased from Bollingtons for more than they were worth, lacking in functionality for their intended use and deposited at the Tip.

During the break, Dad sat down on an old cracked toilet bowl he had dragged outside. He lit a cigarette to really clear his lungs and began to examine a piece of broken wood on a loop of string that seemed to hold some special fascination for him. Meanwhile, Pete remained inside having found something of interest. He had discovered a long gray canvas bag and was looking inside, "Wow!" he exclaimed with melodramatic thrill, "look at this."

I rushed over as he extended the open bag for my observation. Inside were the brushes that Dad used to sweep the chimney, black with dusty soot, and at the moment I saw them I realized I had been had. Pete banged the loose bag with the flat of his hand sending a billow of powdery black clouds directly into my face. As I ran outside to stick my head in the water barrel, Pete laughed hysterically.

This was actually a good thing, because if he had not engaged himself in this wickedness, he would not have triggered a series of events that would eventually reveal the elusive sheet of canvas. As Pete started laughing he momentarily lost his balance and stumbled backwards kicking over the old oil lamp that was obscuring the very edge of a pale green canvas tarpaulin. Our joy at finding the groundsheet was overshadowed by the despair of realizing that it was at the bottom of a different pile of garbage.

We applied ourselves to this latest assignment with renewed enthusiasm, but this wore off quickly when we found a long smooth piece of wood that used to be one upright half of a six foot ladder. It was wedged horizontally, straight through the middle of the pile, binding the heap together and discouraging its deconstruction. Dad wrestled with it for about a minute before angrily volunteering me to hold up one end of it while he untangled the unraveled roll of chicken wire that was trapping it in place. Dad's end suddenly came free, which surprised both of us. With little concern for me he casually pushed it aside and continued his digging. That left me standing like a pole-vaulter, holding the ladder shaft level with the ground, trying to gracefully divest myself of this awkward encumbrance. I lost the struggle along with my equilibrium and the other end of the pole knocked over a biscuit tin that was perched unsteadily on top of an old car radiator. We should not have been surprised that the contents were not the as advertised shortbread treats but instead a collection of old bent rusty nails, which were now scattered over the dirt floor. The mess I created was not really noticeable amid the rest of the disorder so I didn't bother cleaning it up. Instead, I backed away to join Pete, who was amusing himself watching Dad lose his temper with the chicken wire.

Dad grappled with the pile like a man possessed by some evil spirit, growling under his breath, throwing stuff around wildly. Finally when it all got too much for him, he stopped and yelled at us to help him with a new plan.

The canvas was taunting us from beneath a bent and discolored bed frame, which was piled high with about another forty-five minutes of difficult, dirty and dangerous work. Dad grabbed the small visible corner of the tarp, and instructed us to do the same. We kneeled down next to him, and immediately screamed with pain as the old nails that I had spilled dug into our knees.

We all pulled together. Grunting and sweating and straining we managed to move it about an inch. Then the avalanche started and we were forced to jump out of the way to avoid being buried alive. We stood aside and again waited for the dust to settle.

Mum appeared and said cheerily,

"How are you getting on out here?" She then looked around witnessing the carnage, started to say something, thought better of it, and left.

No one could go on. Dad sat back down on the toilet bowl to catch his breath; Pete suggested that we lie to Rodger Pilchard and say that the search proved fruitless. I agreed.

Instead of answering, Dad got up and looked around the barn, scratching his head for a few minutes and then walked away. He returned several minutes later carrying a car-jack and a length of rope as he walked purposefully over to the ground sheet burial mound. He placed the car-jack under one corner of the bed frame and turned the handle until it lifted off of our prize. He then threaded the rope through one of the brass eyelets round the edge of the sheet and stepped away from the pile. Again, he motioned for us to join him and together, using all the remaining strength we had, we tugged the old sheet free, and collapsed in exhaustion.

Dad carried the canvas out into the sunlight and shook it open for inspection. It was dusty and looked well worn in places. There was some white paint spilled on one side and three of the eyelets were missing, but it looked intact and was deemed suitable for Rodger's purpose.

The subject of our frustration was folded and thrown on the floor beside the door, and I was given strict instructions to deliver it to the Pilchard residence at the earliest possible opportunity.

Pete commented that he thought it extremely fair if we suggested to Rodger that we were expecting to be compensated for all our trouble, especially since Guy Fawkes Night was approaching, and we would be in need of fireworks. Dad insisted that we would do no such thing, that this was just part of being a good neighbor, and adding that he felt sure Rodger would do the same for us. But he was unable to convince Pete, and so gave up trying.

When we went back in the house Mum had a cup of tea ready, hot and sweet. We drank it in subdued tiredness and ate biscuits which helped to restore our enthusiasm for life. We then took turns bathing our soiled and aching bodies in hot soapy water. I was not at all happy at having to bathe unnecessarily. Friday was bath night and anyway, I was satisfied that my dunk in the water barrel outside rat barn had been quite a successful cleansing operation, not to mention refreshing. I think that I may have been able to convince my mother of the need to postpone the bath one more day had it not been for the scheduled trip to visit Granny this afternoon.

Granny was Mum's Mum and so named to differentiate her from Dad's Mum, who was always referred to as grandmother. We would have to perform this Granny visiting duty each Saturday afternoon driving over to her small two bedroom terraced house in the center of a nearby market town. Because we combined the tedious duty with a shopping expedition for some necessary supplies, the entire trip would take several hours and eat up most of our Saturday.

We ate an early lunch, during which Dad once again broached the subject of Pete's hair.

"During our trip to the town today, you must get a haircut."

Pete said nothing, but continued to shovel green beans into his mouth.

"You must get a haircut today," Dad repeated. The word "must" was emphasized and spoken slowly.

"I don't need one yet," said Pete, casually continuing his assault on his vegetables.

"Yes, you do," insisted Dad.

Mum knew better than to get involved. She had previously argued that the best footballers had short hair but Pete, having much more information on the subject was able to refer to a picture of a popular footballer with a mop of long black hair. Mum tried again about a month later with the same argument but this time substituting motorcycle riders for footballers. Pete, referring again to photographic proof in one of his magazines destroyed the argument quickly thanks to a trendy Italian rider. Sadly for Mum this also gave additional weight to Pete's desire for a leather jacket.

Dad once again issued his demand, "You WILL get a haircut today."

Pete grunted.

"What did I just say?" asked Dad glaring at Pete.

"OK," said Pete, "I'll get one." Then in barely a whisper he added, "even though I don't need it."

This caused something in my father to snap and Pete was sent to eat alone in the cold hall balancing his plate on his lap.

We finished lunch and closing the door behind us set off up the path toward the waiting car. After a few steps, Pete again fell into his parental agitator roll, behavior that came very easily to him because of his obstinate and contrary nature. He could always be relied on to adopt an opposing viewpoint on almost any subject or opinion.

"I think I'll ride my motorbike today instead," Pete said casually.

Dad had been expecting this moment ever since the trip had been announced, and in an equally casual tone, he replied, "You're going, like it or not."

But Pete, having been reminded that attending this excursion was not optional, was not giving up so easily.

"But I don't feel well," moaned Pete, with a practiced painful expression, and bending forward slightly held his stomach with both hands.

Dad insisted that Pete would feel much better if he got in the car and much worse if he did not!

A sudden spark of inspiration jumped into my brothers eyes.

"What if I'm sick in the car?" Pete asked.

"We'll use Granny's garden hose to clean you, and then you can clean the car," was Dad's ultimatum.

Temporarily forgetting about his imaginary illness, Pete suggested that we go to a different town, one that had some nice sewing shops that Mum would enjoy. This latest attempt to solicit maternal support fell on deaf ears.

Dad had now finished the negotiating process and was taking direct action. He took a few angry strides toward Pete, who quickly stood up, agreeing that he would without further ado, come with us. Unfortunately, this time Pete had misjudged my father's capacity for reason and it was too late to resolve this conflict peacefully.

Dad did not slow his approach. Instead he circled round behind Pete and shoved him in the general direction of the unoccupied car seat. Pete pretended to trip but he could see that Dad was in no mood for this so he once again trudged silently and slowly to join the rest of us. Dad assisted him with another shove and then grabbing Pete's elbow firmly, threw him into the empty brown vinyl seat next to me.

An expression of contentment flooded Pete's face, now that he had succeeded in angering my father, whose reflection was frowning in the rear-view mirror as we set off down Mud Lane. Mum tried to make some polite conversation about how nice the ivy looked this year, and how she hoped Mrs. Snobbit's leg was better, but Pete tried to begin another dev-ilish game, this time with my mother.

"I don't want to go to Granny's," said Pete.

"Well, we have to," Mum replied.

"Do you want to go?" he asked me.

"No," I said.

"Do you want to go, Mum?" he asked trying to gather a groundswell of support for his cause.

"No I don't," she said, "but it's just something we have to do."

"Why?" he asked.

In an effort to end the debate Mum said,

"Look, we'll go see her, have a cup of tea and then we'll leave."

Pete had lost the battle, and was determined to sulk about it. He sank lower in his seat and stared out of the window, frowning at the passing scenery.

The trip took us along narrow, winding country roads through two other small villages, and after several miles Dad loosened up and became cheerful and easy going again. Sadly this amicable frame of mind was short-lived because while Dad was cooling down, Pete was getting bored, and Pete was living proof of my mother's constant warning that "the devil finds work for idle hands to do."

Neither Mum nor Dad had a driver's license. They both learned to drive before any regulation or proficiency test was required, so we had no proof that they were actually any good at operating motor vehicles. It is true that they had never been involved in an accident but that may have been just a matter of luck. Mum seemed fairly capable behind the wheel, but Dad felt that her abilities deteriorated during the spring when the flowers began to bloom and her attention was distracted. On the other hand, Dad considered himself an expert at handling an automobile and cited several jobs he had taken as a professional driver as proof. Personally, I thought that his skills in this area were adequate as long as all went well.

Traveling with my father was always an adventure. He planned any trip according to a strict schedule worked out beforehand. It involved an extended session on his throne, with a map, notebook and pencil. He would calculate how long the trip should take and where he needed to be at any given time. He would take into account the time of day, traffic patterns and weather conditions, all of which resulted in the calculation of a start time for the mission. As long as he was on schedule everything would be fine, but if we slipped behind due to events not factored into Dad's equation, he would begin to drive faster and take more chances. The most entertaining journeys occurred when we were off between three and eight minutes. Any more than that and things started to get frightening.

Dad always drove vehicles of questionable mechanical reliability, and because of this he was overly sensitive to abnormal bumps and rattles that might be emitted from his less than dependable transportation. This particular car had a more unique collection of audible anomalies than any other vehicle we had owned, including the Pork Pie van. The left rear suspension made a knocking sound whenever we went round a corner, the brakes squealed if applied too quickly and the engine made a whining sound until it was warm. Once on a straight road most of these noises disappeared, but the constant wind noise coming from the passenger window that made Mum sound like she was permanently hissing, continued to annoy Dad. It was probably the most annoying thing in the car, besides Pete.

Typically, we would be traveling along peacefully, Dad would be happy and all would be going well. Then Pete would begin to imitate a mechanical problem with the car. Sometimes he would tap something metallic on the exposed metal of the door or click the door handle rapidly. Once when we were traveling to Yarmouth on holiday he tapped his penknife on the ashtray lid for nearly ten miles and almost gave Dad a nervous breakdown. Pete once explained to me that in order for the trick to be successful, the artificially generated sound must be rhythmic, and approximate the road speed or engine revs. Pete was very good at this since he possessed a good understanding of the inner functioning of engines.

This time he began to tap his foot on the floorboards as if listening to a pop song. He started this dull thud just as Dad pulled away from a stop sign, and gradually increased the tempo as the car got faster. Dad, alarmed, began looking anxiously around the car. His neck jerked and he looked in the direction of the gearbox, a second later he snapped his head around to look down at the pedals on the floor. This frantic search of the vehicle's interior continued as he tried to locate the source of the sound. Failing to identify the problem he slowed down, whereupon Pete's tapping slowed. Dad slowed even more, and so did Pete. The car was now stationary.

"What the...?" Dad cried out. In a flash he was down on his hands and knees looking under the car for an explanation. Finding none he stood up and thoughtfully rubbed his jaw.

Dad belonged to a generation that took pride in their appearance and would not make a visit to town without dressing accordingly. This meant clean, pressed trousers and a freshly washed shirt, but now standing beside the car we could all see a very serious stain on the right knee of his gray flannel trousers – One result of him kneeling down and crawling halfway underneath the vehicle to inspect the supposed faulty underside. We knew it was only a matter of time before he saw it and, that he would not be happy when he did.

He looked toward the heavens as if to assign blame and silently mouthed several words that I am glad Mum could not hear. He climbed back in the car to complain to us, whereupon we adopted expressions to indicate the appropriate degree of horror, and this made him feel better. What he did not know was that the horror we displayed was not for the soiled trousers, but for the large black oil stain down the back of his formerly clean white shirt. We should have probably said something to him but nobody was brave enough. Not even Pete.

Dad wiped away at the contaminated cloth over his knee with the only thing he could find, which was the rag used to clean grime off the window. This made the stain worse and only added to his rage. Feeling like he owed us an explanation, he mumbled that something might have been caught up underneath the car, which had now fallen off. Checking his watch against his handwritten schedule, he made a "Bahhhhhh" sound, and putting the car in gear, pulled briskly back onto the road, narrowly missing an old lady on a bicycle.

As our speed increased, the mysterious thumping returned, quietly at first, and then louder. Panicked now, Dad stopped suddenly and the brakes shrieked. This took Pete completely by surprise and he tapped once too often.

Dad turned slowly. His face was red and his eyes were the size of dinner plates. He spoke very slowly through a mouth that barely moved.

"Was...that...you?"

Everyone heard Pete swallow a nervous swallow, and he just nodded.

Normally, during a car trip, Pete's irritating exploits would excite my father until he'd shout, "Don't you make me stop this car, boy!"

When we heard these words alarm bells would go off. It meant that Dad was close to the breaking point and all future attempts to provoke him must stop immediately. But the car was already stopped, which deprived Pete of his early warning system, and Dad was already getting out of the car and heading for Pete, who immediately locked his door.

Dad reached into the car through his front door, and deftly unlocked Pete's. With one fluid movement he opened the back door and extracted my distressed sibling. Given the difficulty we had getting Pete into the car, I was surprised by the ease with which he came out. He was dragged up the road just out of earshot, and he and Dad had one of their "little talks." When Pete returned he was silent, even thoughtful, and would neither look at, nor speak to any of us for several miles. I had strained my ears to hear what was said during their heated exchange, but all I could make out was Dad saying something about "...and they'll never find your body down that well...."

Our schedule had now been thrown off by several minutes, which meant that we were in for a death defying white-knuckle ride. Mum and I were as silent as Pete, as Dad pushed the old car to the limits of its design capabilities. We overtook a milk van, just before going straight through a crossroads without stopping and almost ran over three nuns as they tried to cross the road.

Dad always believed that it was better to be a little late in this world than a lot earlier in the next, but he was now finding it hard to follow this highway creed. A tight left-hand bend on two wheels, and two amber traffic lights later and we were back on schedule.

By now the additional traffic brought out by market day provided a pleasant diversion for all of us and thanks to Dad's unorthodox driving style, we arrived at Granny's house a few minutes early. This was good, because a beer delivery truck was occupying the parking spot outside her house, and we used up our time credit, to locate a spot in front of the corner shop, run by a Pakistani family that was well known for selling stale chocolate bars.

At Granny's front door Mum twisted the metal mechanical bell and Granny, wearing her coat and hat, immediately opened it. She carried a brown glass bottle with a colorful label matching the insignia of a local brewery. Swallowing the last mouthful of brown ale she placed the empty bottle on the hall table, and looked at her watch impatiently.

CHAPTER 5
A VISIT TO GRANNY

"I thought you'd never get here," said granny who always answered the door with indignant criticism about our tardiness. She did not always have a bottle in her hand but it would not be far away. She would want to leave immediately, but Mum would talk her into delaying the shopping excursion until we had at least been refreshed with a cup of tea and some biscuits.

She lived on a street of terraced houses, each adjoining the other, and each a carbon copy of the adjacent property. Granny's house was distinguished only by a blue front door that would not be repeated for another five houses. From the street the houses would represent a continuous repeated sequence of doors and windows embedded in unbroken red brick, and crowned with a single sheet of gray slate tile, property demarcation was by evenly spaced chimneys, each emitting wisps of coal smoke. This was the working class neighborhood of a busy factory town.

Granny's house was dimly lit, smelled of mothballs and was full of old paraphernalia that she referred to as antiques, but to Pete and I it looked like the ingredients of a typical Bollington's sale. Downstairs a living room and dining room had been converted to one larger room, by a distant uncle with only mediocre construction skills. This room overlooked the street, and housed the television set, birdcage and Granny's prized collectibles.

A lean-to kitchen on the back wall was home to the cooking effects, and a door led to a steep flight of stairs to a coal cellar, dark and dirty, which, for obvious reasons, Pete and I were never given access too.

Granny was the oldest person we knew except for Grizzly McKenzie, the mad Irishman who lived at the bottom of Mud Lane. Granny had never been sick a day in her life, which was remarkable considering that she ate and drank some of the most detrimental substances known to man. Her diet consisted of the cheapest lumps of gristly fat she could find, along with anything else that happened to be either on sale or waiting to be thrown away at the local butcher's shop. This mix would usually be fried up in a single pan and would acquire its flavor from whatever the cooking grease was last used for, which might range anywhere from pancakes to kippers. Dessert would always be something sticky, rich in all the substances that the world's smartest doctors told us led to a short and problem filled life. Granny apparently neither knew nor cared about this.

She would drink beer, sherry, and most any other kind of alcohol, but favored the cheapest form of Irish whisky available. It smelled like a curious combination of the stuff that Dad used to clean his paintbrushes and the ointment which Mum would dab on our grazed knees after a bicycle crash.

Along with the drink, a deck of cards was her other standard issue equipment. A lace tablecloth over a side table served as the playing surface onto which she would constantly deal hands of cards. She could play every card game I had ever heard of and many I had not. On the rare occasions when I had spare change, I would bravely engage her in a game of what I foolishly thought to be chance. As I soon learned, Granny was able to shift the odds in her favor, by memorizing not only every card in the game, but also the order in which they were played. We would play out a hand and get down to the final moments, suspiciously eyeing each other with both of us holding only one remaining card. I would be holding something like the king of clubs, close and well guarded. I would feel fairly sure that it was unbeatable. Granny would be holding her solitary card face down, almost casually. I would be considering the best and most theatrical way of revealing my winning card, to produce a victorious conclusion to the contest. Then Granny would casually flip her ace face up.

"Let's see your king of clubs beat that." She'd say triumphantly.

During cold winter evenings my mother would often tell of memories she had as a child, involving her parents in 48-hour three card brag marathons. During these extended sessions where paychecks were gambled and lost in crowded smoke filled rooms, the deck would be changed every hour or so. This was because within that short period of time, the backs had picked up enough individuality in the forms of creases, marks and scratches from Uncle Doyle's "special" ring, that all present could look at the back and determine the face of each card at the time it was dealt.

Gambling was Granny's biggest hobby. She would bet on anything. She would take any wager, providing that she could successfully negotiate the odds.

I once saw her take a bet on the color of the hat of the next person to walk past her window, on a path outside that was busy with pedestrian traffic. She won. And Pete had to pay up.

In the morning Granny would get up as soon as she awoke – about five a.m. By six she would have finished consuming her grease soaked breakfast and would have started on the laundry, then she would do a little gardening before having lunch at ten. We arrived at about two in the afternoon, by which time she would be eager to complete the shopping jaunt and get home in time to have her tea, calculate her winnings from the racing and football results, and go to bed.

During our obligatory Saturday visit, Mum and Granny would exchange the latest gossip while Dad performed miscellaneous household maintenance. This part of the trip was not particularly necessary since Granny, despite her advanced years, was the most self-sufficient woman I had ever seen. Not only did she take exceedingly good care of her own affairs, but also those of her younger neighbors who lived on the same street. And she did voluntary work at the old people's home, the blind association, and she even helped out behind the bar at the working-men's club next to the Pakistani stale chocolate shop.

Besides the deck of cards and the glass of rotgut whiskey, Granny's only other companion was Joey. Joey was a blue-green budgie that resembled a baby parrot. Budgies were a popular pet among older people because they were readily available at almost any pet store, and because they ate only a few seeds a day, they were cheap to feed.

Joey was a noisy little bird. This annoyed most of us, but Granny, by carefully controlling the volume of her hearing aid managed to tolerate the fowl quite well. When she did decide to permit the squawks to shatter the peace and quiet of the small room, she insisted that she could understand the staccato avian language.

Joey would squawk loudly and Granny would look at him, nod her head vigorously, and with excited enthusiasm reply, "Yes...Yes!"

Another screech and Granny would look at Dad and say,

"Listen, Dad, he's talking to you," and then back at the bird, "Yes... Yes!"

Dad would look up with a mouth full of biscuit crumbs and nod politely and curtly towards Joey.

Joey lived in a chrome wire framed round topped cage supported by a single steel pole. A single span of round wood across the interior served as his perch. The choice of wood as a construction medium was probably an attempt to try and fool the bird into thinking it was a branch, thereby creating the illusion that he was living happily in the wild, inside a shiny steel tree. Joey shared the cage with Jimmy. Jimmy was about the same size as Joey and similar in color, but made of plastic with springs for legs. His feet would be snapped onto the perch, and he would sit there all day motionless, looking wistful, with eyes fixed upon some imaginary horizon. Occasionally Joey would do a little sideways shuffle along the perch to where Jimmy sat, and peck him viciously. Jimmy would sway back and forth on his spring legs but other than that, he would show no sign of interest in Joey. I think that both Joey and Granny were beginning to suspect that Jimmy was not a real bird.

Usually Joey would be allowed to enjoy the relative freedom of the room and flit around perching on any available surface. His favorite places being the side of Granny's card tray, where she would hand feed him seeds. He also enjoyed settling on the top of a picture frame that enclosed a replica of a painting called The Laughing Cavalier. Mum never failed to point out that the eyes in the picture would seem to follow us wherever we went in the room. Pete and I remarked that Granny's eyes did the same thing because she was so concerned that our antics would result in the destruction of one of her precious artifacts.

A short while later, we were on our way to the marketplace.

The first stop was a china and glassware shop that Mum loved to visit, Dad and Granny joined her inside to look at some of the expensive breakables, while Pete and I were ordered to remain outside. Of course Dad soon became bored and lighting a cigarette, suggested we walk a short way up the street to the Ex-Government Shop.

It was a wonderful place where one could purchase military surplus equipment at bargain prices. There were defused bombs, cartridge belts, binoculars, flare guns, camping equipment and all manner of fascinating items to capture our imagination. Upon hearing our excited voices the owner would appear, a jolly old lady whom we called "Mrs. Army." She knew us by name, and I got the feeling we were some of her favorite customers, probably because we contributed a sizable portion toward her rent each month.

Mrs. Army began to point out items that she thought would be of special interest to us. She took Dad over to a corner to show him some mountain climbing gear, but he had all the necessary equipment for that particular hobby and was now looking at an old short wave radio. Pete and I were left alone next to a rack containing an impressive selection of durable and practical clothing, most of it green or camouflaged. This is where Basher Middleton's brother Jonathan bought his parka.

Jonathan was a Mod. Most of the teenagers were divided into rival gangs called Mods and Rockers. Mods were picky about their appearance, paying close attention to their hair and their trendy clean suits. Rockers were picky about their motorcycles, and that seemed to be all. They were generally anti-social, and took great pride in looking dirty and scruffy. I had not taken sides yet, but thought that when the time came, I would probably favor the Rockers. There were two main reasons for this. The first is that my brother was a Rocker and I did not feel like fighting him every day over philosophical differences. As an added benefit, there were the motorbikes.

In sharp contrast to the motorcycles were the scooters, which were the favored transportation of the Mods. This was the other reason I wanted to be a Rocker.

Scooters were, in the opinion of my elder sibling, small imported Italian motorized death traps. The engines were enclosed behind tin panels, which both distracted from their beauty and made them sound rather too much like a hair dryer. The wheels were way too small and looked as if they belonged on some kind of child's toy.

Scooters were much slower than motorbikes, and you would think that this would make them safer, but quite the opposite was true. Pete had ridden one and commented that there was no engine between your legs and no fuel tank to wrap your body around, making balance and cornering difficult. In addition, instead of the footrests found on a real motorbike, there were pedals like those found in a car. Pete likened the riding position to sitting on a small chair balanced on a wheelbarrow traveling at sixty miles per hour. One of the problems with this form of conveyance was that when the warm dry Italian air, for which these inherently unstable machines were designed, was replaced with cold wet weather and icy roads, the dangers to the Mod were self evident. Damage to the body, and more importantly damage to the clothes were both problems to be overcome. Even if it were possible to reach the desired destination without falling off, the devastating winter elements could destroy that trendy suit. The fashionable solution to this problem was the parka.

The parka was a military issue waterproof canvas coat that was lined for warmth. It had a hood with a fur edge, a drawstring to keep out the cold and large pockets that could be used to store edged weapons and other anti-rocker apparatus. Some of the appeal of this garment certainly stemmed from the knowledge that it had perhaps seen battle, and on this point, Jonathan's parka excelled. In the back to the left of the coat's spine and level with its shoulder blades was a bullet hole! This made Jonathan the envy of all the local Mods.

On one occasion when the coat was draped over the seat of the unattended scooter, Benito and I, wrapped in awe and wonder examined it. I had never seen a bullet hole, but Benito's ancestors in his native Italy had seen and caused many, and it was his considered opinion that this garment's alleged damage was homemade. His theory being that the hole was produced by a screwdriver and something like a red felt pen had been employed to provide a convincing simulation of blood. But I wasn't interested in parkas today. I had found something of much greater interest.

For several weeks now I had joined Brian and Ryan Pilchard, in a thrilling, if not somewhat dangerous, amusement. The Pilchard boys had, it seemed, decided that if they were lucky enough to reach adulthood, they would both become professional parachutists. I was not sure that the workplace had a significant demand for this type of skill, but went along with their plan to begin training early.

The end of El Paso situated closest to the house provided a perfect setting for this self schooling because the wall, in its state of partial decay, provided jumping off points at various heights from two feet to about twelve feet. It was possible to start training at a very low altitude and gradually progress to the top. The landing site was either soft grass or mud, depending on recent weather conditions, so either way it guaranteed a soft landing. The parachutes were a Pilchard creation and consisted of an old white bed sheet that had been cut roughly square. At each corner and halfway along each side, twine had been tied through holes made in the cotton. The other end of each string was tied to an old leather belt.

The operation was simple. The belt was buckled around the waist, the sheet was gathered up in outstretched arms and the daredevil would assume a position at the appropriate spot on the wall. The correct technique was to throw the sheet high into the air as if launching a kite, and as it filled with wind, leap off the wall and drift safely to the grass below. The parachute was not very effective in ensuring the graceful descent we had all witnessed on television, but we all believed that it did slow our downward plunge enough to allow us to jump from a higher level than would normally be possible.

There were six steps or jumping positions on the old wall, spaced roughly every two feet. The graduations were marked accordingly using some chalk borrowed from one of the Rolonzios. Brian and I had both jumped from the six-foot mark. Ryan, being somewhat smaller had only progressed to the four-foot mark, but his confidence was building and we felt sure he would soon be ready to advance to the next level.

Pete and I looked at the treasure before us. The object lay between a box full of white shirts that proudly displayed a royal navy insignia and a rack of black leather boots, and would certainly allow all of us to attain the next level on the parachute wall. A handmade sign on yellow cardboard indicated that anyone willing to part with five shillings could be the proud owner of a real parachute. Beneath the sign was a stack of four or five tightly stuffed green canvas bags. I remarked to my brother that the product claiming to be a parachute did not look at all like any parachute I had seen on television. They were the wrong shape and not much larger than the bags directly across the aisle that claimed to contain gas masks. An elderly couple were currently scrutinizing these breathing aids, each with one firmly in place over their faces, while they inspected each other for leaks and general aesthetic appearance. I could not possibly imagine what disaster they were expecting, but they seemed to be satisfied that these would provide the appropriate degree of protection.

Pete pointed out that the bags in front of us were slightly larger than the gas mask bags and that the color was a darker green. I had to admit that he was right, but still maintained that they didn't look large enough to be parachutes. Pete lifted one from the pile and looked at it from all sides. He claimed that the only way to be sure was to inspect the contents and immediately popped open two studs that were holding it all together. The covering fell away in four sections to reveal a tightly packed ball of a thin white cloth from which protruded a flat piece of canvas webbing colored with a bright yellow "V" pattern. Pete interpreted this pattern to mean 'Pull me' and reached for the brightly colored tab.

Mrs. Army, who had moved on from the short wave radios and was now trying to interest Dad in a portable gas stove, looked over just in time to see Pete grabbing for the loose strap, and she panicked.

After that, everything seemed to happen in slow motion. The shop owner half turned and her right hand extended toward us, palm first, fingers upward. The portable cooker's instruction booklet she had been holding began to flutter to the ground and her jaw dropped open as she started to say something that started with "Don't..."

The remainder of her sentence was lost as a whooshing sound followed and an explosion of soft white fabric enveloped the gas mask shoppers who were standing behind us. The lady fell backwards in fright, collapsing into a large cardboard box full of camouflage netting. Trapped in the box, she flapped her arms and legs around wildly. The black rubber mask with its two round ocular portals, made her look like some huge inverted bug stranded upside down, unable to reorient herself. Meanwhile her husband was thrashing about savagely, beating the gentle soft mounds of silk in an attempt to escape. He appeared over the edge of the wrinkled cloth just long enough to scowl at Pete through two large fogged up lenses, and then tripped over a pile of brass four-inch shell casings which clattered loudly to the ground and rolled all over the store.

It was now obvious that the package did indeed contain a parachute, and that it was deployed by means of some spring loaded mechanism. We tried to ignore the commotion being caused by the irate elderly couple as the man tried to help his wife to her feet, and concentrated on examining this new discovery.

We could tell now that it was much smaller than the full-size canopy that we were expecting, and was not that much larger than the Pilchard's bed sheet, but it was round, and properly dome shaped with many more strings, and it looked perfect for my needs. The size wasn't a problem. I was not that heavy, and planned to jump only a few feet, not a few thousand. The harness was disappointing though, consisting only of a wide canvas strap in a loop, but I imagined that it would fit comfortably round my chest and under my arms, and represent a notable improvement over the Pilchard leather belt design.

I truly followed in my father's footsteps, when it came to understanding the importance of having all the right equipment for the job. Dad threw himself into every hobby he had with irrepressible enthusiasm. When he became interested in mountain climbing, he begged, borrowed and purchased from Bollington's more specialized equipment than most professional mountaineers ever owned. To scale a small hill, he would take more gear than Sir Edmund Hillary needed for six months in the

Himalayas. The Pilchards were just the opposite. They would attempt an ascent on Everest with a clothes line, a handful of tent pegs and a couple of cheese sandwiches. But if I was ever to make skydiving my career choice, the silky mass that had now settled on the floor before me would be ideal for the job. The only problem was that I didn't have five shillings.

If I had possessed adequate funds I would have willingly given everything for this beautiful device. As it was, I had only a few pennies to my name. Pete would usually come to my assistance, but being a professional motorcycle racer consumed most of his limited income. I also knew that Dad was not going to finance my dream either, since it violated his basic principles about borrowing and lending money. I wondered if this one time I might be able to persuade him to deviate from his strict financial philosophy, but reading my mind he looked at me sternly.

"Never a borrower nor a lender be." He advised.

I had to have it, but could see no way to get it. It was true that I could get a job. That's what my brother had done, to provide himself with petrol money, but this invariably involved getting up early on weekends and engaging in long hours of hard labor. Even if I were to attempt this as a fund raising solution, it would take time. I needed this parachute now!

Mrs. Army arrived on the scene and began to help Mr. and Mrs. Gas Mask. Many shopkeepers would have been quite annoyed by an incident like this, but Mrs. Army was a kind soul. She expressed her good-natured apologies to the couple and wished them a fond farewell as they hurriedly left the shop. As I watched I saw Mr. Gas mask make a rude gesture to all of us as he exited.

Mrs. Army began to gather up the silk in her arms.

"I should have warned you sooner," she said with an understanding smile. When Dad attempted to repack the untidy bundle, she told him to stop worrying about it, that he was wasting his time since it was designed for a single use and could not be restored to unopened condition. She said something about it being used to drop small packages to ground troops. Then she said that she would put the mess in the back room out of the way, since no one would want to buy it in this condition. Fortune had truly and suddenly smiled on me.

"Can I have it?" I said quickly, before she had taken a step.

"Of course you can!" Mrs. Army beamed. Then holding the prize to her side just out of reach she leaned forward, closed her eyes and added, "For a kiss!"

I suppose her reaction was understandable. After all I was a handsome and very charming lad, and up to that point in my life, still unattached, but despite this I was gripped in horror. My desire for the parachute was equally matched by my reluctance to kiss this woman. I was after all English, and didn't even kiss my mother. I was raised to view public affection as a sign of weakness and had no desire to get my lips anywhere near sweet old Mrs. Army.

Besides the embarrassing nature of the request there was also the added danger that my friends would find out what I had done, especially with Pete there to spread the news that would ruin my reputation forever. I looked at the parachute again and visualized myself floating effortlessly through the air, the Pilchard boys staring up at me with envy. I had to have it, regardless of the cost.

I looked at her through one eye, and hoped that my face portrayed a calm and friendly countenance, rather than the shocking panic I felt inside. Why would she want to make me go through this horrible experience? I had no choice. I quickly leaned forward, pecked her on the cheek, grabbed my parachute and ran for my life.

As my feet touched the pavement outside, I wiped my mouth across my sleeve, and the wind stole my reward. It somersaulted off down the path propelled by a brisk winter breeze, and enveloped two pedestrians, rendering them immobile. For the second time in three minutes I watched as flapping arms attempted to break the captors free. Fortunately, this time the pedestrians were Mum and Granny, who had finished their business in the china shop and had made a calculated guess as to where we would all be. They separated themselves from the canopy and stuffed it into a carrier bag, a task made especially difficult because of the aforementioned inclement weather, and the large spring still attached. This struggle lasted several minutes, as everyone expressed a differing opinion about how best to package the thing, but finally we had the beast contained and were able to head toward the market.

We stopped outside a red brick building and luckily for Granny and Pete it housed not only a bookmaker, but also a barbershop.

Granny immediately disappeared into the bookies to place a bet on the 2:45 at Doncaster. I never understood her system for picking horses. It was based not on form and previous performance, but more on the sound of the jockey's name, or the color of the animal he rode. Despite this haphazard selection process she was remarkably lucky. Granny would probably remain in here until someone went in to retrieve her.

"Right," said Mum, "I'm off" and disappeared up one of the rows of market stalls to buy some essential provisions.

"Now," said Dad, turning to Pete, "Haircut."

"But ..." Pete was about to begin some ploy to escape the barber's scissors, but Dad was having none of it.

"No!"

"How about if..." Pete tried again.

"No!" Dad was firm. "You will get a haircut today, even if I have to tie you in the chair."

Dad escorted Pete into a barbershop and took special care to pay the white-coated barber personally, so as to avoid the excuse that Pete used on his last visit. After imparting some strict instructions on military style haircuts and serious threats if Pete did not reappear with one, we left my brother sitting in the leather chair in front of the mirror. I was pleased that the restraining straps were not needed this time, but felt disappointed at the sight of Pete, clearly distressed, angry, even a little afraid as the vaguest suggestion of a tear appeared in his eyes.

I followed Dad into a newsagent's shop, and while he struck up a conversation with a short bespectacled man at the counter, I searched the shelves for any publications on Guy Fawkes manufacturing techniques, but alas, I could find none. Dad soon appeared again with an *Exchange and Mart* and some pipe tobacco.

The *Exchange and Mart* was a thick magazine printed on cheap paper, and was used as a general forum for anyone wanting to buy or sell anything. In other words, the perfect magazine for my father. Each week he would buy this periodical and eagerly scan its pages in search of the ultimate deal. It was rare that these purchases actually delivered what they promised, but that did not deter Dad from repeating his foolishness. He was especially fond of household cleaning chemicals advertising themselves to be "super strength" or "new scientific formula" but seldom did these ever turn out to be superior to that which could be purchased from the corner shop.

"Can we go to Busky's?" I asked enthusiastically.

"Perhaps," answered Dad in his non-committal style.

I waited patiently for our family to regroup, Dad read his *Exchange and Mart*, and eventually when we both became bored we walked along the first row of market stalls. We had no need for underwear, cleaning brushes, or small wooden carved animals being sold by a turban-wearing Indian man. We did however stop at "Marvin's used books" and picked over the dog eared paperbacks, their covers torn and pages yellowing. I looked for several minutes but could find nothing of interest. Dad, predictably enough, found several things of interest and soon become engrossed in a copy of Famous peaks of North Wales. There followed a short battle of wits while the price was bargained down to an amount acceptable to both parties, and then Pete appeared.

"What happened?" asked Dad, suspecting the worst.

"What do you mean?" replied Pete innocently.

"You were supposed to get a haircut," said Dad.

"I did," said Pete, and then went on without taking a breath to say how he thought the barber had done such a good job.

"Well, it doesn't look like it," complained Dad.

"What do you mean?" countered my brother, "the back is much shorter and the sides are nearly gone."

I had to admit that I'd never have guessed that any of his precious pelt had been removed.

The inevitable hostile exchange ensued intending to establish exactly how much hair had allegedly been removed, and my father determined the answer to be "not enough."

We all accompanied Pete back to the barbershop, as Dad had ordered him to return and reclaim his, or rather Dad's, money. Surprisingly the barber gave the money up easily, saying that he did not feel at all comfortable charging for such a small amount of work. He did however request that Pete find another person to cut his hair in future. On several previous occasions I had seen the performance that Pete gave in a barber's chair, and could well understand the shop owner's comments. I privately thought that Pete's plan was to get banned from every barbers shop in the county and thus protect his shaggy and sacred locks.

I was very much afraid that Pete's antics over the haircut had jeopardized our visit to Busky's.

"Dad, can we go to Busky's now?" I asked, hoping against hope.

"If...," he explained slowly while his piercing gaze shifted back and forth between us and paused to make sure he had our undivided attention, "...if you behave yourselves for the rest of the afternoon we will go there last."

By promising this reward at the end of the day our obedience was almost guaranteed. Then he added, "And you," looking at Pete, "will go to Mrs. Wiggins on Monday."

Busky's was too big a lure to pass up and so Dad was able to easily gain our agreement.

While we waited for Mum and Granny to finish their market mission we visited a sweet shop. We were torn between buying chocolate or saving our pennies for something of lasting value from Busky's.

Mum was late meeting us under the oversized antique timepiece at the top of the market square, and Dad had his nose stuck in the book on Welsh mountains when Mum walked up to us carrying two bags of shopping.

"I found a good price on carrots," Mum stated.

"Here's a picture of Glyynfyllewelan," replied Dad.

"I thought they might be nice with some shepherd's pie," continued Mum.

"Yes, I think Roger Pilchard climbed it last year," continued Dad.

"Can we go to Busky's now?" I begged.

Dad bought us all ice cream, which we had developed the skill of eating in any weather, as we waited patiently for Granny to gamble away the remainder of her old age pension. Surprisingly, we did not have to go in and get her. She left the gaming establishment of her own free will, having actually won, and joined us as we devoured the remainder of the iced treat.

With my anticipation growing with every step, we started toward Busky's, making a slight detour back to the newsagent, because Mum had promised to buy Mrs. Snobbit a *Bull Monthly*. We waited for her and Granny in the recessed doorway of the adjacent shop, which sold chemistry equipment. I was always fascinated by this stuff, and desperately wanted a chemistry set for Christmas. I believed that given sufficient time I could equal the great work of Dr. Frankenstein, or repeat Dr Jeckyll's historic achievement.

Busky's was situated in an old Victorian arcade. Many of the frosted glass panes in the roof were cracked and looked as if they had not been cleaned since the place was built. The elaborate wrought ironwork was tarnished and dirty. The street was too narrow for cars and being protected from the normally unpleasant weather should have been a perfect shopping precinct, but for some reason it was not well visited and most shops were closed and boarded up. Many of the buildings had signs in their windows advertising that they could be rented, but a newsagent and The Electric Appliance Emporium, hung on in desperate loneliness.

Dad called Busky's Toys and Games a "shrine to cheap plastic rubbish." The shop sold toys, games and jokes of the inexpensive foreign variety. A visit to this place was one of the few things that made the trip into town tolerable. It continued to absorb most of my pocket money each week and we viewed a visit to Busky's with the same level of importance that devout Muslims viewed a pilgrimage to holy Mecca. Pete and I both had a few coppers that were burning holes in our pockets, and we knew we would find something in the Joke shop that would be of use to us.

The front window was packed with appealing products, barely a square inch remained that was not covered in colorful enticements, all at very reasonable prices. We went inside through a glass door that when opened, collided with a small brass bell that hung from the ceiling. At last we were inside this magical place and were now able to feast our eyes on a vast selection of toys and practical jokes. There were big fake rubber ears that clipped over small real flesh ones, phony money, whoopie cushions, badges that squirted water at your enemy and rings that would make a buzzing sound when you shook hands with someone. It was an

"Aladdin's cave" for children, selling invisible ink pens, spy telescopes and fake devices to create the appearance of having a nail through the finger or an arrow through the head.

After spending a few minutes in here, our meager finances had been replaced with valued effects. I wanted to purchase a packet of three stink bombs but my economic prosperity did not run to such extravagant luxuries so I bought a peashooter instead. It was made of thin shiny rolled tin with a blue plastic mouthpiece – a good investment since I knew that Mum's pantry would provide an unlimited supply of ammo.

Pete bought a pair of red tipped Dracula fangs to wear during the upcoming Halloween festivities.

That concluded the shopping trip and I trudged wearily back to Granny's house dreaming of shooting Pete with my pea shooter while he sipped a hot cup of tea through vampire fangs. Granny apparently had some other kind of fortifying beverage in mind, because she stopped at the Pakistani grocery shop and bought another bottle of the cheap Irish sheep dip that she, without humor, referred to as whiskey.

We reached Granny's house, cold and tired, and found comfort on her large couch, and warmth from the gas fire. I wanted desperately to bring my parachute in for closer inspection, but Dad seemed to think that the combination of an antique collection, a large spring and an inexperienced operator "would only lead to disaster."

Granny placed a tea tray on her card table, and we waited for the kettle to boil. The budgie was then released to stretch its wings, and on the second pass it tried to attack Dad before landing next to the tea tray to enjoy the remainder of the wrestling match which was now playing on television. Granny did not hear very well, so the ear splitting noise of Mick McMannus being thrown around a wrestling ring prevented any normal conversation. The budgie did not seem to mind the din from the television. Possibly it was as deaf as Granny, which would explain it not hearing Pete's suggestion.

Pete's hands were idle and once again the devil was at work. He leaned over to me and suggested that I test my ability with my newly acquired peashooter by attempting to hit Joey with a projectile.

I carefully removed the weapon from my pocket. Looking round and finding no appropriate ammo, I asked Granny if she had any dried peas. She didn't understand at first, which was probably because of her reluctance to use a perfectly good hearing aid. Eventually she looked from me to the peashooter, back at me and around the room at her irreplaceable collectibles. She waved at Mum and when Mum looked over, Granny simply pointed to the peashooter in my hand. Mum took away the peashooter and Granny went into the kitchen to bring the boiling water for tea.

Pete was still bored and taking full advantage of Dad's preoccupation with Mike Marino delivering a flying forearm-smash, he had now removed Joey's plastic cellmate from the cage. He pretended to make Jimmy peck the back of Mum's head until Mum hit him with a newspaper. Realizing that no human was going to tolerate his petty annoyances, he began to annoy Joey. Placing the fake bird halfway behind a cushion, he kept peeking it out at Joey, who was naturally intrigued by the seemingly lifelike movements of his usually static companion. He fluttered over for a reconnaissance mission, and cautiously approached the cushion cave that Pete had constructed as an ambush site. He slowly edged forward trying to get a glimpse of Jimmy, shuffling toward the dark interior with his little green head bobbing back and forth nervously.

Granny reappeared with a pot of boiling water, and Pete quickly ended his devious strategy to capture Joey.

Granny placed the pot of tea on the table to brew and retrieved her copy of the football pool form. Each week she would gamble on the combined outcome of nearly a hundred football matches. The wrestling match had reached its climactic yet predictable conclusion and they had carried poor Mick out of the ring on a stretcher. Then the sports announcer commenced calling out the football results and people all across the country started marking their copies with little crosses to calculate their degree of success at becoming rich. Halfway through the third division, the tea was ready.

As I sat down to enjoy the brew, I heard a slight crunching noise as I destroyed Joey's plastic plaything that Pete had just thrown onto my seat. I don't think Pete intended to kill Jimmy, he probably just wanted me to become startled upon contact with the feathered fake and hopefully deposit the hot tea on my lap. But children seldom comprehend the possible consequences of their actions and this time disaster had struck.

Joey had not yet realized that Jimmy was dead. Granny did, but was so immersed in her football results that she simply waved at my mother and pointed at me in much the same manner as she had with the peashooter incident.

A few minutes later Dad was marching me back down the cold street to the nearest pet shop, which luckily was not far. It was getting dark now and it started to rain, which did not do very much to improve my father's temper. Neither did the presence of Pete, who had joined us to delight in the fact that this time it was I, instead of he that was in trouble. My brother and I both agreed that it would have been quicker and easier to take the car but Dad refused on the grounds that he was unwilling to loose a good parking space. We got to the pet shop just before it closed, and emptied out Jimmy's broken remains on top of the glass counter. The shop owner picked up one of the largest pieces, and scrutinized it. The left side of Jimmy's head extending down to his shoulder was then compared for color and size to one of several similar decoys lying on a layer of straw in a brown wooden box. Pete commented on how lucky it was that part of the head survived, because that would allow us to match the eye color properly. This was Pete's idea of humor.

Again, we walked all the way back to Granny's house, this time with the added joy of being both cold and wet. Upon our arrival Pete created a diversion by offering Joey one of the chocolate biscuits from Dad's plate, and I clipped Jimmy number two onto the wooden perch of his new home.

Joey fluttered over to the cage. We all held our breath. My relationship with this bird was already strained, following an unfortunate incident that occurred last Christmas, and I was worried that if he realized Jimmy number two was a ringer, he might never squawk at me again. Joey sat on the perch, shuffled over to Jimmy and pecked him a few times causing Jimmy to rock back and forth on his spring legs. Joey screeched.

Granny smiled and said "Yes...," and all appeared well.

A potential disaster had been averted, order had been restored and life would go on for Granny, Joey and the new plastic impostor.

We drank another cup of tea while Granny reviewed the day's racing results, and then left so that she could go to bed. Dad's schedule suffered a minor set back because of the rain, and he was still upset at my carelessness surrounding the death of Jimmy.

Passing through one of the villages on the way home we noticed a fun fair was setting up, and we begged Dad to allow us to visit it. The rain had now stopped and his mood had improved slightly, but he still declined.

"No! Because you made a lot of trouble with the parachute and the broken budgie," he said.

"Well, can we go on another night?" I asked.

"We'll see," answered Dad.

Pete and I immediately launched into a whining tone and beseeched him.

"Aoooww, pleeeese."

It didn't take more than two or three minutes of this painful petitioning, before Dad agreed.

"Alright," he said, "we'll go on Thursday."

Pete rewarded this kindness by spending the next several miles banging his knee into the back of Dad's seat, a diversion that never failed to result in disciplinary action. He began his torment slowly at first with just the occasional bump, and little or no pressure, as if it was an accident that he could not avoid. Initially Dad tried to ignore this in order to prevent another altercation, but Pete was persistent and the pushing became more frequent. When we stopped at a cross roads in a nearby village, Dad informed Pete that he would be walking home. Something about his tone told us all he was serious, and the knee banging stopped.

We did not drive directly home. Dad made quite a lengthy detour to drop off the box of "miscellaneous sundries," at Bollington's. All items for bid had to be submitted before Sunday night, so that prospective bargain hunters could view them before the actual auction on Monday.

I suspected that this mission was the reason we did not have time to stop at the fun fair.

CHAPTER 6

DISTRESSING NEWS FROM MRS. SNOBBIT

I awoke to the sound of my brother revving his motorcycle followed shortly by the sound of Dad yelling about making too much noise on a Sunday morning when people were trying to sleep. My first thought was of how I did not have to go to school today, and then the joy became quite blissful as I realized that today, I could take my parachute on its maiden voyage.

It looked as if the weather was going to be good for skydiving – the rain of last night had now stopped leaving behind a clear but cold day. I jumped out of bed and ran to the window. Up by El Paso, out of earshot, Dad was lecturing Pete with a fierce expression and outstretched finger that could quickly be converted into an open palmed slapping hand if the need arose. Dad began waving his hands around the way he always did when making a point, and I followed the direction of his pointing finger, from Pete to the bike to the old toilet to the house. From Dad's sweeping gestures I concluded that Pete was being instructed to put the bike away and go in the house for breakfast.

My eyes strayed further, followed the lane up the slight rise and toward where my good friends and parachuting partners the Pilchard brothers lived. There was no sign of a vehicle in front of their house, which I assumed meant that they were not at home. That was a pity since "goggle-eye" was currently in their possession, and I would certainly need it before my big jump. Goggle-eye was a crash helmet that was considered an essential part of our skydiving paraphernalia. We had made a rule that for any height above four-feet, the jumper must always wear goggle-eye.

The helmet had once belonged to a friend of Dad's who used to race motorcycles. It was white and when worn looked like an inverted bowl on the owner's head. On the front, a pair of large oval stick-on vinyl eyes had been added, to emulate the headgear of a popular racing driver. The helmet had been given to my brother several years ago, but it was too big for him so he found little use for it. It had hung unused and gathering dust on a rusty nail in one of El Paso's interior walls, until one day Pete had attempted to remove the stick-on eyes. He got halfway through the job and changed his mind, leaving one solitary large oval eye that constantly looked to the left. From that point on the helmet was known as goggle-eye. Pete eventually sold it to Squeaky Norrington for much more than it was worth.

Squeaky's real name was Norbert. He was given the name Squeaky because of a bicycle he owned, which after being ridden through the floods by Benito had developed a coating of rust and a corresponding squeak. Squeaky was not a particularly bright child, slow on the uptake, and his mind always appeared to be struggling to keep up with the conversation. His parents were also rich. Not as rich as the Maudly-Creechoms, but they had more money than anyone else in Mud Lane. This made the Norringtons an easy target for anyone wishing to raise some additional cash by disposing of a broken, worn out or unwanted toy. A visit would be paid to Squeaky and an attempt would be made to part a fool and his money.

Squeaky's brother James, older by almost ten years would have intervened in many of these unfair transactions to protect Squeaky, but he had long since left home to join the Army. We believed that this was merely a desperate attempt to escape Mrs. Norrington's overbearing personality. Squeaky's father worked in a bank in the nearby town where Granny lived. He worked long hours, mostly I think because of Mrs. Norrington.

Mrs. Norrington's affluence was well disguised by her unusual appearance. Despite her wealth she liked to make her own clothes, but she was not very skilled at her many dressmaking endeavors. Rather than select the correct material, the thrifty nature of Squeaky's mother drove her to use whatever she could find on sale, and she would often be seen around Great Biddington wearing a blouse with mismatched and uneven sleeves, sewn from someone's old curtains. Nobody minded this except Squeaky, because she also insisted on making his school outfits, the embarrassing patchwork of materials and irregular sewing making Squeaky the subject of much hilarity.

I hurriedly dressed and went downstairs. It appeared that Pete, Mum and Dad were already engaged in a contest to see who could finish their meal first. I sat down and drank some of the steaming tea that Mum had begun pouring for me as soon as she heard my footsteps on the creaky old stairs. I ate some cereal while Mum delivered a large oval plate piled high with toast. I raced my brother to make a grab for the largest piece and smeared the surface of it with a generous portion of Marmite. Dad and I were the only two people I knew of on the planet who liked Marmite, enjoying its rich texture and savory taste. To everyone else it resembled the black sticky tar that the county council would spread on the roads every few years, or the dark tacky substance on the back of Mrs. Leecham's dress after she sat on the garden seat.

"Did Rodger Pilchard like the sheet?" Dad asked taking another mouthful of toast.

"What sheet?" I asked.

"The canvas sheet that we found yesterday. You were to take it to Rodger. Did you?" Dad's question reminded me that I had of course forgotten all about it.

"I thought you meant Pete was going to do it," I explained.

"No," corrected my father, "I told you to."

"I'm sure you said Pete," I insisted.

"He didn't ask me," protested Pete, anxious to become involved in the first argument of the day.

"He did," I argued.

"You go!" shouted my mother over the noise of our squabbling, and pointed directly at me to eliminate any chance of misunderstanding.

"Why me?" I whined.

"Because you have to deliver Mrs. Snobbit's bull magazine, it will be no trouble for you to drop off the sheet to Rodger Pilchard on the way."

I was disgruntled at having been assigned this new chore, but kept quiet in case any more were added to the list.

"Don't forget," said Pete, with a theatrical grin.

"I won't," I said, and tried to kick my dear brother.

"Dad will be angry if you do," he continued.

My father interrupted, "Dad will be angry if you two don't shut up and let me read the paper."

After breakfast, Pete went to his motorbike shed to perform some modifications he felt sure would yield an extra mile per hour or so, and Dad went to inspect his tobacco crop, and at last I had an opportunity to examine my new parachute. The only problem I saw was the large spring attached to the underside of the white cloth dome, but I thought Pete, with his mechanical wisdom and extensive tool collection, would be able to surgically remove this. So, gathering up the silk in my arms and grabbing the Snobbit's *Bull Monthly*, I set off toward El Paso.

I explained my spring problem to Pete who said he could fix it as soon as he was done performing some minor adjustment on the back wheel of his motorbike. I threw the Bull magazine down on the ground as I walked off to the Rat barn to collect the sheet.

When I returned carrying the loose bundle, Pete was involved in a lively conversation with Mario Rolonzio. Mario was the eldest Relonzio, a criminal, and Benito's mentor. Mario passed down to Benito all the traditions of dishonesty, sleight of hand and deception, just as he has received them from his father. Outside on the gravel driveway a green bicycle with a flat front tire lay on its side. I presumed that the bike was currently in Mario's possession, although I also realized that this did not mean that it actually belonged to him.

I shook out the sheet and several nails fell out from its stained and wrinkled folds. I remembered the incident yesterday when the upturned nail tin emptied out onto the dirt floor of rat barn.

"You idiot!" my brother barked.

"Why?" I asked.

"Because those nails could cause a puncture in my bike," said Pete.

"Or mine," said Mario.

"You mean another puncture," said Pete to Mario.

I picked up as many of the nails as I could find and turned my attention to the crumpled ground sheet. I began to fold it in half, then into quarters, eventually producing a manageable package. I placed it on a large rock and sat down only to discover in a most painful manner that there was one elusive nail remaining in the folds of the canvas.

Mario was leaning casually on the door frame and leafing through Mrs. Snobbit's bull magazine. In the center was a double glossy page depicting two large black bulls, seen in profile each facing the other. The only difference we could detect between the two animals was that one was wearing a red ribbon rosette, while the other wore a blue one. The ribbons looked like the ones that Billy Tadcome had on his living room wall, which existed as proof of his exceptional skill at playing darts in the Red Lion. We all laughed for a moment at the thought of how dangerous it might be if the two creatures gracing the pages of this magazine were admitted into the Red Lion dart's team. Then we wondered how they picked one bull as being better than the other. Mario thought that there was probably a series of tests that the bulls must perform that probably involved some timed running event, and that additionally there would be some jumping contest. Pete said that he thought Mario's opinion about this was "rubbish." Mario tossed the magazine onto the floor and defiantly claimed that back home in Italy they did things very differently.

"Here it is," said Pete.

He slid a steel tobacco tin over the cracked cement toward Mario who dumped the contents onto the ground. The puncture repair kit included some rubber patches and glue along with several other odds and ends. Mario unscrewed the glue cap and was testing the contents for freshness when Pete also handed him a bicycle pump, two tire removal levers and one of Mum's spoons.

In response to Pete's stern warning about not losing any of the pieces, Mario started to remove the front wheel. When this was done he slid the tire levers under one side of the flat tire and worked the spoon until the black rubber inner tube was exposed. Using the pump he added new air to the tube, which already displayed several patches, and then carried it over to the water barrel outside rat barn to look for the tell-tail trail of small bubbles.

Without warning, Dad appeared at the front door and yelled loudly, "Rodger Pilchard..."

I picked up the canvas and held it high enough for Dad to see. He nodded.

"And Mrs. Snobbit..." Dad added at the top of his voice.

I snatched up the Bull magazine and yelled, "I'm going!"

"You idiot!" said Pete.

"What?" I asked, not realizing that Mario had been using the publication as a work bench and that I had inadvertently spilled the puncture repair paraphernalia onto the ground. The contents of the tin were now hidden in the gravel mingled with the remainder of the lost nails. It was time to make a quick getaway.

I had to pass the Pilchard's house on the way to visit Mrs. Snobbit, but there was still no car outside so I decided to visit Mrs. Snobbit first.

She lived at the end of Mud Lane. Just past her property the paved road ended and it became a dirt cart-track that farmers used to get to their fields. The only traffic would be farm tractors hauling a variety of agricultural contraptions, humans on foot who could be collecting berries to make pies or homemade alcoholic brews, and my brother who used this as his motorcycle-scrambling track. It was possible to reach two other nearby villages using this primitive thoroughfare and was quite a pleasant walk if you did not mind thorns, mud and wild animals.

Mrs. Snobbit's house was sparingly furnished, but comfortable. From what I could gather, most of her time was spent in one of two rooms, the kitchen and living room. Like most village folk, the kitchen served as an all-purpose room, and the living room was reserved for special occasions.

Usually when I visited I would stay in the kitchen and talk to the old lady over the well-scrubbed oak table.

Mrs. Snobbit was a skinny woman, kind and slow in speech. Her gentle and deliberate manner of communication was intended to put visitors at ease and make them more likely to disclose some vital piece of village gossip, which was the currency in which Mrs. Snobbit dealt. Although she lived on the very edge of civilization she knew more about the day-to-day activities within Great Biddington than anyone else. Mrs. Snobbit's husband had a sister, and according to her, the Snobbit family had lived in the village longer than any other inhabitant. Mr. Snobbit once claimed that the Snobbit presence in the village pre-dated the invention of dirt. Her sister June, lived in a brick house round the corner from the Eagle's Nest pub, which was convenient, because that's where she spent most of her time, sharing a brace of bar stools with Billy Tadcome.

Mrs. Snobbit had few visitors, yet she came to control a vast collection of news, stories, rumors, and personal history. Her secret was not in the number of visitors she had, but in the quality of data that each possessed. The people that did stop by and talk with her were critical links in a village spy ring that permeated the very fabric of local society. It was generally believed that her intelligence information came from a network of informants that used St. Mary's Church as their operations base.

Mrs. Blinkton was the main contact. Along with Mrs. Crippin, she was in charge of the flowers at the church, and had a multitude of social interactions with several of Great Biddington's key personnel. The updates that she received and passed on to Mrs. Snobbit every two or three days came from three main reporters: Mrs. Collins, Mrs. Diggsmore and Pauline Spinner. Each of them had their own network of contacts, and in this way Mrs. Snobbit was able to preside over the entire spectrum of village gossip and re-distribute it as she saw fit.

Mrs. Collins, who ran the post office and corner shop, was able to provide valuable facts about local commerce and communication between the villagers and the outside world. Mrs. Diggsmore, the schoolteacher, was able to offer the latest on the local children, and often some very revealing tales about their parents. But the most interesting contact by far was Pauline Spinner, the wife of Pete, who was the landlord at the

Eagle's Nest Public house. It was the publican's spouse who provided the juiciest and most scandalous gossip from the more dubious elements of the local population. Any missing chatter, that had not been reported by Mrs. Blinkton would be supplied by either the milkman, the paper boy or the postman, as they made the daily deliveries to the Snobbit household.

Mrs. Snobbit made her visitors very welcome, and always had an ample supply of hot tea and chocolate biscuits. The shortbread or chocolate treats would have already been sprinkled with truth serum and placed invitingly in the center of the table.

Her data extraction skills, refined over the years, would then be brought into play. She never offered nor expected anything for free. If she required information from you, she would first offer a fragment of common village knowledge to gain your trust, then probe delicately for the specific piece of news she needed to make a story complete. Those who visited her in search of news would always have to supply some piece of inside information in order to get it. Everything was available for trade, with the old lady collecting the pieces of a puzzle which would complete a particular news story she was following. At Christmas, Granny would visit her and this represented the only deviation to her typical system. Since Granny, not being a resident, had no interest in anything to do with the village, she would provide news of her own hometown in exchange for seven or eight glasses of Mrs. Snobbit's sherry.

The high point of Mrs. Snobbit's intelligence-gathering career came one morning when she discovered a dead body seated in a car across the road from her house. The police were called and as she waited for them to arrive, news reached her of a pair of Christian fanatics who were advancing up the lane trying to force innocent people to join them in praise. Since they did not attend St. Mary's, Mrs. Snobbit did not consider them real Christians, and consequently had no time for them. She certainly did not want them interfering in her murder investigation. When they finally arrived at her house she chased them off with a broom, only to find that she was chasing off the detectives who had been called to investigate. While Mrs. Snobbit was apologizing to the police officers the "dead man" woke from his hangover and drove off home.

I sat down at her kitchen table, and helped myself to a biscuit.

"Oh, how wonderful," she said over the sound of the steam driven kettle whistle. She held the Bull Magazine like some priceless antique, and put the periodical safely to one side for her husband Len.

Len Snobbit worked at Potter's farm. No one knew exactly what he did or why it took him so long, but he was seldom home. Like most farm workers, the job was hard and the hours were long. Mr. Snobbit would leave home before it got light, and would not be seen again until he drove his old blue car back up the lane for his lunch. After lunch he would return to doing whatever it was he did and would not be seen again until returning home after dark.

"How have you been?" I asked.

"Well, do you know, my leg has been showing signs of getting better, but of course, this damp weather doesn't help at all."

She now felt that she had surrendered some information and was due some in return. I should have picked up on this but my attention had been captured by the tin of chocolate biscuits resting on the table.

We sat in her small kitchen in silence, just Mrs. Snobbit, me and the chocolate biscuits. I became acutely aware of the ticking clock, the smell of soap powder and farmyards, until after an eternity she broke the silence.

"And how are your Mum and Dad?"

"Oh, fine." I told her.

The game was now afoot. I had supplied her with some information and according to the rules I could now ask something of her.

"May I have another chocolate biscuit, please?"

We both understood that this now meant that I had exchanged my right to some privileged gossip in return for a sugary treat. She pushed the plate toward me and her eyes fell on the canvas sheet. I could see that she did not want to ask me directly what this was for, since this would spoil the fun. Instead she preferred to hint around the subject. Thinking that it may be something to do with Pete she inquired,

"And how is Pete's motorbike?"

I replied that it was running well, and that Pete had now removed the exhaust pipe to increase the noise it made. Mrs. Snobbit was delighted at this revelation since she could now report to the congregation of St Mary's that Pete had slipped down another rung on the delinquency ladder, but it brought her no closer to the purpose of the canvas sheet.

She tried a different approach by asking me where I was going next, and I told her I had to visit Rodger Pilchard.

Recognizing this valuable trading token, she responded by telling me that the Pilchards were going on a camping holiday to Scotland in a couple of days. It did not surprise me that she knew this. Rodger Pilchard had borrowed a camping stove from Bobby Sikes, whose wife was a good friend of Bob Bascome, and whose son delivered newspapers to Mrs. Snobbit. A slight smile crossed her face as she made the Pilchard-Scotland-Camping-Ground-sheet connection.

"Are you going to the firework's display this year?" she asked.

"Yes, I expect so," I told her.

"It should be a lovely affair," she said. "There will be lots of food there. Allen Tidwell and Gordon plan to be there, and they are donating some meat and according to Mrs. Crippin, you know, who plays the organ in the chapel and does the flowers for the church, they are going to bring some pork pies. You must tell your father because oh, you know how he loves pork pies."

I lost interest in her monologue, and I was not paying very much attention until off in the distance I heard her say something about a Guy.

"Excuse me, Mrs. Snobbit, but what did you just say?" I asked.

"Well," she said, "I was just saying that Pete up at the Eagle's Nest was going to donate some beer and there will also be some lemonade there, and..."

"No," I said, gently interrupting her, "you said something about a Guy."

"Yes," she continued, "the Maudly-Creechoms are building a Guy this year; they were working so hard on it yesterday. The Gurneys are helping them. Oh, it should be a lovely one."

I almost spat a mouthful of tea over the Bull magazine, which would have been tragic since Mr. Snobbit kept all the past issues in chronological order and pristine condition.

So, the Maudly-Creechoms were building a Guy this year. This was dreadful news and I sat there for a moment, dumbfounded.

I did not hear the car arrive, but the sound of Len Snobbit's voice snapped me out of my shock. I fumbled a farewell to the old couple and wandered out into the daylight, dazed and concerned by this new development. From behind me I heard Mr. Snobbit grumbling that the centerfold of this month's Bull magazine seemed stuck together with puncture repair glue.

On Friday as we had walked home from school to the sound of Oscar's squelching feet, Benito had proposed that we build a Guy. It was unlike Benito to suggest something that involved such an investment in time and energy, but the payoff would be worth it. Now it appeared that the Maudly-Creechom family was contemplating a similar project. This was no coincidence. Oscar was the connection. Although not an active participant in the conversation that night, Oscar's ears were one of the few parts of his body not caked with mud and he certainly had no problem overhearing Benito's grand design. The problem was that although the plan hatched by Benito was a good one in theory, so far we had done nothing about realizing this objective. We had planned to start on the project in a few days, but now it appeared that the Maudly-Creechoms had stolen the idea and were forging ahead with their own design. They had also enlisted the help of the Gurney brothers, which would certainly provide the necessary manpower.

This news was made particularly distressing because this wasn't just a few other kids from the village making a Guy, this was the Maudly-Creechoms making a Guy. The Maudly-Creechoms were our archrivals and were the richest family in the lane. Their house was bigger, they drove better cars, and the two children, Horace and Jane, also known as Maggot, were always dressed in clean clothes and held themselves to be slightly better than most of the village, and significantly better than us. They were generally disliked by most people, and especially disliked by Billy Tadcome, who filled the role of Great Biddington's philosopher and drunk. Once, we met Billy sitting by the churchyard in the process of sobering up. He had just received word that his unemployment check was going to be discontinued, and for some reason he blamed the Maudly-Creechoms for this. Billy called them the "aristocracy," which sounded like a foreign word but none of the Rolonzios had heard it and they were all foreign. Billy explained that it meant they were rich, and descended from the people who burned poor Guy Fawkes. He then proceeded to rave on for a while about coal miners and unions, until someone got rid of him by saying that they were giving away free beer at the Red Lion.

Squeaky Norrington was under considerable pressure from his mother to befriend the Maudly-Creechom's, but he enjoyed our company more. So nobody really knew how loyal he was or what to do with him. Oscar and Willis had not yet decided where their faithfulness lay. They lacked the Pilchard's strength of character to stay uninvolved and since their arrival in the village we had watched them with interest to see with whom they would align themselves. As they came to know us better, they had decided to spend more time with the Maudly-Creechoms, and it was now clear that they had decided to fully join forces with our opponents. At first, I thought that this decision was encouraged by Friday's calamity involving Squeaky's quicksand and Oscar's clumsy attempts to cross the stream, but then it occurred to me that these two families were very similar and probably deserved each other. When I thought about Oscar betraying us by divulging our strategy to build a Guy, I didn't feel so bad about the stream-crossing incident.

But the fact that the Maudly-Creechoms were now trying to compete with us was a serious problem. Whoever completed the task first could get the best donations from the villagers. This seemed fundamentally unfair since the Maudly-Creechoms were already rich. It looked as if we were going to have to step up our efforts, and enlist the other members of our gang if we were to complete our Guy first.

But now I had another more pressing problem. Sunday lunchtime was something Dad was very strict about, and I had spent so long in Mrs. Snobbit's house that I was already late. I knew I would suffer the wrath of my father if I did not arrive in a timely manner.

A usual meal in our kitchen would consist of boiled meat, boiled potatoes and boiled vegetables. It would be served on plain white china and eaten quickly and functionally. If we requested seconds, we would be treated like Oliver Twist. Once a month Mum would buy a bottle of orange cordial that could be mixed with water to create a refreshing beverage, but this would only be consumed during Sunday lunch. It would stand on the cupboard by the sink and taunt us the rest of the week. If we stared at it longingly and complained of thirst, Dad would sometimes allow us to drink some of it, but usually his response was that there was an endless supply of "free water" in the tap.

For dessert, we would be treated to something else boiled.

A formal meal on the other hand was a lavish affair, with tablecloths and real metal cutlery. These would only occur on holidays like Christmas or for special events when we had company. My parents were gracious hosts, and always reserved the best for our guests. We would start with soup – a vegetable or tomato variety. This would be followed by a salad, made with lettuce, carrots, peas and tomatoes, all fresh from the garden. The taste sensation would be complete by a sprinkling of oil and vinegar dressing. The main course would be beef, chicken, turkey or sometimes all three. There would be roast potatoes, fresh steamed vegetables and mint sauce. We would then pause to allow this abundant feast to digest before continuing with treacle pudding, which would be consumed with sweet yellow custard while we waited for Mum to wheel in the dessert cart. This would be filled with cake, apple pie, ice cream and French pastries. We would then pick at the cheese board while my mother made coffee.

We all enjoyed these events, but no one more so than Dad, who loved food, the way a man ending a hunger strike might. I have never seen him refuse food and I have never seen him complain about the taste of any particular menu item. Once I heard him say that Mum's gooseberry and prune pancakes were not as tasty as the last time he had some, but no one took him too seriously since he was on his fifth helping.

During these formal dinners, Pete and I were instructed to follow two strict rules of behavior. F.H.B, and F.U.O.B. And that is exactly how Dad would remind us, if he felt that we were straying from his code of mealtime conduct. He would catch our attention, look us directly in the eye, point his calloused finger at us and say "F.U.O.B."

It is important to understand that because of the improved quality of food during one of these official dining extravaganzas, Pete and I would tend to eat not only more than usual but much faster too. This created the potential embarrassing danger of us running out of food before our guests had consumed their fill. If this situation looked imminent, Dad would instruct us to F.H.B.

F.H.B. was code for "Family Hold Back," and served as a reminder for us to slow down. We resented this restraint, feeling that everyone started at the same time, so why should we have our rations cut just because someone can't keep up?

F.U.O.B. would sound equally cryptic to guests but we knew that it meant "Fill Up On Bread," This rule was self explanatory and we considered it unfair that Dad was treating these strangers as if they had paid for the meal.

My brother and I did not care for bread, so we complained about how hungry we were in front of the guests. This was done in the most sorrowful tone we could muster, and invariably prompted the guest to offer us that last helping of roast potatoes.

Dad realized that he must strike at the root of the problem by removing our hunger before we began the meal. He issued a directive known as the "three slice rule." A clever plan, but it did not work for long.

Pete soon discovered, and was quick to let me in on the secret, that the old oval dining table sat on a square base that had a ledge running down each side. This was only accessible from under the table, and was not at all obvious to the casual observer. The ledge was only two or three inches wide but that was sufficient to hold a slice of bread or two, or three.

Our trick was simple. When we arrived at the table we would take a piece of bread, and a statement in a loud voice would accompany this action. "Having the first piece of bread Dad." One or two bites would be taken in an overly theatrical manner and we would wave around the remainder of the slice to make sure everyone saw us with it. Then, as our keepers became distracted with conversation, we would carefully let our hands slip below the levels of the table and slowly without looking execute our well-practiced maneuver. The slightly nibbled bread would be placed under the table and up on to the ledge. After a sufficient pause to check that we had avoided detection, we would proudly proclaim, "Having the second piece of bread, Dad."

Dad soon became irritated by the attention grabbing announcements, and instructed us to stop. He monitored our slice consumption by placing a special plate containing exactly six slices, which was to be used only by us.

This continued for several months. As time passed we were sure that Dad suspected something. We would catch him sneaking sideways glances at us during the bread cycle of the meal, and he would ask us for a bread count while he locked us with his piercing gaze. But he was unable to pin anything on us. We were careful that each time we performed "operation bread ledge" we later returned to the scene of the crime to collect the partially eaten food, for redistribution to the cat.

I think we could have continued to deceive him had it not been for a chance encounter between the table and Mr. Smith, a particularly fat visitor who came once or twice a year to eat us out of house and home. On this particular occasion, Mr. Smith, having eaten the last piece of cheese and swilled the remainder of his coffee, attempted to stand and leave the table. Being the unfortunate victim of one too many glasses of sherry, he underestimated the enormity of this task and lurched suddenly sideways hitting the table. The table did not move that much but it was adequate to dislodge an old discarded piece of bread crust that unknown to Pete and I had somehow escaped our detection and remained there for unknown ages.

"What do you think this is?" asked Mum in a puzzled tone. At first neither parent could determine its origin – it was certainly a very hard substance. Dad supposed some type of stone, but Mum favored the notion that it was ceramic in origin. Dad argued that ceramics are usually glazed, and that this looked very porous. Mum defended her position by remarking that its shape looked too even to be naturally occurring stone.

Mr. Smith, who had been standing silently rubbing his sore hip, and suppressing a belch, casually remarked that part of the shape resembled teeth marks. That's when Dad and Mum simultaneously changed their expression from puzzled wonder to a mix of understanding, embarrassment and anger.

It was several months before we were allowed to eat with the grownups again.

CHAPTER 7
THE HOBBINS / CRIPPIN
ENTERTAINMENT HOUR

With my lunch consumed, I was out the door and heading for the Pilchard's house. The first thing I had to do was report to my comrades and impart the parachute news. The recently acquired information that the Maudly-Creechoms were also building a Guy weighed heavily on my mind and I became concerned that it might have a profound effect on our fireworks money collection. Obviously something must be done about this, and I resolved to visit Benito as soon as my business with the Pilchard brothers was concluded. I walked briskly up the lane toward Brian and Ryan's house, lost in my thoughts. So preoccupied was I by the Guy news that I failed to notice Rodger Pilchard's car returning home. It was almost driven by Rodger, who was twisted round attending to something in the back seat. I glanced up from my pondering and got a good view of the back of his head through the windscreen of the car that was heading directly for me. Fortunately, he turned in time to see me, and for one long moment time became frozen as we stared at each other, each of our faces mirroring the surprise in the other.

He turned the steering wheel sharply to the left as I leapt out of the way. His sudden evasive maneuver caused him to re-chart his course across his own front lawn narrowly missing two of his wife's favorite rose bushes. As he drove by, our gazes were locked again, but this time my face was contorted with anger while his showed one of those "where the blazes did you come from?" expressions. For a long time now Mrs. Snobbit had thought that Rodger drove like a madman. From the moment this latest near miss occurred, the facts of the incident were destined for her ears. The story would inevitably be passed along through her network of undercover operatives and would be delivered, with only the slightest exaggeration, to provide the final piece of proof that would confirm forever Rodger's driving reputation as "dangerous and foolhardy." And him with a family too!

As Rodger sped off up his driveway, I noticed Brian and Ryan looking over their shoulders at me through back window of the car, their laughter was obvious and to a certain extent, understandable. I walked toward the car that had now stopped and arrived there just as Rodger was getting out. He looked at me long enough to mumble something under his breath. Several of the words were,"...just like his brother..."

The two Pilchard boys now had the small vehicle's driver's seat pushed forward and were both trying to exit through the same door at the same time. Ryan was carrying a notebook while Brian had the pencil, and they were engaged in a dispute. I greeted them both and was immediately informed about their father's opinion of my supposedly ineffectual mental state. I responded with a few quotes from Mrs. Snobbit about their father's inability to operate vehicles, and the boys continued with their argument. I was certain that the subject of their heated discussion was surely whether their father was guilty of attempted murder or whether my almost superhuman reflexes had saved my life, but I soon realized that they were concerned with something else entirely.

Brian was pointing to a sketch on the notebook, which I recognized as a map of the area where Mud Lane joined the High Street that ran through Great Biddington. What I couldn't recognize were the series of dotted lines that ran across the map. As I listened to their intense bickering, it became apparent that they were discussing the orientation of "The tunnel"

"I've been looking for you two," I said.

"We had to fill the car with petrol ready for the trip to Scotland," Ryan responded.

'What are you doing now?" I asked.

"We're trying to find out where the tunnel goes," replied Brian.

"How are you going to do that?" I said.

"We're going to crawl down it."

"Why do you care so much about where the tunnel goes?" I inquired.

"What do you mean?" asked Ryan.

"What does it matter where the tunnel goes?" I tried again.

They looked at me with blank expressions. In a moment of inspiration Brian said, "Because it's there?"

I knew that this was repeated from something he had heard his father say when his mother had asked about their father's mountaineering escapades, and realized that there wasn't much left to say about it.

"OK," I said, changing the subject. "Do you know anything about making Guys?"

"No," said Ryan. "Why?"

"Because it's there," I said trying to be clever, I then realized that this response made even less sense than when it was applied to the mysterious tunnel.

I had to admit that although we were familiar with almost every hedgerow, ditch, stream, bank, and tree in the surrounding area, the below ground features, like the tunnel, were more of an enigmatic element to our geographical understanding. Although I didn't know the layout of the tunnel, I well remembered its construction the previous year as a solution to the terrible floods that every two years or so would inflict their watery devastation upon us. There had been no flooding since the completion of the construction project, but there had been no weather conditions to fully test it either.

"I'm sure it ends up at the sea," Ryan insisted, as the two Pilchard brothers continued to debate the destination of the drainage tunnel.

Ryan's opinion that the pipe made a more or less direct routing to the seashore about one hundred and fifty miles away, was to my mind ridiculous. His argument was based entirely on his sighting of a similar pipe, during a recent visit to the seaside at Great Yarmouth. Brian being older, wiser and far more knowledgeable on the subject of drainage insisted that it connected with an existing pipe, to emerge in a ditch about eight hundred yards away. The only thing they did agree on was that the only way to know for sure was to crawl down it and investigate. They vowed to do this as soon as they returned from their holiday in Scotland, and this appeared to bring them some resolution on the subject.

"I've got a new parachute," I said.

This snapped them to attention.

"What kind of parachute?" Brian wanted to know.

"A real one," I replied. "I got it in town."

"Can we see it?" asked Ryan.

"Yah," I replied, "It's at home. Pete is fixing it for me."

I was excited about the prospect of showing it off to them and so we all set off toward my house. Besides, Brian and Ryan had been told by their father to collect the canvas sheet from Dad.

On the way, we met Benito, who was walking up the hill toward us.

"Where are you going?" he asked.

"Looking for you," I said. "What are you doing?"

"Hiding," he replied.

"Who from?" We all wanted to know the answer to this one.

"Father O'Leary," replied Benito.

"Oh," I said, We all understood.

"You know what I just heard from Mrs. Snobbit?" I asked him.

"How would I?" he replied. I ignored his response and continued.

"The Maudly-Creechoms are building a Guy."

"Oh no!" he said, slapping his fist down in the air onto some imaginary surface. "How much have they done?"

"I don't know," I answered. "I think we have to get the rest of the gang involved."

Normally, gang business would not be discussed in front of non-gang members, but the Pilchard brothers had on many occasions proved themselves capable of keeping a secret. Anyway, they were usually so wrapped up in their own bizarre world of skydiving and cave exploring that everyday matters did not concern them.

"We can't let them win," said Benito.

"I know," I replied. I just wasn't sure how to proceed next.

"We're going to need a trolley," said Benito.

It was true. Being overwhelmed with the task of creating a Guy, I hadn't considered that we also needed transportation to haul it round the village.

"Do either of you have a trolley?" asked Benito of the brothers. I knew the answer would be no. Even if the Pilchards had owned a trolley, it would have three or five wheels and be built with some weird configuration that would render it totally useless for our purposes.

"No," they replied, shaking their heads in unison.

"With any luck, Crumb might have a trolley," I suggested.

Benito and I were the nucleus of a small gang, which included Chucky Billings, Basher Middleton and Crumb Carrington. Occasionally our ranks would swell to accommodate others who would temporarily join us at play, but Chucky, Basher and Crumb were the most common associates.

Crumb or Peter, as his mother knew him, was a useful member of our small group – he provided comic relief and had a vast collection of useless junk, which if he continued to accumulate, might one day rival my father's. Crumb also possessed some considerable mechanical skill and in his backyard he had a fine collection of bikes and trolleys in varying stages of repair. He excelled at finding those highly sought after items like trolley wheels and nonstandard bicycle handlebars.

"Hmmm," said Benito, "how long have the Maudly-Creechoms been building it?"

"I don't know," I replied.

"We need to have a meeting about this," said Benito.

This was the ideal day to do it. Great Biddington was usually quiet on Sundays with people enjoying a much-needed rest, or going to church. The Pilchard family didn't go to church. They claimed to be atheists, and so did not concern themselves with such lofty matters. Benito and

I were not atheists but neither of us had plans to spend any time in church today. If we were to build a Guy we would need all the free time we had and could not afford to spend the day pursuing our respective religious obligations.

The path to eternal salvation favored by my family was Church of England, and because of this we would normally have attended Sunday school. Fortunately for us, the vicar, who was the closest thing we had to a Supreme Being in the village, had recently suggested to my mother that my brother and I discontinue our attendance there.

Sunday school was a concept that I could never really understand. If it was in fact "school", then why not roll it into one of the normal boring school days leaving Sunday free for far more important things. If it was somehow significant that it occur on Sunday, then why not move one of the regular school days to Sunday and free up a valuable weekday? It made no sense. It was not that Vicar Hobbins had nothing to do on Sunday, in fact, as I understood it, Sunday was one of his busier days. In any event, someone, probably the Queen, started it and all the village kids of God-fearing parents were supposed to go. Sunday school was held in the chapel, which was located opposite Binford's shop and next door to Mrs. Wiggins's small shop selling plant pots – a location feared by my brother because Mrs. Wiggins supplemented her income by attempting to cut hair.

I could not fathom why this event was held in the chapel and not in the school or better still, the church. We would have preferred the church since it was a large stone building with a thick wooden door that that allowed the inmates to pretend that they were in a castle. I am also not sure why our small village needed both a church and a chapel, exactly what the difference was or what influence each had on one's eventual planned trip to heaven. With so many of my spiritual questions remaining unanswered, it is not hard to see why I did not take to this way of life.

I could not relate in too much detail the events that transpired within those hallowed walls because I only attended on three occasions, but from what I saw it would begin with Vicar Hobbins arriving wearing a long black dress. Although we laughed openly at this bizarre attire saying that the vicar dressed like a girl, secretly we admired how much it made him look like a vampire! He would take his place in the pulpit beneath a large wooden statue of Jesus. Reaching into his pocket the vicar would produce a pair of gold-rimmed bifocals and balance them on the bridge of his nose, allowing him to read to us the words of divine guidance from a large leather-bound bible. He would intermittently lift his eyes halfway through each sentence to scan the audience and check for attentiveness. The reading seemed to last for hours and be delivered in such a monotonous tone that no one really paid attention. At the end of the reading he would tell us what he thought it meant. This would be followed by a highly critical monologue designed to remind us what rotten, sinful people we were, and then we would all have to sing about it.

Mrs. Crippin would then arrive and seat her self at the piano with her back toward us. She was heavily involved in numerous aspects of Great Biddington's daily life. She assisted serving lunch at the school during mealtimes, she helped with the flowers at the church, and she apparently fancied herself something of a sacred musician. We calculated that the vicar was at least one hundred years old, and Crippin looked as if she could have been old enough to be his grandmother, especially when she put on a pair of bifocals almost identical to his. This left us to conclude that either Christianity was bad for the eyes or that these special religious spectacles were issued by God to assist in reading the tiny print contained in the prayer books. When Crippin was satisfied that the murmurs had died down to an acceptable level and that the assembled masses were ready to enjoy her divinely inspired music, she would angle her head back, squint at the music sheet and bang out a chord on the badly tuned piano. This was our cue to start singing.

And what singing it was. As the discordant cacophony began, it became immediately apparent why this event was held in the chapel, it being a free standing building set back from the road so that the off-key warbling was kept away from the delicate ears of local inhabitants. The singing would begin like a gramophone record slowly starting up, rising in both pitch and volume, and would then grind along reluctantly, with the same degree of enthusiasm normally reserved for a visit to the dentist. Each child in the congregation sang a slightly different variation of both tune and key, and no two seemed to be at the same point in the song at the same time. This dreadful dirge would continue until Mrs. Crippin struck the final chord, and the vocalists would just sort of drift of into silence in the same way that bagpipes, at the end of a solo, groan out their last dying breath.

It was only Crippin's unintentional comedic vigor during this performance that provided any relief from the boredom we felt at having to participate in this ceremony. She would attack the piano keys with a maniacal gusto that we found quite remarkable for her age. Of course it did not take long for my brother to begin imitating her and making comparisons to the mad and masked organist in "Phantom of the opera."

At the end of each line of the hymn, Crippin would rotate her head almost an entire one hundred and eighty degrees to ensure that all present were as emotionally involved in the proceedings as she was, and at the same time, show us all how humorous she looked. After about half a second she would jerk her head back around and attempt to re-focus on the sheet music, giving us the welcome opportunity to laugh behind her back. Since we were able to predict with absolute accuracy the exact moments of her scrutiny, we were able to synchronize our laughter perfectly with her exaggerated movements, thus avoiding detection and therefore punishment.

The collection plate would then be passed around. As the plate approached us we would hold out the few coins given to us by our parents for a contribution, rattle the change already in the plate and put the gob stopper and chocolate money back in our pockets.

Then Vicar Hobbins would once again take center stage and we were all supposed to pray together. More often we would bow our heads and whisper jokes to each other. It had not taken Pete long to invent several variations of the vicar's name.

"Vicar Dobbins," he whispered almost inaudibly, but I heard it and a sudden short amused breath escaped from my nose. Sam Tropit had a plough horse on his farm called Dobbin, and for an instant I had a vision of the overweight mare, wearing the vicar's black dress and holy spectacles. In turn, Pete found my reaction entertaining and began to chortle quietly himself.

"Vicar Nobbins," he said between chuckles, trying another variation of the preacher's name. I found this equally amusing and now had the desire to laugh out loud, made worse by the solemn silence and the fear that everyone would hear me. Pete fired his final shot.

"Vicar Hob-nob." He said this quite loudly. Since he was already laughing himself, he had lost the ability to control the volume of his own voice, and several other members of the congregation heard him.

I burst into laughter, along with three other rows of highly amused children. The vicar's sermon immediately changed directions.

"...And Jesus said unto the assembled masses.... Will you boys behave yourselves?"

This made vicar Hob-nob sound ridiculous and the remainder of the assembly now joined us in our merriment.

The following week, we discovered that the large round thick cushions, used for kneeling in prayer, resembled a motorcycle's back wheel. Pete was the first to point this out and also the first to tip one on edge and sit on it. He grabbed the polished brass handrail of the pew in front as if it were the handlebars of his imaginary dirt bike, and began to imitate engine noise. In no time at all I mounted up, as did Crumb Carrington who was sitting the other side of Pete, and Basher Middleton, who was sitting next to me. We gunned our engines like an unholy quartet of rockers and once again the pulpit lapsed into silence. The vicar was angry, and I think wanted to curse at us. Nothing about his reaction suggested that he practiced what he preached, and after the class was over he took us to one side and threatened us with severe punishment involving fire, misery and eternal damnation. Basher said that it was enough to put you off motorcycles forever, which gave Pete the joy of participating in another argument.

By the third week we were able to sing some of our own words to the hymns. This was too much for Vicar Hob-Nob to bear and the vicar quietly suggested to my parents that we move to another village. And that was how we escaped from the vicar's tyrannical supervision, and our souls were delivered into eternal Sunday morning freedom forever, and ever, Amen.

Although I complained about my religion, Benito had it much, much worse. Benito was "technically" a Catholic, but many believed that a boy with such a sinful nature did not really belong on consecrated ground. My father said that he was surprised that Benito did not burst into flames whenever he entered a church. Despite the fact that Benito came from a religious background that was very different from ours, we shared some common ground regarding spiritual beliefs. These were best described by the phrase "playing is better than praying." For this reason, Benito was about as keen to go to Mass as we were to go to Sunday school.

I remember one lazy evening, when we were sitting on the church wall beneath a large oak, with a good vantage point to see the motorcycles arriving at the Red Lion. Our conversation turned to discussing things that waste time. Naturally I nominated Sunday school as the best example of this, and I shared with Benito some of the secrets of our religious practice and the mysterious beliefs surrounding it. He looked at me with astonishment. I expected him to console me by supplying words of comfort and supportive understanding. Instead, he had quite the opposite reaction.

"I don't know what right you have to complain," he said with the indignation that comes from the sudden realization that his parents had picked the wrong god. I had seen this look once before when Crippin, who was distributing the dessert during the school lunch, was temporarily distracted and accidentally gave me an extra large helping of jam tart.

Benito had been quite happy with his portion until he saw my gargantuan slice. His gaze shifted back and forth from his plate to mine displaying utter disgust. What followed was a lengthy attempt by him to convince me that I would not like the jam tart because he had seen Crippin accidentally spill some vinegar in it. When that approach failed, he tried to bargain me out of my share by offering me some chewing gum, which he had not yet bought. He then employed a strategy overburdened by sympathy and rambled on about how Mario had stolen his breakfast that morning. I listened to his tragic tale as I looked down at the oversized desert, and in a moment of clarity realized that I really did not enjoy the taste of jam tart very much. I considered this for a moment within the framework of Benito's hunger pangs before deciding that there was a matter of principle involved, and I forced it down.

'You know what I have to go through every Sunday?" he asked.

I explained that I did not, but that it could be no worse that listening to Vicar Hobbins babbling on.

"Oh no," Benito said with outrage and horror," you can't imagine how terrible it is."

He then went on to describe a dreadful ordeal where the priest conducted the entire affair in some foreign language known only to him and the Pope, and where the audience was encouraged to join in for certain lines of the sermon. The biggest annoyance for Benito was that just when he got comfortable sitting down, quietly bored, almost asleep, the congregation would have to stand up. By the time he had shuffled to his feet, it was time to sit down again.

I listened to him raving on about having to eat little biscuits that tasted like stale cardboard and watch the priest drink blood. He soon had me convinced that this was not something that a child should be exposed to. I think it was on that day that the seeds of discontent were sowed in Benito's mind, an event that would eventually lead to his self-imposed excommunication.

The Rolonzios were the only Catholic family in Great Biddington. There was no Catholic center for worship despite the large quantity of Rolonzios that were obviously in such desperate need of it. They did not have a car and so seemed doomed to burn in hell. The solution to this spiritual deficit came in the form of Father O'Leary. Father O'Leary was a priest from a nearby village called Nether Biddlington, and each Sunday he would drive over to Great Biddington in a large shiny black car to collect the entire Rolonzio household, and take them to Mass. Benito put a great deal of effort into avoiding Father O'Leary.

CHAPTER 8
RYAN GOES SKYDIVING

"So, are we going to try the parachute or not?" Brian was growing impatient. The discussions about our Guy problem were of no concern to him – and he wanted to view my latest purchase.

"Yes," I said, "let's go and get it."

"Oh, don't forget that Dad asked us to get that canvas sheet as well," said Ryan to his brother.

We walked on down the road toward our house. Benito clearly was not happy about this plan, since he was, after all, in hiding, and this route brought him closer to his own house, thereby making discovery more likely. As we walked, he kept stretching his neck upwards as if the extra height would allow him to spot his pursuers before they saw him.

It had not always been this way. Benito used to be a loyal follower. He followed Father O'Leary the way Mr. Rolonzio followed Manchester United football club. Each Sunday Father O'Leary's big black car would roll up the dusty lane and slow to a halt outside the gate leading to the Rolonzio residence. The back door of the car would open and down the concrete path they would come.

Mrs. Rolonzio would be in front dressed in black. Immediately behind her would be the tallest of her children, Big Gina, and then each of her other eight or nine children would follow arranged by height. This organizational pattern of progressively shorter Rolonzios created a human slope from Big Gina to Angelina. Because Mr. and Mrs. Rolonzio were in the habit of having one child a year, the slope was remarkably even, which made it easy to spot any sinful family members not present.

Mr. Rolonzio would never be present. In his life Catholicism took a back seat to football. Each Sunday the best football game of the week was televised, and although it did not start until much later in the day, the head of the Rolonzio household was going to take no chance that may lead to him missing a minute of this important event. He said that he felt God would understand, but I thought he was a little fanatical in this regard. My brother once heard him say that he thought Jesus must support Leeds United, since his robes were all white and the same color as the Leeds players uniforms, but this supposedly powerful following did not explain the teams gradual slide down the first division following a recent string of defeats.

Mario was also absent from the line-up. There appeared to be no particular reason for his reluctance to accompany the rest of the family to church, and unlike his father, he offered no badly thought out excuse. He simply did not go. He used to attend each and every Sunday, but then he reached that age when he decided he would no longer have any part of it, and by that time he had achieved a certain reputation for violence, so the priest did not question his decision.

Benito was rapidly approaching the age when there would be one less devotee in the Rolonzio clan. One more seat at Mass would be left empty, and Father O'Leary would weep for one more lost soul as the victor became apparent in the battle for Benito's salvation. But the war was by no means over. There would be a period of several months when he would, each week, try to avoid this spiritual excursion. During this time his attendance would gradually dwindle away to nothing, and in the end his efforts would be repaid as he attained the same status as his older brother and become a free man.

We had now reached the edge of our property, and climbed up on top of the wall on the Ricketson's side of El Paso. This was to avoid entering our property in full view of any holy emissary. We walked in single file along the narrow edge of the wall until we reached the out buildings where Pete's motorbike was kept. Pete, and the motorcycle had gone but I was happy to see the modified parachute lying in a crumpled heap by the door.

"Is that it?" asked Brian rushing over to pick it up.

"Let me see," I snatched it from him, wanting to wait no longer to inspect my brother's handiwork at removing the spring. He had done a very clean job and no sight of the steel coil remained.

"That's wonderful," said Ryan. "Let's go and try it."

"Yes," said Brian. "I can't wait."

"Well you'll have to," said Benito.

"Why?" asked Ryan.

"Because it's too risky," came the simple response.

"Oh, I'm sure the new parachute is completely safe," said Ryan. "It's a real one, you know."

"I don't mean the parachute is too risky," said Benito.

I understood Benito's concern. I was as eager as the brothers to try out the new silk safety device, but the test area was located on the other end of El Paso, and would have been in full view of Father O'Leary as he arrived to pick up the rest of the Rolonzio household. We all agreed that it would be unfair to subject Benito to the risk of capture and we postponed our jump until the coast was clear. As an alternative plan we decided to hide out in our tree house.

It was built in a giant gnarled oak tree that was perfect for climbing. The twisted limbs allowed it to be everything from a rocket ship to a cliff face for mountaineering. It was a gathering place for our gang from the time when we were very young and it never lost its appeal. In summer it was densely foliated, but now the brown twisted branches were starkly visible, and offered little cover. The trunk proceeded skyward with a profusion knot-holes and branches situated perfectly for an easy climb. Further up, the tree branches spread out parallel to the ground forming a support of strong limbs. We had covered these branches with a couple of old floorboards that made a platform for easy sitting, and upon this structure the clubhouse was built. A single rope swing with knots tied in it to aid grip, was attached to the platform and hung down almost to the ground.

We climbed up into the tree and once inside took up our positions, with Benito electing himself as look-out, and Brian and Ryan seated cross legged on the floor performing an envious in-depth examination of the parachute. I took a position by the doorway, and tried to play host by offering everybody one of Mrs. Snaggins pilfered apples. The Snaggins' chickens didn't take kindly to intruders and although not brave enough to attack they were able to sound the alarm that would bring Snaggins running, so the removal of apples from Mr. Snaggins chicken encampment had to be executed with extreme precision.

I felt very much at home in the treehouse, amid the peacefully creaking wood and the soft rustling of the parachute, hidden away from the world in my own private den. Many happy memories had been forged in this place, but as is inevitable with unsafe construction in high places, there were also fearful times, which when recalled, would quicken my pulse and cause me to unconsciously rub the site of some ancient injury.

The tree house had started life as a simple platform, but eventually it had had been expanded into the comfortable and well-concealed place where we now sat. It was actually Joey Cave's idea. He was a master tree house builder, and had achieved ample notoriety in his profession. He had personally constructed seven different tree based dwellings and served as an advisor to many more in neighboring villages. We were fortunate to have access to his design skills, and equally fortunate to have access to Dad's immense collection of junk to use as construction materials. It took no more than a couple of hours to locate a fine collection of treasures: two large pieces of plywood, some old floorboards, a window with some of the glass missing, a large triangular piece of blue carpet, a waterproof plastic sheet and all the necessary string, rope, nails and glue with which to construct our high altitude hideout and headquarters for our gang. A tin bucket on a rope served as a means to transport items too difficult to hold while climbing.

'Any sign of him yet?" I asked.

"Nope," replied Benito.

"Do you want me to take a turn as lookout?" I asked helpfully.

"No, It's OK," Benito said.

"Well, let me know if you change your mind," I offered.

We all waited patiently inside the wooden walls. I felt that we had done a fine job decorating it. There were pictures of pop stars and football heroes, and Benito had pinned up a large picture of Frankenstein chained to a stone wall. We had a collection of old comic books for entertainment, and a flashlight for emergencies. Mum had donated a small wicker basket in which we kept a constant supply of apples, and we had a plastic telescope from "Buskys" to keep a watch out for unwelcome visitors. It was this that Benito now peered through, ever vigilant for the arrival of Father O'Leary.

The Pilchards were lost in admiration and wonder as they continued to examine the parachute, and I was busy relating to Benito the horror story that I had to endure to get it.

'There he is" exclaimed Benito. We all scrambled to share a peek through the cracked lens of the telescope. A freshly washed and polished black O'Lery-mobile cruised ominously up Mud Lane and slowed to a halt just beside Benito's front gate. The rear window was lowered about half-way and an arm became visible extending a skeleton like finger to beckon the faithful. Even from this distance we could hear the commotion from inside the house as the believers scrambled to ready themselves, and predictably, it wasn't long before we heard Mrs. Rolonzio crying out Benito's name. Benito, in turn, responded with a mischievous chuckle. A moment later her panic stricken cry was heard again. This time Benito slowly reached down and carefully selected an apple, which he casually inspected closely before taking a bite. Next, the collection of Rolonzios of various shapes and sizes were dispatched and ran from the house in all directions like rats escaping from a smoke filled barn. This was obviously a search party sent forth to find the absent Benito.

Benito's self-imposed exile from the Catholic Church was now entering Stage Two. Stage One was characterized by his realization that he did not want to go. This reluctance was expressed every Sunday as he spent the hour leading up to his departure vehemently arguing with his mother before finally being dragged forcibly, and often screaming, into the waiting car. As he became more secure in his role as a religious dissident he entered Stage Two. This involved him adopting a more strategic approach to avoid his date with the heavenly father. The plan was to slip out of the house unnoticed and remain hidden until the group could wait for him no longer. In the end they would go and he would stay.

Escaping from the house was easy. He skillfully used his knowledge of the turmoil that constantly surrounded his family to slide out of view. While his mother was busy readying the numerous children for the dreaded expedition, Benito would be busy setting everything up. He was at the very least non-cooperative, and attempted with his every move to create diversions to take everyone's attention off him. Usually this involved hiding items that were essential to the trip. His mother's purse, his sister's hat, his little brother's shoes. Just at the point when all affected participants had worked themselves into a frenzy attempting to locate the missing items, Benito would nonchalantly kick the television's power plug out of the wall. This caused his father to panic, and excitedly recite an endless string of Italian curse words. Benito would then step quickly and quietly out the back door and disappear over the fence.

In the coming weeks Benito would enter Stage Three, which I called the defiant stage. It would involve him openly defying his father, mother, priest and God by simply refusing to join the rest of the family on their pilgrimage. But for now, he would have to hide out like a wanted man until his family's search efforts were exhausted and Father O'Leary's car left.

"They're looking for me," he said. "Carminas checking in the coal shed now."

The family was urgently calling Benito's name, and for the next few minutes we giggled at his daring escape.

"Is that your Mum calling now?" I asked, recognizing the voice.

"Yeh," he said, "she's yelling out of the bedroom window."

The direction of the desperate cries changed and Benito said, "Now Big Gina is riding Mario's bike up the lane to look for me."

A minute later he said, "I think they've given up."

Eventually I regained possession of the telescope and I could see the somber procession advancing down the concrete path toward the open door of the waiting car.

I felt as if I was witnessing a true miracle of the Catholic Church as one after another, all the Rolonzios crammed themselves into Father O'Leary's car. I tried to visualize a seating plan that would accommodate so many and could not, leaving me with the notion of a magic trick. I imagined the Relonzios entering the car and then all escaping through a secret trapdoor in the floor like clowns in a circus vehicle, or simply leaving through the adjacent rear door in the style of an old comedy film. Ryan made a comment that the sight of Benito's family driving off in a big black car did nothing to dispel the playground rumors that the Rolonzios were secretly involved in the Mafia. Benito said that there was no such thing as the Mafia, but the behavior of his family convinced us otherwise.

In the distance we heard the roar of my brother's motorcycle, which was a convenient distraction because I sensed that Benito was uncomfortable discussing the Guy issue with the Pilchard boys present. We scrambled out of the tree-house and positioned ourselves in the thick branches to get a good view of Pete's victory lap. As usual, he appeared rounding the bend between the twin poplar trees that stood in front of rat barn, the rear wheels throwing up loose dirt and gravel. The sound grew louder as he rode over the grass beside the rows of brussels sprouts and banked hard as he avoided the pole that held up the clothes line. He cornered the tobacco plantation, rode under the tree, made a tight one hundred and eighty-degree corner with the back of the bike sliding to obliterate the weed patch that Dad called a lawn, and then he retraced his route toward the old stone barn where he would stable his mount for the night. But he never reached the barn. My father stepped out from behind the hedge and held up his hand like a policeman directing traffic. This was a bold and daring move since Pete despised using brakes. Fortunately for both of them, Pete was able to stop.

The young rider was then told for the second time that day that he must not ride the bike round the garden because my mother found the noise offensive.

Pete countered by saying that Mum did not mind at all since she believed that the vibrations from the machine dissuaded moles from taking up residence in the top soil.

Dad pointed out that we did not have a mole problem. Pete pointed to a pile of black dirt.

Dad began to angrily explain the difference between a molehill and one of Morris the bulldog's recent excavations. Pete was smiling, not only because he knew it would irritate Dad, but because he had been successful at steering the conversation away from forbidden motorcycle riding practices and toward some other subject guaranteed to make Dad's blood boil. We would normally have gathered to watch the heated debate until its inevitable conclusion where my brother gets hit, but Brian and Ryan wanted to test drive the new parachute, and had to soon return to help their father pack for the holiday trip.

We hurried on past, quickly arriving at the jump site at the end of the old stone barn. The wall was constructed of broken-down limestone and was indeed a treacherous place. It was half collapsed which allowed for easy hand and foot holds during the ascent, but these places had a habit of disappearing in a cloud of rubble and dust as the intrepid skydiver gained altitude.

Then an argument started about which of us would try the parachute first. Good arguments were made from all present, except Benito, who as he put it, didn't have much interest in killing himself, and so declined to be in the jumping line-up. In the end I prevailed as the successful test pilot, the key point of my argument being that it was my parachute. The Pilchards watched enviously as I strapped the green canvas webbing around my chest and under my arms.

I began to carefully climb the loose stone structure. Benito followed behind carrying the parachute canopy as if it were a bridal train. I was now at the "six feet" mark. This is as high as I had previously jumped from, but felt that my new equipment should allow me to descend safely from at least ten feet so I continued upwards into the sky. The scratched chalk mark on the stone where I now stood indicated ten feet. As I shifted my weight for the next step, the stone broke free beneath my left foot. We all watched for what seemed like an eternity as the stone tumbled to a crash below. This brought me to my senses, and to some extent shook my confidence. This was after all an un-tested and experimental device. After a few moments of pause I decided that it was better to make the first jump from a lower altitude. I protested my decision despite Benito's insistence that I should go all the way to the top. Returning to the eight-foot mark I assumed the "get ready" position and waited.

As a gust of wind picked up, Benito threw the white silk into the air and I leaped into the blue yonder. I found myself quite surprised at the speed of my descent. The ground rushed up at me with a suddenness that I was not prepared for and I landed with a jolt, severe enough to cause me to fall over, but I was able to save face by turning the fall into an impressive looking roll. I climbed to my feet, a little disappointed that my descent was not as slow and graceful as I expected, but I tried not to let this show, and although in pain I walked without limping.

Everyone immediately began to tell me how good it looked and how fortunate I was to posses such a professional looking device. As the congratulations continued I found it harder to be honest with myself and the others, and began to embellish the event with fabricated detail. Brian and Ryan were hanging on my every word as I related the feeling of free fall and weightlessness, about the sensation of floating effortlessly on the breeze, and they stood wide-eyed with envy as I explained that the landing impact was barely noticeable.

An argument then broke out as to which of the brothers would go next. For some reason Benito was still not keen to try it, which left the two Pilchard boys to squabble between themselves. Ryan, the smaller Pilchard won the argument and donned the device that would transport him safely back to earth. With the white parachute tucked under his arm, Ryan eagerly climbed up the dilapidated and decomposing wall. He soon passed the four-foot mark that indicated his previous best. Carefully picking his way up the steep rock face he passed the six-foot mark. We all exchanged a concerned and puzzled glance wondering how high he would ascend, but he was in his own world – his eyes glazed with determination, and he continued until he reached the eight-foot mark. In an attempt to dissuade him, I said this was an impressive attempt for a boy of such slight stature, but he countered that his lighter weight would allow an even slower descent than I experienced. He crouched at the eight-foot point trying to pick out a good landing spot. For the first time he seemed slightly hesitant and looked back down the wall at the lower elevations. Benito reminded him that it was getting late. Ryan shuffled his feet to find a good take off position. Benito now held the canopy, ready to throw it into the breeze.

I will always wonder how well the parachute would have worked for him, if it had opened properly.

Ryan jumped off the wall. Benito would later say that Ryan should have warned him first. A momentary increase in the volume of my father's voice, still protesting the finer points of mole dwellings, captured Benito's attention so he never actually threw the parachute into the air. Ryan did not get far before realizing that he was still tethered to the ball of cloth in Benito's hands. The strings went tight with a popping sound, and Benito instinctively held onto the bundle, which he now viewed as some kind of safety line. This had the effect of pulling Ryan back toward the sheer face of the wall, which he tried to grab, but instead slid down it vertically. There was a ripping sound as his shirtsleeve and arm caught on one of the sharp stones in the wall. Benito, realizing that he could not save the boy, let go of the parachute. Ryan tumbled backward and cried out as he hit the ground. He rolled onto his left side, clutched his grazed arm and cried. While we all waited to see if Ryan would ever walk again, Benito suggested that Brian now try out the parachute. It was several minutes before Ryan would let any of us near him, several weeks in the case of Benito.

Mr. Pilchard was not at all happy that his two sons had not returned to help him load the car for the holiday trip. When he saw his youngest son, tearful, limping, bleeding and with ripped and dirty clothes, he immediately began to yell at Brian. Of the three of us, Brian was perhaps the most innocent of the crime for which he was currently accused, but I was content to let him take the brunt of his father's wrath, since I reasoned that he was more used to it than the rest of us. It suited me quite well that I was not the focus of this anger. Mr. Pilchard had harbored a vindictive grudge against me ever since the incident involving my cricket bowling practice and his living room window. For a number of reasons Benito was equally unpopular with the Pilchard patriarch, so even though it seemed unjust for Brian to be wrongfully condemned, we said nothing. We stood silently, occasionally nodding in agreement with Mr. Pilchard as he chastised his eldest son.

Ryan was then taken inside the house to be cleaned up by his mother, and we were all enlisted to assist with packing the holiday equipment. Mr. Pilchard had taken my father's suggestion to heart and the small boat had already been securely tied on to the roof of the car.

Eventually all the camping supplies, foodstuffs and a cooking stove were loaded inside the car and all the clothing, blankets and sleeping bags were thrown into the boat on the roof. Mr. Pilchard turned to Brian.

"Now where did you put that canvas sheet?" he asked.

Brian looked at me for an answer. Not having one I looked at Benito.

"Well?" I said.

Benito replied that he remembered Ryan having it just before his unfortunate encounter with the stone wall, but we all knew that this was a lie. Just at that moment a slight breeze picked up and I felt the first few drops of rain as I tried desperately to remember when I last saw the canvas sheet. I remembered having it when Mario was fixing the bicycle tire, but did not remember seeing it after that.

"I think it might be lying next to Pete's motorbike toilet," I addressed the senior Pilchard directly. "Should I go and see?"

He said, his anger mounting, that unless we did something quickly the bedding would be rain-soaked. His solution to this problem was to angrily decree that the boat must be unloaded and the bedding placed in a dry location until either the rain stopped or the canvas sheet was located.

In the next few minutes we all realized that throwing the bedding up over the side of the boat was a much better technique for loading it than it was for unloading. The threat of a downpour made us struggle desperately. We had the boat about halfway unloaded when Mrs. Snobbit arrived carrying the elusive canvas. I then recalled leaving it in her kitchen as we discussed Bulls, Guys and groundsheets. Mr. Pilchard said a few words about the deficiencies of my mental state and once again we began to load the bedding. This time all available personnel were employed to sling the sleeping paraphernalia back into the boat. Mrs. Pilchard and Ryan helped with the last couple of bundles and Mrs. Snobbit tried to memorize each item as it was loaded. Lastly, the canvas was stretched over the top of the boat and lashed down securely. Then it stopped raining.

As Benito and I walked home, we talked about what an unpleasant father Mr. Pilchard was, and how he did not have much patience with children, even well-behaved ones like us. We walked down Mud Lane in the stillness of the approaching dusk, and our conversation had once again turned to matters of the Guy Fawkes.

Benito restated that we not only needed to build our own Guy Fawkes, but also required a transportation device with which to carry it around from house to house on our begging mission.

"OK," he said, "I'll build the Guy, and you make the trolley."

"How are you going to build a Guy on your own?" I asked curiously.

"I've got lots of brothers and sisters." He said with undeniable logic.

The implication was that the Relonzio clan would pull together and assist in this project, but I found this scenario unlikely. I had never seen them do anything together except fight, but I trusted that there was a plan buried deep inside Benito's conniving brain.

Constructing a Guy Fawkes required extensive raw materials, and a good deal of skill. Benito had neither. Transportation, on the other hand, required only a trolley.

The simplest trolley consisted of old pram wheels bolted to each end of a small plank of wood. The pilot would sit on the wood and hang on for dear life as other playmates pushed the trolley as fast as they could. As trolley-building skill grew, a steering mechanism might be added along with a more elaborate seat. Some were even painted. I knew that Crumb would probably have a trolley and said as much to Benito. He did not immediately take to this idea since including another person would mean dividing the spoils of our mission three ways instead of two, and if Crumb joined us then Basher and Chucky would also come along and that would mean sharing the money with them as well. This argument continued most of the way home but finally Benito agreed that the trolley was essential to the success of the plan.

It was nearly dark when I arrived home, and I was welcomed by the sound of an argument in progress. I did not need to open the door to hear my father any more clearly, but since it was fairly certain that the object of his reprimands would be my brother, I rushed inside to enjoy the entertainment. Dad was pacing in circles round the kitchen table talking angrily about the way things were when he was our age, and I hoped that I hadn't missed the toilet up at the end of the garden story. Pete sat in a chair by the window gazing at the ceiling, which only caused Dad to become more exasperated. His anger was momentarily focused on me for arriving home late, and then thankfully, soon redirected to the rightful recipient of his wrath.

"The point is," he said, as if explaining to someone half Pete's age, "You can't go around with hair halfway over your collar. If I had done that at your age, my mother would have killed me."

"It's not over my collar," said Pete tilting his head forward to artificially raise the hairline at the back of his head. When he did this a mop of his dark mane fell forward over his left eye.

"And now you can't see properly," added my father, very near the end of his rope.

"Yes I can," argued Pete. "There's the sink over there."

Dad was no longer prepared to continue the discussion.

"Tomorrow you will go and visit Mrs. Wiggins and come back with a reasonable haircut. IS THAT CLEAR?"

Pete ultimately nodded his agreement, feeling that he had found a loophole in Dad's argument by use of the word "reasonable." We sat around the kitchen table and Mum begun to serve supper. As she carried the last plate of food to the table, she looked through the window as the Pilchard car, with boat on roof, laden with camping equipment sped past, narrowly missing Morris who was being walked by Horace Maudly-Creechom.

"Roger just almost ran over Morris Maudly-Creechom," said Mum, and Dad immediately jumped up from his seat. For a second I thought he was going to get the gun to finish off what Roger Pilchard had started, but instead he rushed over to the radio.

We were all immediately forbidden to talk from the moment Dad turned on the radio in expectation of hearing the weather report. There was only band music playing, but silence had to be maintained in case the weatherman made an unexpected announcement. This was normal during any radio or television broadcasts that might contain any information about news, weather or ships, three subjects about which my father was passionate.

A large, black hard-bound book was then brought to the table and placed alongside Dad's plate of beef and mashed potatoes. He licked the forefinger of his right hand and turned the pages of maps one by one until reaching the well worn image that showed our home in the lower left corner. Moving his finger slowly along a squiggly red line, Dad traced the Pilchard route northbound. Just outside Birmingham the weatherman made his longed for presentation.

The news was not good. Heavy thunderstorms were expected in the north of England, with the worst being near the Scottish border. Dad made a comment about "poor Rodger" but offered his own "expert" opinion that it would probably only last three or four days. After swallowing a mouthful of mashed potatoes he remarked how fortunate it was for Rodger that we were able to loan him the waterproof sheet.

CHAPTER 9

A DAY OF TORTURE

"For heavens sake, will... you... boys ...get...up...!"

Mum had reached the point of desperation. Next would come the threat of forcible removal of the bed sheets and after that the promise of a bucket of cold water thrown over us at close range.

It didn't start out this way. At first we would vaguely hear the knock on the bedroom door and my mother's cheerful voice gently alerting us into consciousness and reminding us that today was a school day. This was her first mistake.

"Wake up boys, downstairs there is a big bar of chocolate, some ice cream and a new bike," Is what she should have said.

Our next experience would be a gentle shaking as Mum tried to revive us. She would tell us that the kettle was on and that we should come down for breakfast. This was also ineffective at motivating us for we knew that there was no hurry. Dad woke early to spend as much of the day as possible engaged in back breaking labor, and I thanked the powers that be, that Pete and I were not cursed with a similar fanatical outlook toward work. In fact, we had quite a different attitude toward anything involving effort. That is why, for the second time in less than ten minutes we went promptly back to sleep.

Round three would commence when my mother realized that you can achieve more with kind words and a cup of tea than you can with kind words alone. She would arrive carrying the hot fortifying beverage. This delivery would be accompanied by strict instructions to consume it quickly.

As the hot tea slowly invigorated me, I reflected on the day's proposed activities. It was always amazing to me how quickly Monday morning arrived, and I was disappointed that it brought with it the promise of school. School was really not very much fun and was quite a distraction from our busy agenda, however, it did serve one useful purpose: It was good meeting point for our gang. Today I would have to approach select members of that gang to aid me in procuring a trolley.

Halfway through my second piece of toast there was the expected knock at the door. Pete and I gulped the remainder of our third cup of tea and slipped into our warm coats, as Squeaky, Chucky Billings and his dog, Spot, let themselves in.

"Ready?" Chucky asked.

"Not really," I said, putting on my coat.

"We don't want to be late," said Squeaky.

"Yes, we do," said Chucky.

Mum threw a piece of half eaten toast on the floor for Spot as I finished buttoning my overcoat.

"Alright," I grumbled, "Let's go."

Chucky was the most recent member to be allowed into our gang. He was not born in our village but moved in next door to Mrs. Snobbit when he was young enough to not be branded as a foreigner for the rest of his life. He was the product of honest hardworking stock, and his strength and eagerness to hit people made him one of the first players to be picked for a football match. His younger brother Mathew, was prone to violence and seldom seen without a rock or a large stick in his hand. We sometimes used Mathew to do our dirty work but for the most part considered him too young to be of use. I grabbed my recently acquired peashooter from the kitchen table and the four of us, along with Spot, set off to collect Benito.

Walking to school followed a strict time tested procedure. Whoever lived furthest from the school, in this case Chucky, would set off first and collect additional school inmates along the way. Squeaky would be first, always eager to set off, then the Pilchards would normally be added to the group, but for the next two weeks they were off having a wonderful time in the deserted and inhospitable northern climes of Scotland. Pete and I would join the group next, and so on until the small clutch of frostbitten juniors reached the dreaded place of instruction.

Outside Benito's house, my brother leaned on the wooden gatepost and argued with Chucky about the weekend's soccer results while I walked briskly up the concrete path, past a rusty bike with several parts missing, and knocked sharply on the kitchen door. There were two frosted glass panes set into the door, the left pane had been replaced with a sheet of plywood after Mario, in a fit of rage had thrown a shoe at Big Gina and missed. As I stood stamping my feet to keep warm, from inside the house I heard the usual commotion, and could see through the opaque window the movement of blurred forms. There was always some sort of disturbance occurring in the Relonzio household. After about a minute of being ignored I looked through the letterbox to see Mrs. Rolonzio walking up and down the narrow kitchen past a sink full of dirty breakfast dishes, with the latest addition to the family laying in her arms and crying loudly. She yelled something in Italian and Carmina, the third youngest, came running with a baby's bottle. Off in the distance Antonella was screaming at someone about a scratched Beatles record.

I'm not sure exactly how many brothers and sisters Benito had – the number seemed to change every time you counted them. The ones I knew the best were Mario, the eldest, Big Gina the biggest, the twins Michael and Frankie, the daughter with a passion for horror films, and Antonella.

Tired of being ignored I opened the door and went inside. I was immediately confronted with the smell of exotic Mediterranean foods. Offering my greetings I pushed passed Mrs. Rolonzio and the baby and went into the living room where Mr. Rolonzio sat listening to the radio. He had set the volume at its loudest in a partially successful attempt to

drown out the surrounding turmoil. Seeing me he bellowed toward the
ceiling in Italian, and within seconds I heard Benito descending the stairs
three at a time.

Benito came in and said something that was inaudible over the din of
the screaming sister, crying baby and deafening radio. He beckoned me
to follow him outside, as he grabbed his coat and we walked to the front
gate. This loud and chaotic occurrence was typical. Most people tried to
conduct any business at the front gate, rather than suffer through the
pandemonium. I was one of the few people who dared go inside for more
that a few minutes.

It was a mile and a half to the school, which could, depending on the
weather or the mood that we were in, take up to an hour. Since today was
Monday, we were going through our weekly adjustment after two days of
freedom to the promise of a week of confinement, boredom and wasted
opportunity.

On the way we paused momentarily to make ugly faces at the Maudly-
Creechom's house. Chucky was by far the best at this. He claimed there
was an annual competition in which the contestants attempted to distort
their faces into a repulsive mask designed to be more loathsome that the
other participants. With great pride he would tell us that his place of
birth was home to several repeat winners. We tried hard not to let our
envy show.

Had the Maudly-Creechom children been visible we would have
called them names or thrown something at them. If Morris had been
present, Spot would surely have launched an attack of her own.

The Maudly-Creechom's impressive stone residence with pea gravel
driveway, behind a white painted five bar gate was the largest house on
Mud Lane. And somewhere behind the neatly edged lawn and perfectly
groomed flowerbeds, probably in the outbuildings that used to function
as a stable, they were constructing their Guy Fawkes. With their inex-
haustible supply of money, they could acquire whatever raw materials
they needed to fabricate a replica of the long dead would-be bomber.
Even had they not enjoyed this advantage, they could have hired slaves
to build one for them, bought one outright or paid one of the working
class to sit on top of the bonfire. This injustice bothered me almost as

much as it bothered Billy Tadcome. It seemed impossible that we could build a Guy to compete, but that was Benito's problem. I was on the trolley detail.

It was my turn to watch out for Grizzly McKenzie, the old drunken lunatic who lived on the corner of the High Street – fortunately it was too early for him to be awake so we were able to pass without incident.

Reaching Joey Cave's house we paraded single file down the garden path, past the neat rows of vegetables planted by his father. Joey opened the door just before Chucky was going to knock and emerged from the house buttoning up his coat. He called a sharp and irritated "good bye" over his shoulder to his mother, the aftermath of an argument we had not heard. As we walked Joey explained that he had been trying to convince his mother that since the usual caravan of cheerless students had not yet passed his house, school must have been cancelled for the day. He blamed our arrival for the failure of his plan, and we all had to apologize to prevent him from spending the rest of the day sulking.

We began to ascend the hill into the center of the village. It started by the village hall a hundred yards up the road from Joey's house, and continued on a steep and unforgiving incline, past the Red Lion pub in a slight sweeping curve, to level out opposite the butcher's shop.

I paused to look back down the hill and over the hedges and fences where a layer of fog had gathered in the lowest hollows of the ground, contrasting the brown soil visible further up the field. In late summer these fields would be awash with the stalks of yellow corn, its surface blowing gently like waves on the sea. By the end of summer sophisticated farming equipment would be brought in to harvest the wheat and corn. The straw would lay in neat rows for us to dive into and wrestle around, and in the bright sunlight we would hang onto the trailers that collected the corn, covering our mouths and noses from the dust with self-styled handkerchiefs like the cowboy outlaws we longed to be. By the end of harvest season, the remaining straw would be burned to clear the fields for the plough. Running along the edges of the burning straw and jumping in and out of the lines of flames was exhilarating. But it was now winter and all of that was gone, leaving behind rows of muddy plough furrows that caked boots and made walking slow and hard work.

We trudged past the Red Lion Pub, then a short walk past the church and the haunted graveyard, past Binford's shop where Mario would steal cigarettes, and we would be at our dreaded destination. Outside the school gate there would be a short, but never missed, affectionate session when Chucky would bid Spot farewell for the day. The dog had been banned from entering the school by Mrs. Diggsmore, who was still stewing over Spot's disruptive actions during last years school play.

Chucky would squat down to her level and scratch the thick fur on top of her head, and Spot would push her nose in the air and close her eyes halfway with pleasure. The two would look at each other and share a connection that I could never understand. On her hungriest day, our cat, Scraps, was never as emotionally supportive. Spot would then roll over as Chucky finalized the ritual with a belly rub before Spot turned back to trot home. At the end of the school day, Spot would always be waiting outside to meet Chucky and the moments of fondness would be repeated.

As we stood outside, a home made poster outside Binford's shop caught my eye. It read: "Join Great Biddington's population for an evening of Fun, Food and Fireworks." The festivities would take place on Sunday in a field on Farmer Wilmot's land. The poster also noted there would be a large bonfire and a ceremonial burning of the Guy. And then I saw it.

"Look at this," I said to Benito.

"What is it?" Benito asked.

"Read." I replied.

Benito traced the words with his finger and moved his lips as he mouthed them quietly.

"…farmer Wilmot……Sunday…..burning Guy….The Guy is being donated by the Maudly-Creechoms."

"The Guy is being donated by the Maudly-Creechoms!" he exclaimed. "Are we the only ones that didn't know about this?"

The Maudly-Creechoms were definitely building a Guy. And the event organizers had agreed to accept the said effigy as the official bonfire Guy.

I didn't mind them being selected as the official Guy Fawkes, but I was concerned that if we didn't build our own, however simple and basic it may be, that the village's loose change would go in the pockets of the undeserving Maudly-Creechoms.

"You better get busy," I instructed Benito.

"I know," he said with a serious nod. "But don't forget your part."

"I won't," I said. "I bet I finish the trolley before you finish the Guy." Benito ignored the challenge.

This was one more wake-up call that we were falling behind in our plan. We had first discussed it on Friday night. Saturday and Sunday, the best time for projects of this magnitude, had passed with no progress on our part, and it was now Monday. We had to make the begging rounds through the village next weekend before the fireworks.

The poster also reminded everyone not to forget the village talent show on Friday night in the village hall. It listed some of the scheduled attractions as Fred Pollard and his guitar, Toby Lawson's poetry reading and the glorious singing voice of Belinda Stuart. These cultural additions were not anything that any of us had any interest in.

Great Biddington school was a large two-room jail-like building constructed from carefully placed oversized and uneven blocks of limestone. It was bordered on two sides by open ground that served as a sports field, and one side by a road. The remaining side bordered Mrs. Jessop's house. Most of her property shared a wall with our fine educational institution, but a narrow alley at the back of the building, led to a high red brick wall that protected Mrs. Jessop's hallowed back garden. And it needed protection, for located in the backyard sanctuary was an impressive collection of very breakable plaster statues of animals. They had been deliberately arranged in a line resembling the targets that could be found at any fairground sideshow booth. This was a good demonstration of Mrs. Jessop's cruel streak, for she must have known that this tempting little diorama would taunt anyone who had ever owned a catapult, in the same way that pasta and tomato sauce would tempt Big Gina Rolonzio.

The outside toilet was located a short walk across the playground, a walk that seemed longer in winter, across an open area surfaced by a cracked, uneven and deteriorating concrete, that served as a playground. Behind the rudimentary and roofless building that provided a convenience to answer the call of nature was a wooden shed were the coal was kept, and a patch of small round pale colored gravel that was perfect for catapult ammunition.

The children were protected from the traffic on the High Street, and vice versa, by a low wall, and a high wire mesh fence. Together they completed the illusion that we were in jail. At the end of the wall, was a heavy black iron gate that swung on two large rusty hinges embedded in the wall. The gate squeaked open as we crossed the threshold into despair.

The noisy gate alerted Mrs. Diggsmore to our tardy arrival. She was one of the two teachers at the school. Younger children would occupy the smaller of the two rooms and it was there that Mrs. Malton would train them to act like normal people. Upon reaching the age of seven, pupils would graduate to the "big" room, where Mrs. Diggsmore would take over as handler. It took some time to become accustomed to the transition from Mrs. Malton's kind and understanding nature, to the cruel and harsh torment that old Mrs. Diggsmore had perfected over the course of her one hundred and twenty years of teaching.

The big room had a high wooden beamed roof with bare light bulbs hanging from the ceiling by brown twisted cloth-covered electrical chord. One end of the room was cleared for group activities like dancing and performing the annual school play. We were currently due to become involved in rehearsal for this year's performance, and I wasn't looking forward to it.

So we began the school week by being immediately reprimanded for our late arrival, something all the other students found entertaining, and after a short commotion we settled down at our desks. I sat at a desk with Benito, which was not such a good idea. It's not that Benito would not let me copy his work, it was that the accuracy of his finished projects would be highly unreliable. Our desk was in the back row, which prevented us from getting to the door quickly, but did have the advantage of being close to the heating stove and more importantly, as far from Mrs. Diggsmore as possible without actually going outside. I liked it because Mrs. Diggsmore's aim deteriorated with distance. Benito liked it because it allowed him to "keep an eye on things."

Chucky sat in the next desk with William O'Flanigan. William came from the top of the village. His father had been killed in the war and he spent most of his time looking after his mother. The only time we saw him was at school. William was a short, swarthy blond kid of Scottish descent who loved to fight, being in at least one violent altercation every month. We had been friends since the second day of school. On the first day of school, I found myself in a confrontation with him over the ownership of a small blue plastic fireman. Benito goaded me into fighting with him and I learned an important lesson about underestimating an opponent. In the scuffle that ensued I lost a piece of an upper front tooth, but left a decent bite mark on William's leg and was able to remove a good handful of his blond curly hair. By the time it was over it was I who had sustained a little more damage than he, but in the end we parted the best of friends.

Crumb sat in front of Larry Moady. Larry Moady was known as Toady for no other reason than it rhymed with his last name.

My brother sat in a special row that was reserved for the kids who would be leaving next year to attend a larger secondary school in a village several miles away. Along with Mario and Dotty Wiggins, they had a special curriculum to help prepare for their future education. They would be taking the entrance exam in the next few months and I expected that Mario would fail, and have to go to some "special' facility."

The desks were made of heavy wood, stained yellow-brown, with age, varnish and dirt. The writing surface could be lifted up to create a shield if one found oneself subject to a bombardment from the front of the class. Inside would be our books and writing implements, but a random inspection of desk contents usually also revealed comics, sugary sweets, and various forms of weaponry. I placed my peashooter next to the flexible wooden ruler that I used for launching small paper pellets at Sarah Crabtree, and closed the desk.

As the school day began we were first forced to listen to an utterly useless lecture about Australia, with particular emphasis being given to the climatic conditions, and the bizarre mode of conveyance employed by the kangaroo. This was followed by some form of instruction that required us to participate in either reading or writing.

I had dozed off but was startled awake when Mrs. Diggsmore slammed the large atlas shut with a bang. She made her concluding remarks about Australian wildlife, and then there was an impromptu question and answer session in which she attempted to sort out the attentive listeners from the rest of us. Taddy Bascome correctly answered a question about rainfall, and then we all laughed at Toady as he incorrectly identified the alligator as a common Australian house pet. I had my "polar bear" answer ready just in case but fortunately I was not called upon.

As predicted, the next lesson involved much more participation – each student was handed one piece of paper upon which we had to write. Of the two principal disciplines, I much preferred reading. I did not see the advantage of writing something when you could convey the same information verbally much more quickly, and without the requirement of any special equipment, which was the other problem that I had with writing. In order to write you first needed paper, and this was strictly rationed by Mrs. Diggsmore, as if she was privately aware of some upcoming global shortage. Each child was given only one sheet as she felt that to give out more only encouraged the youth to make either mistakes or paper airplanes.

Next we were all instructed to open our desks and remove our pens. The pen was a round stick of wood that required the attachment of a steel nib in order for it to qualify as a writing utensil. Excessive nib use would result in the need for a replacement, which had to be requested in person to Mrs. Diggsmore. For such an ordeal she would sit behind her polished black desk with a box of nibs placed neatly beside a garden cane and begin an interrogation to discern the cause of the request. Benito used up nibs at an alarming rate, and we all had to take it in turns to re-tip his writing instrument. The reason for his disproportional consumption became obvious to anyone who had spent a rainy lunch break inside the old school hall, looking for ways to ward off the boredom. On the inside lid of Benito's desk was a beautifully and very precisely drawn rendition of a dartboard. Benito had selected this particular desk on the advice of his older brother, who occupied it when he was at this school. Hundreds of tiny pinpoint impressions told the tale of generations of idle school children throwing their pens at the opened desk lid in search of the high score. This obviously had the effect of accelerating the deterioration of the metal nib.

The ink itself was wonderful stuff. Black and thick, leaving it's indelible stain on anything it touched and therefore had practical joke value, so like the paper, it was strictly rationed the way sandwiches might be in a lifeboat. To carry out Mrs. Diggsmore's bidding, a special student was selected as the ink monitor. I always hoped that I would one day be selected for this prestigious position, but when the call for volunteers came, I was invariably passed over. No matter how quickly I reacted to the announcement, how high I raised my hand, or how loud I snapped my fingers, the coveted post was always assigned to someone possessing better dexterity. To see the look of power on a pupil's face as he walked slowly and carefully carrying the chipped enamel ink jug filled us with envy. One stumble and someone was going home early, one slip and a huge permanent memento would be left that future generations would point to and in hushed and sacred tones talk of "the day that Billy tripped!" The Ink monitor was the most highly sought after of all monitor jobs. Next came the Milk monitor. Each morning the milkman would deliver two crates made of galvanized thick steel wire that each contained twenty half-pint bottles of milk. Two children were needed to carry in the crates and since they had to be surefooted and unlikely to engage in any tomfoolery during the haulage of this delicate freight, I was not selected for this service either. The way I saw it, this job trained you for teamwork, whereas the Ink monitor trained you for independence and to have nerves of steel.

On Tuesday mornings, Vicar Hobbins would visit us in class, presumably to try and catch any sinners that slipped through the Sunday school net. This visit involved his usual lecture, and some hymn singing from books that were stored on a shelf behind Mrs. Diggsmore's desk. The hymnbook monitor was not a very desirable position and no one wanted the task of distributing and collecting the old heavy worn out tomes. It took several trips to allot one book to each of the temporary and tone deaf choir, so the more books you could carry, the quicker the unpleasant ordeal would be over. The best technique was to stack the books up and carry them in front of you, leaning them against your chest, and clamping the top book firmly in place with your chin, but there were two problems with this approach. In the first place, the books were positioned about two inches from a young and delicate nose, and they stank. The awful reek of mothballs was infused with the aroma of the old musty church storeroom where they had spent the last several hundred years. The second problem was that after collecting the books they had to be carried back to their resting place. Any luckless boy staggering carefully down an aisle between two rows of desks, books stacked high, unable to look down at his feet, was just asking to be tripped. It only took a moment to stick out your foot and the unfortunate book bearer would be left sprawled amid the scattered chaos of praise texts. It would be easy to imagine that the hymn book monitor was the most feared of all duties in the school, but there was one far, far worse.

The bulbous cast iron stove from which we so gratefully accepted warmth had a terrible appetite for coal. Anyone observing the class could be excused for reaching the conclusion that as the stove burned lower the behavior of the students improved. However the reduction in heat was not directly responsible for our enhanced compliance. The connection between these two seemingly unrelated events was the coal. In the dead of winter the stove, which also produced the hot water that was essential for scrubbing perpetually dirty hands, would consume up to three full coalscuttles each day as it performed its life support duties. When we ran short of fuel, the fire died down and some cursed soul had to assume the position of coal monitor. There was a noticeable shortage of volunteers for this awful assignment, and so it was allocated randomly according to the behavior of the students. If one were caught misbehaving around the time that the boiler was in its death throws, it was very possible that the recalcitrant pupil would be selected to go and fill the coal bucket.

There were a number of reasons why this mission was so feared. First there was the effort. Lifting the large heavy iron pale was almost impossible even when empty. It was also filthy. Tell tale patches of dusty black remnants would cling to flesh and clothing. Adding to the misery were the subzero temperatures and perpetual precipitation. The coal heap was located behind the toilets, as far from the school's front door as it was possible to get. Dressed in a coat, hat, scarf and gloves made for cumbersome attire, and driving the steel shovel into the coal pit, sometimes frozen and snow covered, was an exhausting struggle. Finally, the worst came when the bucket, now filled to the brim with coal and many times heavier, had to be dragged back to the schoolhouse, requiring the use of two hands and a most unorthodox walking style. The semi-permanent damage sustained by the physical exertion would leave one in agony for days, but the real pain emanated from the jeers and torment from the rest of the class.

As the fire burned low, and our attitudes became more and more angelic, Mrs. Diggsmore employed her sadistic strategy. She would simply wait for a child to request permission to go to the bathroom, then point to the empty coal bucket with a stern look, the meaning of which we all understood. Because of this, an informal contest would develop to see who could postpone a trip to the toilet for the longest time. Quite often, in the afternoon following the consumption of too much water, each of us would sit quietly enduring the discomfort of bloated bladders and resisting the urge to answer nature's call, waiting in agonizing misery for the first child's willpower to fail. When at last some unlucky victim could no longer wait, they would make the fateful request of Mrs. Diggsmore, and consequently, as part of the toilet trip they would have to suffer the hellish coal monitor detail, while the rest of us would then stampede across the playground, at last free to go in peace.

My fellow Mud Lane companions and I were kept inside during the lunch break as penance for our overdue arrival that morning, so it was after school before I was able to talk to Crumb about a loan of the trolley.

I found Crumb sitting alone. He had just been an unwilling participant in William O'Flanigan's monthly fight, and by all accounts it had been a rather fierce battle, resulting in William sustaining some nasty bruising and a torn collar, and Crumb, who everyone agreed lost the bout, ending up with a bloody nose. I had to listen to Crumb complain about William for several minutes before I was able to divert the conversation to the procurement of a trolley.

Crumb was the master trolley builder of the region, and for a modest fee of comics, and/or chocolate, his services could be called upon to build or repair any ailing vehicle. His backyard service depot was a wonder to behold, and any inquisitive youth, could explore the region for days on end. It was usually littered with various trolley and bicycle components and numerous unidentified mechanical parts. Lined up beside his father's gardening shed there was usually a collection of vehicles that could be purchased or rented. I phrased my trolley question to him carefully, emphasizing the deplorable state of my finances.

Crumb scratched his head thoughtfully as he explained that had I possessed the foresight to make this request last week, it would not have been a problem, but now his inventory was sadly depleted. I listened with interest as Crumb explained that just last week he had been in possession of two trolleys. But that was last week. The better of the two was a very fast, sleek sports model with several costly modifications. An attempt had been made to improve on the already impressive speed of this craft by adding strips of black and white checkered tape in the manner of a racing vehicle, and surprisingly this did seem to help.

The other trolley had been much more rudimentary. He called it his "back up." A wide piece of wood, which was cracked in such a manner that bumps would cause the wood to flex and the crack to open and close slightly, causing the pilot's behind to be intermittently and painfully pinched by the dangerous contraption. There was no steering, no seat and no flashy go-faster sticky tape. What's more the front wheels were prone to becoming detached at a time when you least expected it. I suggested that we might be able to fix the wheels and scrounge another cushion to render the seating surface less hazardous, but he just shook his head slowly and explained that even with his vast experience he had been unable to locate the cause of the self-ejecting wheels. Crumb was a highly accomplished trolley and bike rider, and had fallen off them more times than I had eaten hot meals. I had to respect his professional opinion.

"What if the trolley was for a non human?" I said.

"What, like Squeaky?" he asked.

"No," I continued, "like maybe a Guy?"

"Huuuumm," he mused, "there's not much weight in a guy, and he wouldn't complain about the seat pinching his bum. It might work, but we would still need new front wheels."

This was a tough order to fill, as wheels were in short supply at the moment. Of all the trolley making components, wheels were the one element that could not be fashioned from something else. The main "body work" plank could be derived from any piece of wood that we found, likewise string, cushions, and even deluxe additions like lights and rear view mirrors could be scrounged, swapped or borrowed. Wheels were different.

The principal sources for wheels were prams and pushchairs, which small children had outgrown, and once discarded, they were eagerly snapped up according to a system based on the degree of familiarity with the owner. We had been visiting Mrs. Snobbit lately to keep track of any soon-to-be available prams. Mrs. Popkin's youngest of seven would soon be walking, but she would probably keep the pushchair around for the next one. Even if she did decide not to produce any more little Popkins, the current infant transportation would certainly not be obtainable in time for Guy Fawkes Night. Our only option was to visit the holiest of shrines, a pilgrimage to that sacred location where almost anything could be found. We must go to "the tip."

Crumb loved to visit the rubbish tip, and spent almost as much time there as my father. He wanted to leave immediately but today was Monday and on Mondays Pete and I had to visit grandmother. So we made arrangements to go tomorrow after school, and I walked home resenting the fact that my grandmother had deprived me of a joyous evening digging through discarded rubbish.

CHAPTER 10

THE OTHER GRANDPARENT

The walk home was quiet and without other gang members wasting my valuable time, I walked briskly, lost in thoughts of trolley repair and questions about how Benito was going to make the Guy in time. Most of all I was troubled by Benito assigning himself the hardest part of the task. This was not like him. He was a crafty and cunning boy, and like his father, did not engage willingly in work.

I walked rapidly in the direction of the setting sun. The streetlights were just beginning to shed their luminous guidance, except for the obvious hollow shadow caused by the broken lamp outside our closest neighbor's house. Benito was to blame for the inoperable light, having recently scored a direct hit on the bulb with one of Ryan Pilchard's schoolbooks. I reached my front door just in time to hear the excessive volume of dreadful sounds emanating from within my house.

The desperate screaming was clearly coming from Pete and I was sure he must be fighting for the very salvation of his soul. Table legs were being scraped across the kitchen tiles, as if moved by a great force, and then I heard a horrifying smash as something made of glass connected with something much harder. Concerned for the safety of my brother I rushed into the house.

Pete was in a chair with his back to the stove, his face contorted in a death grimace as he again kicked the kitchen table and moved it several inches more. His right foot was swinging wildly at anything within range as he turned his head rapidly from side to side trying to bite my father. Dad was behind him now, wedged between the chair and the stove. My father's large muscular arms were firmly wrapped around Pete in a bear hug, pinning my brother in the chair. But Pete was quick and proved to be a worthy adversary. Suddenly Dad was forced to swing his head backwards to avoid Pete's gnashing teeth, and he lost his grip on my brother's left arm. Quick as lightning, the liberated limb thrashed out, sending another dinner plate crashing to the floor. Dad once again seized the delinquent appendage.

"Now! Now! Do it now!!" Dad yelled desperately to Mum.

My mother dropped the length of clothesline with which she had been trying to bind Pete's legs to the chair and came toward my brother with the most determined look I'd ever seen. In her hand, low by her side in a vain attempt at concealment, Mum held a newly sharpened pair of dressmaking scissors. My brother's eyes opened even wider as the light reflected from the scissors caught his eye. Pete's screams reached a crescendo, and his thrashing around became even more desperate.

There was no doubt in my mind that I was witnessing day number three of the haircut battle! It had started on Friday, continued on Saturday with Pete's halfhearted visit to the barber in town. Yesterday, Sunday, Dad had gone easy on Pete, being satisfied to extract a commitment that he would visit Mrs. Wiggins today after school. If I had to render an opinion, I would say the visit to Mrs. Wiggins did not materialize and that very soon after, a battle of words would have escalated into the use of more substantial weapons. It would not be long before the forcible hair cutting would commence.

A few tufts of hair, some cut from Pete's head, some pulled from Dad's, lay on the kitchen floor. This indicated that the current struggle had been in progress for some time. The combination of Pete's struggling and Mum's fear that she might inadvertently remove an eye or an ear along with some hair resulted in her inability to deliver Dad's prescribed "short back and sides" I sat quietly in a safe corner and enjoyed the remainder of the incident. It lasted several minutes more and then everyone gave up, exhausted and beaten. Neither side was happy. Pete ran to the bathroom to inspect his treasured locks, and my father sat down on a stool next to the kitchen table to regain his breath and roll a cigarette. He opened a large black book and we all fell silent. This was a serious time for Dad and we all knew better than to interrupt him.

He opened the book and used his extended finger to trace a thin red line that progressed up the page. At Birmingham he was forced to continue on a different page, but he eventually found the location where he estimated the intrepid band of Pilchards would be. He now proceeded to stage two of the investigation. He looked at me and jerked his chin toward the corner of the room. Of course we all knew what that meant.

On top of Mum's crockery cupboard next to stove was the radio, which might have found residence in a museum if the broken case had not been repaired with wood screws and electricians tape. I crossed the room, rotated the brown plastic dial and waited for the wireless to crackle into life. Dad had previously, with expert skill, tuned the receiver to the marine shipping forecast and then removed the brown tuning dial with a pair of pliers to prevent Pete from changing the station to one that broadcast pop music. The marine shipping forecast was an unorthodox method of checking the weather, especially since we lived a hundred and fifty miles inland, but Dad insisted upon its accuracy. No one else in the household understood it.

Dad closed the atlas, and leaned back in his chair. Through a cloud of exhaled smoke he made a groaning sound and expressed dismay that the Pilchards would be running into some pretty foul weather as they approached the Scottish border. He then remembered grandmother.

Upon realizing that the self styled barbershop operation had taken up some of the time allotted for visiting our grandmother, we all became a little happier. I was hoping that the venture might be cancelled altogether, but alas, in a panic Dad quickly grabbed his coat and instructed us to do likewise. Mum would not accompany us, as she, like so many other people, did not get on well with grandmother.

"Don't forget to talk to your mother about Christmas," She reminded Dad.

She was not referring to Dad offering grandmother an invitation to the customary Christmas dinner – she was jogging his memory to try and persuade grandmother not to come and visit us this year.

"Yes, I know," said Dad as if he and Mum had already spent too much time discussing this, and he rushed us up the path toward the waiting car.

The Hillman was our current transportation and Dad had not owned it for very long. Despite it's unreliable engine, and leaking bodywork, Dad still referred to it as his "new' car." Prior to Hillman our principle mode of conveyance had been a Ford pork pie van. Although it had high mileage, it was mechanically sound, and Dad had managed to strike a good deal with the local butcher to acquire it. It had the advantage of being able to carry a large payload on Dad's regular trips to Bollington's, and almost every week he would set off to the auction house with a truck-load of good saleable items, and return with an equally large cargo of skillfully negotiated useless junk. It was the ideal vehicle for Dad.

If the pie van had any disadvantage it was the large sign that graced the side panels and back doors of the vehicle that read, "Smith's Pork pies." It was beautifully scripted in gold with a large picture of a steaming pork pie over block-lettered text that read, "The best in the land." There was also a picture of plump pork sausages, visible behind the pork pie. They looked to have been fried to perfection and their swollen crispy skins were golden brown. The skillful artist who created the picture had even drawn wisps suggesting the mouthwatering aroma of well- seasoned meat rising gracefully from the food. Whenever we parked the vehicle we would return to find numerous people gathering around the van demanding that we sell them pork pies. Even our cat would sit and stare at it for hours. Some people, seeing us drive by would actually follow us home and pull up behind us in the driveway requesting the tasty dish advertised on the sides. Dad would often have to open the back doors and show them that the area they expected to be full of pork pies was actually used for building materials, fire wood or the latest batch of Bollington's treasure.

Dad eventually assigned Pete the job of painting over the signs but several weeks passed before he completed the task. Until that time, we continued to fight off hoards of hungry people clamoring for some of Mr. Smith's delicacies.

Prior to the Pork Pie Ford was the Austin.

My father purchased it in a moment of madness after Mum's declaration that she liked the color. In the several months that Dad tried to drive it, we were plagued by constant mechanical breakdowns. The engine made a loud knocking noise that drove Dad crazy, and if you exceeded twenty miles per hour a whining sound emanated from the gearbox and got louder as the car's speed increased. The rear door on Pete's side did not close properly, and I always suspected that Dad secretly hoped that Pete would one day fall out. My job was to gaze out of the back window, which was cracked, and watch for road bumps or potholes. If we hit any, which we almost always did when Dad was driving, the boot would open by itself and anything inside would fall out.

Dad finally gave the car a decent burial by driving it past rat barn and deep into the sea of stinging nettles and brambles beyond. That's where it remained to this day, rusting and overgrown with weeds and creeping vines. It served out the remainder of its life by being a source of engine parts, spare wheels, bolts, brackets and many other improvised solutions to my father's needs.

Dad herded us anxiously into the back seat of the Hillman, as Pete and I exchanged puzzled glances. As we sped off down the lane, Pete looked at me and nodded.

"Bollingtons." He said in a low voice.

Mondays was auction night at Bollington's, and the high point of Dad's week. Obviously he planned to not only visit his mother, but also spend some time out-bidding one of his auction room cronies for the right to take home some worthless, broken or obsolete piece of junk. Dad considered Bollington's much more important than the upcoming maternal visit, since on Saturday he had delivered a box full of rubbish collected from El Paso, and was anxious to view the bidding. But first things first, and the unwanted obligatory trip to grandmother would be, we all prayed, short and uneventful.

Grandmother lived in Lower Marsham, a village only about four miles away, but the drive took longer than expected because we were on the edges of the storm system that plagued the Pilchard's adventure. Halfway through the trip the driver's side windshield wiper decided to go on strike, so Dad was forced to travel slowly and stop often as he handed either Pete or me an old shirt.

"That window needs to be cleaned," exclaimed Dad, pointing at the rain soaked glass.

We would take it in turns to disembark from the vehicle, and stand in the freezing rain to clean the car's front window. We could then proceed onward for another half mile.

Grandmother was a throwback to the Victorian era. She had raised her children with two guiding principles. The first was that "children should be seen and not heard," the other was "spare the rod and spoil the child." These beliefs alone would have made her a mean and domineering woman, but combined with her Methodist upbringing it made visiting her as enjoyable as a measles inoculation or a school arithmetic test.

Alcohol was also off limits, and at least once a week Dad would tell us the story of how, when he was about twenty-six years old, returning home for a visit after a six month trip at sea, grandmother answered the door, caught the exhaled scent of a blackcurrant flavored wine-gum that Dad had been chewing, and made him sleep in the barn. Dancing, too, was to be avoided, as were bright colors and humor – all viewed as steps on the downward road to the devil's playground.

Dad often entertained us with stories of the frequent boyhood beatings, and how as a child he was only allowed to dress in black clothes, which he dare not get dirty. Apparently he spent most of his young life in church or listening to grandmother reading aloud from the bible. This explained why he ran away to sea as soon as he could ride a bike, and spent most of his time in rebellion, frequenting dancehalls, gambling houses and drinking establishments.

We parked at the top of a tree lined hill under the branches of an ancient sycamore tree. Dad turned off the car's engine which caused a moment of apprehension because of the risk that the car would not start again. Dad carefully placed his tobacco in the glove box, and herded us reluctantly up the steps of the old Georgian home. Pete asked Dad if he could stand outside in the cold rain rather than go inside.

Grandmother lived at 43 Bolton Drive, but never much cared for the town of Bolton which she found much too "working class." Her solution to this problem was simple. One day without any warning to the post office she changed her address from 43 Bolton Drive to 16 Sycamore Hill. It took the bewildered postman only a few days to completely succumb to her will.

All laughing and talking immediately ceased as we entered through the kitchen door and passed through the long dark hallway to the parlor where "she" would be. The house was spotlessly clean thanks to a constant stream of neighbors who were motivated by fear of this frail old white haired lady. The intimidating psychological grip she exercised over the local population provided her with several house cleaners and maids, two gardeners, a cook, and a driver who made sure that grandmother's car was the cleanest in the village even though it had not left the garage in seventeen years.

The heavy door swung open to a dimly lit room where grandmother, sat stern and motionless in a high backed chair, chin held high and sharp gray eyes residing behind horn-rimmed spectacles. A brass handled walking stick, leaned against a round polished cherry wood reading table on which resided a large leather bound well worn bible with a tattered gold ribbon marking a passage that we would no doubt have to listen to during our visit.

On the wall were several photographs. One used to be of Dad and Mum on their wedding day, barely visible through the fog as they leaned against their borrowed car, but Mum had been carefully cropped out of this. The rest of the wall decoration consisted of pictures of Methodist ministers from a number of different parishes. A large portrait of Winston Churchill enjoyed a privileged spot over the mantelpiece, and on the opposite side Queen Elizabeth bestowed her royal blessing upon the dimly lit room.

After bowing to Grandmother and saluting Winston, Pete and I sat motionless, side by side like wax dummies on the couch. Only the sound of rain on the window and the occasional crackle of the fire broke the stony silence.

Eventually, Dad tried to start up a conversation. It began by talking about the weather, my father offering an opinion about the Pilchard terrible timing for their Scottish Holiday. Then the mother and son pair once again fell silent. I knew Dad wanted to offer a highly opinionated comment on the offshore fishing strike but politics, or anything perceived as such was forbidden. For fear that we would all be cursed into hell, religion was also a taboo subject. It was difficult to find any common ground. Neither of the two had any interest in sports, Dad did not know any hymns, and grandmother had never ridden a motorbike.

More silence followed as we all listened to the rhythmic ticking of the clock, and my father needlessly stoked the fire twice sending showers of tiny sparks up the chimney. According to the schedule that had been perfected over years of grueling visits, after about ten minutes Dad stood up and went to the kitchen to make a pot of tea. This left Pete and I alone in the room with grandmother. She looked at us for an uncomfortably long time before turning away to gaze at the walking stick beside her chair.

Quite unexpectedly, Pete, mustering all the courage he had, rose slowly to his feet and spoke in the most polite tones I'd ever heard from him.

"Please, Grandmother, may we play with some...toys?"

The last word was squeezed out and Pete grimaced.

Grandmother just looked at us with a frozen calculating half smile. After an eternity of clock ticking and steely-eyed scrutiny, she responded with a surprising,

"Yes Pete, you may."

This indeed was a rare treat. Grandmother had obviously judged our behavior suitable to reward us by opening a box containing some of the toys that Dad played with as a child.

We knew the routine. We must play without fighting, we must play on an area no larger than a pocket-handkerchief and we must play in silence. When finished, we must clean up and return all the toys to their original position in the box. This seemed simple enough and Pete ran off to get the treasure chest as I heard the sound of the kettle whistle from the kitchen.

The box contained three wooden blocks with the original lettering worn away, four lead soldiers, three of them too bent to remain vertical, and one kneeling down with a rifle but missing a head. There were several pieces of a jigsaw puzzle, and also a black leather boot lace that had been tied to the wheel of a small model car. We didn't know why. Even by the humble toy standards that we were accustomed to, this was a miserable collection.

Pete immediately grabbed two of the blocks, and forming a wall, placed the lead soldiers with heads behind it. This left me with one block and the headless rifleman. Simultaneously we both grabbed opposite ends of the bootlace and began a silent tug of war. As we strained against each other and I leaned back for additional pull, Pete let go of his end and I rolled backwards breaking both the fighting rule and the pocket-handkerchief play area rule. Before I could recover or Grandmother could unleash judgment, Pete had hit my wooden block with a soldier.

"Boom!" he shouted.

Grandmother fixed us with an icy stare.

"Perhaps the boys would like to play outside for a little while?" It was more a statement than a question.

Despite the cold rain anything was preferable to staying inside the parlor, for the Bible readings would soon begin.

We made a mad dash down the brick pathway to the barn. Inside we turned on the light and sat down on some apple crates to survey our surroundings in search of entertainment. The large barn served as a general storeroom for everything Grandmother did not want in the house. Some furniture, unbroken and with decent upholstery, stood in the corner covered with a dustsheet, and along one wall was a shelf containing some plates and dishes. All in all, Grandmother's junk appeared to be better than our good stuff.

We passed the time with idle chatter and brotherly arguments about motorcycles and football, and it wasn't long before we regretted being evicted from the warm house. We had avoided a sermon but also missed out on a cup of tea and perhaps even some cake.

Grandmother was known for her fruit producing trees and in an act of unselfish charity, often distributed the imperfect specimens to the financially less fortunate. All that remained this late in the season were cooking apples.

Eyeing the apples, Pete selected what he thought was a tasty one. It took him only one bite to discover that there is no such thing as a tasty cooking apple. His protruding tongue betrayed the fruit's sour taste and without hesitation, he threw the partially eaten fruit at me, hitting me on the shoulder. Intending to return the compliment I reached for a large dark green specimen, knowing that the color was a good indication of the fruit's firmness. I turned to acquire my target only to see the barn door swing closed as Pete ran out into the rain.

I gave chase, rushing out, the apple ready to be launched like a cricket ball, when I saw that Pete was no longer running. Something had caught his eye. He was crouched behind a bush looking in through the parlor window where Dad sat patiently with Grandmother. I quietly approached and together we saw that Grandmother now had the Bible on her knees and was reading aloud. Dad sat with his head slightly bowed, and every now and then he would nod to appease his mother. We both knew that Dad could not stand this for very long and that signaled that the end of the trip was imminent.

In anticipation we went to wait by the car. Dad soon arrived, breathing a sigh of relief and immediately lit a cigarette as he climbed behind the wheel. We pushed the car down either Bolton Drive or Sycamore Hill, until it started, and then leaped in as the engine began to pick up. Dad was off down the road driving at a hell-for-leather speed – he had to reach Bollington's before the bidding war began. Precious junk purchasing time was a-wasting.

It continued to rain heavily, and the roads were soon filled with frequent puddles of deep standing water, but this did not dissuade my father from driving at a speed that even unnerved Pete. On we raced through the wet darkness. Pete and I just sat silently in the back, gripped in fear. There were no playful fights between us, and none of Pete's irritating pranks designed to annoy Dad. We just thought it best to sit quietly and hold on to the door handles, Dad sat hunched forward, his face only a few inches from the rain spotted windshield, driving like a man possessed. I think that if Dad had realized that his reckless driving was responsible for Pete's good behavior, he would have always driven like that.

Dad hurried inside the auction house, ordering us not to leave the car as Pete and I had been banned from entering Bollington's. On our last visit, Pete, being unable to keep quiet or still, accidentally bid several times for a set of plumbing tools and a bucket full of old rusty keys. Afterwards in a mad dash to evade my father's pursuit he knocked over a hat stand and two reading lamps. Thus we now sat in the car patiently waiting for the inevitable. We didn't have to wait long.

Dad soon appeared carrying another lawnmower.

CHAPTER 11

NEW WHEELS

Tuesdays always broke the monotony of a boring day at school by providing us with an even more tedious start to the day – on Tuesday mornings we were blessed with a visit from that pompous twit known as Vicar Hobbins.

He would arrive in his long black gown which was always flapping wildly in the frosty breeze, promptly at nine o'clock to lead us in prayer and impress upon us the wisdom of his considerable years. Mrs. Diggsmore would appear and both blow a whistle and clap her hands rapidly. This was universally understood to mean that we should stop playing and come inside so that the Vicar could begin to bestow his biblical wisdom upon the disinterested masses. It was the type of experience that only my Grandmother would enjoy. His monotonous droning sermon was always about how thou shalt not do something or other, and how if thou did-est do-eth, the wrath of the almighty savior would be upon us for forty days and forty nights. But it would not be this way today.

Metal toy guns were an indispensable piece of equipment for any self respecting lad, and these devices were given an impressive and realistic sound by inserting roll of "caps" to provide a suitably loud gunshot emulation. Even though each roll contained one hundred of the tiny explosives, caps were always in short supply, mostly because these tiny bombs were often used in a manner inconsistent with their design objectives.

Basher our most rotund and lethargic gang member had purchased several rolls of caps yesterday, on his way back home from a fishing expedition with Chucky and Taddy Bascome. I was astonished that he still had some left, considering his favorite use for caps was to place an entire roll on the ground in front of him, and jump onto it. This produced one of the more satisfying effects, but it was not an economical nor long-lasting use of the product.

A little before nine o'clock found us milling around the playground waiting for the arrival of the Vicar. Benito, Crumb and I were reviewing our master plan to build and profitably exhibit a Guy Fawkes. We had however made no progress in this ambitious venture and Benito, who had assumed responsibility for the manufacture of the Guy, had not even started on its construction. To add to our problems, Crumb and I were still short a set of wheels for the trolley. Benito was somehow able to convince us that everything was under control and that instead of doubting his ability to deliver the Guy Fawkes to us, we should focus on finding the much needed wheels for the trolley. Our planning session was cut short when Benito's eyes lit up in seeing Basher idly fondling his last remaining roll of caps.

It did not take him long to convince Basher that we could make good use of the caps, and in the process provide all our classmates with a little entertainment. Basher looked at his munitions thoughtfully, and then stared at Benito. Benito hastily offered the loan of Crumb's catapult for one week as payment for the caps. After a short but heated negotiation Benito agreed to include six of Chucky's marbles. Basher finally agreed.

Benito sprang into action, hurriedly grabbing the tiny roll of ammo. He immediately summoned Basher and Big Gina Rolonzio, and had them grasp the iron bars of the gate. The hinges were brown with rust and the gate when opened or closed emitted a loud squeak not unlike the squawk of Granny's feathered sidekick.

Basher and Big Gina were then instructed to lift the gate slightly, but it proved too heavy. Even with Gina's gargantuan strength, it wouldn't move. Two more bodies were thrown at the problem. Chucky Billings, who was given the lower rail to grip and Crumb who because of his superior height, grappled with the upright bars above Basher's head. All the while, as he directed the operation, Benito was folding the caps into a small tight bundle and positioning himself closer to the gate hinges.

The Vicar was almost upon us, and once again, Benito barked the order for a synchronized lifting effort. This time the gate moved just enough to provide a small space in the hinge between where the gate met the frame. Benito, not knowing how long this opportunity would linger, quickly pushed the pile of caps in the hinge gap. He then grabbed a section of the weighty gate and with everyone's combined effort, eased it very gently down to a resting position, pinching the caps and Crumb's finger as he did so. Because old "Hob-nob's" arrival was imminent, Benito's final order to scatter and act naturally was whispered quickly. We all complied, and I took up a relaxed position leaning against the drainpipe on the corner of the hefty stone steps. I started to whistle casually, certain that this conveyed an image of innocence.

The aging clergyman rounded the corner to the school entrance and just as he had thousands of times before, pushed hard to open the gate. The weight of the stationary gate was not sufficient to explode the caps, but the rusty grinding friction of the moving hinge was. With a force at least equal to one of Basher's jumps, the caps exploded with a deafening boom.

The shocked-out-of-his-wits vicar had half collapsed onto one of the school dustbins. One hand was open with claw-like fingers stretched wide across his heart and the other made a white knuckled fist which was tightly wrapped over the silver crucifix that hung around his neck on a chain. He was panting, trying to catch his breath, while simultaneously muttering some very unholy exclamations.

Hearing the commotion, Mrs. Diggsmore double-timed it down the stone stairs to provide aid to the injured and retribution to the guilty.

She took the Vicar's elbow and assisted him through the arched doorway, and we followed them inside, our mirth now rapidly turning to concern over the possible penalties involved. Benito, being used to much more severe retribution at home, announced that since today was Halloween this had been a good test to prove the strength of the vicar's nerves.

Hobbins was led inside to sit beside Mrs. Diggsmore's desk, one bony hand still clutching the silver cross. A first-aid kit now lay open on Mrs. Diggsmore's desk. The vicar carefully waved some smelling salts beneath his nose as our teacher stood like a statue before the class with her arms folded and a look of extreme disappointment on her face.

Our faces were scanned for signs of guilt, but the great Inquisitor saw only expressions of purity and innocence. When this approach failed to produce a culprit, each of us was asked to render our personal version of the affair. This was much more successful. Benito had seen the whole thing from afar and was able to identify Barry Ogden as the perpetrator. Barry would have suffered a dreadful penalty had he not in turn blamed Crumb, who was in turn convicted based on the large blood blister now appearing on his finger. Crumb was rewarded for his misdeeds with extra homework and had to write on the blackboard 100 times "Thou shalt not frighten thy vicar."

Mrs. Diggsmore repaired Crumb's finger with a band-aid and we all sank into what promised to be another dull and uneventful school day.

During the arithmetic lesson, which consisted of most of the class endlessly repeating the eleven times tables, Crumb and I were at last able to continue our trolley planning. We kept handing back and forth pieces of paper with drawings detailing how we would attach the wheels that we would surely soon own, to the remains of the broken trolley.

As usual, our lunchtime passed with noses pressed against the wire fence overlooking the road, dreaming of freedom. Then suddenly our silent vigil was interrupted by the sound of a scream. We all ran toward the source of the dismay and discovered a small group had already gathered in a tight semi circle for a ringside seat to the event. Basher bulldozed his way through the crowd and soon discovered that the scream was emanating from a tearful Graham Smith who had decided to provide a little post meal entertainment for us by wedging his forefinger in the keyhole of the storage shed.

"Calm down Graham, I'll help you." said Chucky stepping forward.

But when Graham's eyes focused on the rusty blade of the broken pocketknife that Chucky had found under Mr. Snobbit's car, the volume of his cries for help alerted Mrs. Diggsmore. She immediately confiscated Chucky's treasured dagger and banished him to the furthest reaches of the playground. I liked to think that our gang, Benito, Chucky, Basher, Crumb and I were among the most creative and resourceful in the school, and this was soon to be proven. Chucky had already been sent away for trying to help and although this did not seem fair, we were exposed to injustices of this sort so frequently that we had learned to take it in our stride.

"Please, Mrs. Diggsmore" Crumb was the first to speak up, "we could get a stick and sharpen it with Chucky's knife and then we could push it in from the other side of the lock, and push Graham's finger out."

"Don't be silly, Crumb," replied Mrs. Diggsmore as she inspected Graham's reddening flesh. Graham winced.

I raised my hand. "Mrs. Diggsmore, if we all grabbed Graham's arm like a tug of war rope..."

I didn't even get to finish the sentence, suffering an instant dismissal of my cleverness.

Basher's recommendation was that Mrs. Diggsmore walk down to the post office and purchase some caps and we could explode the finger loose, but Mrs. Diggsmore pretended not to hear this.

Instead she ran inside to fetch the first-aid kit that was still on her desk. Benito then decided that he could regain some credibility by solving the matter personally. Without explanation or discussion he simply grabbed Graham's trapped appendage and with a swift and forceful movement yanked his hand free. The good thing was that the digit had now been removed intact but Graham reacted to this surgical necessity by screaming, which only served to hasten Mrs. Diggsmore's return. As she appeared at the doorway she saw Graham holding up his injured hand, which now had a small trickle of blood on the forefinger. Graham's good hand was pointing squarely at Benito.

Benito was sentenced to six whacks with a wooden ruler across the knuckles of his left hand, deliberately chosen so that the resultant injury would not limit his literary expression. He spent most of the day in a dismal state but his interest increased in the afternoon when we had to endure a lecture about the Roman Empire. He seemed to delight in hearing about the battles fought by his blood thirsty ancestors.

After what seemed an eternity, school was over. This day was especially good because Mrs. Diggsmore made an announcement. There would be some workmen an the school tomorrow making changes to the bathroom, which involved turning off the water supply. Therefore school would be closed. Everybody cheered and we were given letters to take home to our parents proclaiming the happy news. With that, Mrs. Diggsmore wished us all a Happy Halloween, the bell was rung and we bolted for the door like rats leaving a sinking ship.

Crumb and I set out along Church Road in the direction of the Tip. It took about half an hour to reach Tip meadow, but it was not an easy half hour. A heard of angry cows gave chase and I ripped my trousers hastily scrambling over a wire fence. Then Crumb stepped in a tractor wheel rut half full of water soaking his shoe, but in due course we reached the long green field known as Tip meadow.

The Tip was a wonderful place. It had started its interesting history simply as a large hole in the ground. Billy Tadcome said that it was a bomb crater from World War I created during one of the Japanese balloon attacks. We saw no reason to disbelieve him. The Tip had certainly been around for as long as any of us could remember and over the years bushes and small trees had grown round the perimeter disguising its true purpose, but those aware of the treasures hidden within were usually well rewarded for paying a visit.

The Tip served the local community as the place where people deposited what they considered rubbish, and others found what they thought to be useful, functional and best of all free goods and supplies. Many of my father's most prized possessions came from the Tip. Sometimes larger prizes could not be delivered or retrieved on foot and evidence of tire marks were often seen. Such tracks were an indication that an unusually large or heavy prize was up for grabs. Grizzly McKenzie was able to acquire his cast iron double bed following a tip from Mrs. Snobbit that there were new tire tracks in Tip meadow. Miscellaneous repair parts for farm vehicles and cars were always available and kept half the village mobile.

The best thing I ever saw anyone find at the Tip was an armored breastplate from a Roman soldier. This was found in the very center of the Tip, in what was called the "yucky zone." It contained the deepest and darkest layers of the old crater, and was especially treacherous due to frequent flooding in the center, which mingled with the old oil cans and rotting vegetation. The best riches were to be found here because most people considered them to be irretrievable, only the bravest and most resourceful were able to claim prizes from the yucky zone. Benito and Basher had spent three days building a bridge and crossed the last six feet using ropes to reach the antique armor. To verify the authenticity of their find, an expert was called upon in the form of Mr. Cranly from the bakers shop. Within a few seconds he was able to authenticate that it was in fact a heavily padded, reinforced jacket once owned by the local dustman, but the deluded archeologists continued to prize the artifact as it provided excellent protection from arrows and catapult projectiles.

My brother claimed that his most memorable find was our cat. He was on a routine reconnaissance mission looking for bike parts, when he discovered the small straggly creature, skinny and hungry as it tried to devour one of Grizzly McKenzie's cast off shoes. The cat was subsequently and aptly named Scraps, and her attitude and temperament in later years was no doubt a product of her harsh upbringing.

Crumb and I pushed through a gap in the bushes and surveyed the contents of the rubbish dump, our eyes anxiously scanning the junk for signs of wheels. There was the back wheel of a child's tricycle, and an old car wheel with no tire, but no sign of our desired prize. Just when I was about to give up all hope, Crumb let out a shout of joy.

"Look! There!" Crumb was now jumping up and down and pointing with his bandaged finger to a spot in the heart of the yucky zone. Sure enough, half submerged in unidentified brown sludge was a pram wheel.

We climbed onto an overhanging tree branch, then with a grappling hook fashioned from a bent piece of metal, attached to a piece of rope, we went fishing for the wheels. The wheels were firmly stuck in the mud and we both began to speculate that the other end of the axel was trapped under some other piece of junk. The line needed more length so we attached an old bicycle chain which added about three feet. Ultimately we were successful, but it required the force of both of us to drag our prey free of the filthy quagmire, while taking care not to fall from the branch into the same disgusting ooze.

On the way home we clambered down the steep sides of a grassy river bank and used the flowing fresh water to wash the muck of our new prize. The wheels were on a good straight axle, and both turned freely and they appeared ideal for our purpose. There was an even covering of rust over the entire assembly, but that was also true of everything else we owned.

We walked proudly with wheels in hand and so enthralled in our trolley planning that when we walked past the front gate of the Maudly-Creechom's house, we almost missed a very disturbing sight.

Next to the barn beside the driveway was a red and white striped deck chair and making themselves busy around it were Horace and Maggot, Oscar and Willis and a fifth member of their ranks, Squeaky Norrington. Oscar was holding a tattered yellow straw hat and Maggot was trying to wrestle an old shoe onto the figure sitting in the chair. We climbed the gate to better determine the facts of the situation. It was not Mr. Maudly-Creechom's servant in the chair. It was by all accounts a Guy Fawkes. It was still missing its head, and the legs and arms were not yet stuffed, but it was well on its way. This was another sudden dose of reality that I didn't want.

"Do you think Benito will make ours in time?" I asked Crumb. I could feel the desperation.

"I don't know," he replied. "Benito's always got a few tricks up his sleeve."

"I know," I said," but he hasn't given us any proof that he is doing anything about making one."

"Why would he lie about it?" asked Crumb.

"I don't know," I said.

This was not a good end to the day. There were two factors that would determine the amount of money that could be collected from a

Guy parade. The first was the quality of the Guy. Since the Maudly-Creechoms were already engaged in this pursuit it was practically certain that theirs would be a superior effort probably even having hair and a beard. We could not hope to match this degree of detail in the short time we had to complete the project. The second thing that would affect income potential was timing. The first to finish and exhibit would get the lion's share of the donations, and we, or should I say Benito, had not even started ours yet.

Upon our arrival home Crumb took my bike and cycled off home. Halloween was not a night you wanted to be out alone, and he rode off quickly before the sun finally set and the monsters came out. He would be busy tonight with the extra homework he had been awarded for orchestrating the caps in the gate stunt. I went in to tell Mum the happy news about the plumbers and the school. Mum had, of course, refused to believe that the note we brought home excusing us from school tomorrow was genuine, and had consulted with both Benito's and Squeaky's mother before accepting the validity of Mrs. Diggsmore's blissful notification.

"Can I go out tonight and look for ghosts?" I directed the question at my mother, thinking that she would be more likely to lend her support than Dad.

"No," she replied, without looking up from the cooking pot she was stirring.

"Well, Dad?" I tried another approach. "it is Halloween you know."

"Your mother has said no," he replied without looking up from his newspaper.

"Why not, Mum?" I was hurt and disappointed. Clearly she did not understand the need to rid the village of the evil powers of darkness.

"Because you have school tomorrow," replied Mum.

"But I don't," I reminded her. "Remember Mrs. Diggsmore's note?" Mum was now caught in her own trap, and I rushed in with some additional pleading.

"Ooowww, pleeeease," I begged.

"Well who will you going with?" she asked.

"Benito and Chucky," I said, then added, "and Spot will be there as well."

"Where would you go?" was her next question.

"I don't know," I said, "We'll probably just sit at the bottom of the lane."

Mum stirred the pot endlessly. Dad turned another page of his newspaper with a loud rustle. I waited in the silence for an answer. I knew that Chucky was probably having the exact same conversation with his parents. Benito would just be sneaking out of his bedroom window to crawl across the porch roof and down over the top of the coal shed.

"Well, all right," my mother finally conceded. "But don't be late."

"I won't," I reassured her.

"What will you do if you see a ghost?" asked Dad.

I was afraid that if I told him that we intended to engage the apparition in battle and drive it from the village, he might reconsider his decision to let me go.

"I expect we will just run home as fast as we can," I said.

"Good idea," said Dad, which told me I had answered correctly.

I finished my tea and grabbed my coat.

"Don't get into trouble," my father called out from behind the newspaper's sports section.

I walked briskly towards Benito's house. It was dark now and I didn't like being out alone. I quickened my step past the broken street light outside Mrs. Snaggin's house, and paused outside the Relonzio residence. There was a strange chill in the air. Benito had planned to escape without permission and had asked me not to knock on the door. That suited me well because even on Halloween the inside of the Relonzio residence was scarier than the outside.

A rustling in the hedgerow was much louder than it should have been and I strained my eyes in the darkness to see. I could just make out a dark shape, but reasoned that it must just be a shadow caused by the pale moon peering through a broken cloud. But wait, now it was moving! I felt uneasy and wished that Benito was here as well. Without warning Benito burst through the hedge.

"I got it," he said, proudly holding up his brother's catapult in the half-light.

I recovered quickly and felt even better when we heard Chucky and Spot coming down the lane. Chucky was whistling, which was something that he rarely did. Chucky Billings was a superstitious boy and so I considered him not a very useful member of our small band of devil hunters. Spot, on the other hand, had proved to be fearless on many occasions and was a welcome addition to the group.

We set off toward the center of Great Biddington and the churchyard, which was our final destination. There was an eerie dampness in the air, and a thick blanket of fog, especially by the bridge where we stopped to pick up catapult ammo. We all knew well that trolls were known to live under bridges, and so Chucky, Spot and I kept watch while Benito collected the smooth wet pebbles from the streambed.

Halfway up the hill, we met out first ghost. Spot began to emit a low growling sound, and we stopped our nervous talking and listened. A ghostly murmur was coming from the darkness ahead of us. Chucky bent down to reassure Spot that all was safe, but Spot now had her ears down and was barking, a vicious drooling affair with plenty of exposed teeth. The unseen ghoul, hearing Spot's warning, began to make a horrible groaning noise. The creature moved slowly, lurching around in a crazed stumble.

"Get him, Spot," Chucky said, his voice trembling with fear. Spot leaped forward to accost the demon. We ran after her as Benito tried to load the catapult as he ran. Spot had the ghost down on the ground and was gnawing at his trouser leg. She was summoned back to Chucky's side as we ran quickly up the hill to escape.

We soon reached the church and with extreme caution approached the double iron gates that led to the graveyard. I expected that of all the places in the village it would be here that we would encounter some ghastly guardian of the underworld. We crept along the outside of the church wall slowly, and silently with Benito in the lead. He peered carefully through the iron gates.

"There's one," he whispered. I leaned forward to look. Sure enough, in the dim light I could just make out the form of a figure clad in a robe of ghostly gray, rattling the door handle of the church.

"It's trying to break into the church," I said, shaking.

"Let me see," said Chucky. He and his family attended church regularly and the sight of something wrenching on the doors of his holy sanctuary, upset him. Not wanting to risk Spot for such a dangerous mission he grabbed Benito's catapult and loaded it with a brown rock.

Mustering all the courage he could, Chucky pulled back on the slingshot, stepped in front of the church gate and released his projectile.

"Die, you evil creature from hell!" he shouted.

The ghost was at the church door when the shot whistled past its left ear and hit the oak door. We ran off into the misty night, leaving behind the echo of footsteps.

We followed the church wall round the corner and entered the graveyard through the side gate and prepared ourselves for encounters with both zombies and vampires, knowing that they favored surroundings such as these. We arrived at a bench that had been positioned to afford a good view of the cemetery and sat down. This would be a good observation point to check for werewolves and the undead should they suddenly emerge from their tombs and try to sneak up on us.

"Look," said Benito," startling us. "That old gray ghost that was trying to get into the church is going into Crippin's house now."

After a few minutes during which we heard no screams from the Crippin house, we decided that the ghost had gone up to haunt Mr. Jessop. This was indeed proving to be a very active night for the spirits.

It wasn't long before Benito started to try and scare Chucky.

"My sister said that when the moon's full, one of the graves here opens up and a ghost comes out."

"Which one?" asked Chucky.

"One over there," said Benito pointing to a moss covered headstone.

"What ghost is it?" he asked.

"I think it's old Peppy Rollins. He died about ten years ago."

"Why does he come out?" inquired Chucky with a slight tremor in his voice. He was tightening his grip on the catapult finding a sense of security in its metal form.

"They say he was murdered, and now his spirit can't rest," Benito whispered.

"Who killed him?" asked Chucky.

"I don't know," said Benito, "maybe it was...." he paused as if he had just heard something and then ... "YOU!" he blurted out as he grabbed Chucky's arm.

We all jumped, including me who had heard Benito do this at least three times before. Then just as we all laughed, enjoying the release of tension, a low moaning sound came from the oak tree near the church wall.

"What was that?" I asked.

"I don't know," said Benito.

Then we heard it again. It was a long painful cry, hollow and empty in the darkness like a murder victim's last breath.

"Its Peppy Rollins," said Chucky. Spot began to answer the moan with a toothy snarl of her own. Chucky again put his hand on the dog to settle her.

"Look," said Benito.

"What?" I asked urgently.

"Did you see it?' said Benito.

"No," I replied, staring toward the place where we heard the ghostly groan.

"You're just trying to scare us again," said Chucky.

"I'm not, I really saw something." I could hear the fear in Benito's voice, and that scared me.

"Look, there it is again," he said.

We all saw it this time, a white formless shape that seemed to float slowly behind a line of gravestones.

"It's Peppy Rollins," Chucky repeated, his voice trembling.

We jumped behind the bench to hide, and peered over the back to watch the unreal vision before us. Chucky made a sort of whimpering noise as Benito snatched the catapult back from him, and loaded it with a shiny rock from his pocket.

We looked on in horror as the shapeless figure seemed to glow in the darkness as it drifted along. Then it made that awful cry again as it turned toward us. Chucky and I were frozen in fear, but Benito, peering over the back of the churchyard seat, bravely pulled back the elastic of the catapult as far as he could and released the shot.

The apparition cried out in pain as the stone hit him dead center. There was a flapping sound as the ghostly figure struggled to avoid the next projectile. Benito loosed of a second shot, but as the figure struggled to remove the bed sheet, it was not Peppy nursing a wound but Crumb. Basher giggled and snorted from behind a nearby grave.

A few minutes later, we were all laughing again. It seems that Crumb and Basher had decided to dress up as ghosts and wander the village scaring whoever they could. They had been reasonably successful at this despite the red welt that Crumb had sustained to his chest. Benito explained that had it not been for the damage that his knuckles had sustained in school today, the shot might well have killed Crumb.

Basher said that if that had happened, we would not have to carry Crumb far to bury him. A very sensible response I thought.

CHAPTER 12

BENITO THE TRAITOR

Dad was rushing to finish his cup of tea. Today he was involved in some local work helping Joey Dobbins put a fresh coat of paint on Dickey Braithwait's roof, and he was enthusiastic to make an early start.

"Why are you in such a hurry, Dad?" I asked.

"Because the sooner I start, the sooner I finish," he said, handing down his time tested wisdom.

I believed that you should never rush to something as unimportant as work. I agreed with Billy Tadcome who said that you should never do tomorrow what you can put off until the next day.

"And, "Dad added, "I've got some stuff to do at home this afternoon."

"What's that dear?" Mum asked.

"I'm going to build a tobacco drying machine," said Dad, his voice full of excitement.

"So it is going rotten then," said Pete.

"No, it's just that this will be faster," replied Dad, saving himself the embarrassment of admitting the truth.

Mum and I finished breakfast together and talked. The village was buzzing with the news that last night as Mrs. Crippin was locking the church door someone had shouted and thrown something at her. I told Mum that it was probably the ghost that we had seen. She looked doubtful.

The thoughts of falling behind schedule on the Guy Fawkes project was weighing heavily on my mind. Crumb was coming over today to help make the trolley repairs, and I decided that we must approach Benito and demand proof of his progress.

Crumb rode up on my borrowed bike, with Benito sitting on the handlebars. The two dismounted, and the bike was thrown haphazardly on the side of the road. He had ridden my bike all the way from his house towing the two-wheeled trolley behind him. The front of the trolleys, which did not yet have wheels, was tied to the back of my bike seat with about two feet of rope. Just then the sound of dogs barking attracted our attention, as Willis Gurney appeared, running down the lane brandishing Morris's leash. Morris was barking, as was Spot who chased a few feet behind.

"Hello, Willis," said Benito, being uncharacteristically pleasant.

"Hello?" Willis answered suspiciously.

"So," Benito casually asked Willis, faking a total lack of interest, "what are you going to do for bonfire night?"

"Maudly-Creechoms and us are building a Guy, good one too!" he said.

"Yeh?" asked Benito, carefully probing for information. "Are you going to take it round the village for money?"

"Oh yes," replied Willis, straining now to hold the dog lead as Morris had caught the scent of something interesting, probably Scraps. "The Maudly-Creechoms are going away tomorrow and won't be back until Sunday morning so we will do our penny for the Guy on Sunday before the bonfire party."

"Ooooh." Benito thought for a minute, he needed one more piece of information "How will you take the Guy round the village? You don't have a trolley, do you?"

"No," Willis replied, "I think Mrs. Maudly-Creechom will sit it in the back of her Jag and drive us around."

This was typical of rich people, and it made my blood boil. Crumb and I had to spend time digging through muck to find parts to make a trolley while the Maudly-Creechoms got chauffeured around in style. Still, at least Benito was thinking of us when he inquired about the availability of a trolley from the Maudly-Creechoms. I am sure that if they had one, he intended to try and steal it for us.

Benito walked away with Willis. We all thought that Benito favoring Willis's company to ours was a little odd, but had learned that Benito moves in mysterious ways. Mum made tea for us both and then Crumb and I retired to the barn to assess the extent of the damage to our future Guy transportation.

The main plank that served as the chassis was cracked, and the steering was non functional, but since a real person would not ride this conveyance, it did not matter. The real problem was the replacement of the front wheels. Major refurbishment was needed. The front of the broken bodywork would have to be removed with one of Dad's saws and then we could simply fix the wheels directly onto the new front. All that would then be required would be a seat for the Guy.

We found a rusty saw with a broken handle in El Paso, borrowed a hammer from Pete and located a handful of six-inch nails. We did a fairly decent job of removing the broken part of the board, and then attached the wheels by driving in a row of nails across the edge of the main seating board, laying the axle of our newly acquired "pram" wheels next to the protruding fasteners and then bending them over to keep the axle in place. We rolled the trolley back and forth a few times to test it, and although neither of us dared to sit on it, we decided it was suitable for our purposes.

I had remembered seeing a two-legged dining room chair in the rat barn, and sent Crumb in to get it, being careful not to mention the rats. He emerged hurriedly and visibly shaken, and although he had been able to recover the chair, he also brought with him tales of "something moving around in the darkness."

"Probably only Scraps," I assured him, and we resumed work attaching the modified chair to the trolley.

All that remained was the paint. We carefully examined Dad's paint supply and found a can labeled "Black." It was the perfect color, so we opened the can using the saw blade, only to find that it was, in fact more of the ugly green paint that Dad had in abundance. Lack of brushes caused us to improvise the application of the green covering using sheets of crumpled up newspaper and bunches of feathers, donated by Mrs. Snaggin's backyard chicken farm. Following various painting experiments we finally settled on two separate techniques. For even surfaces, the best finish was obtained when I poured paint directly from the can onto the wood, and Crumb spread it evenly with a piece of cardboard. For the wheels and tires we had to resort to the chicken feathers, thrusting the paint-laden feathers into the moving wire spokes. Although messy, this proved to be a quite decorative – there was even some improvement to Crumb's ugly shirt. The final result was hardly professional, but as my father used to say, "A blind man on a galloping horse wouldn't know the difference."

Benito had been predictably absent while there was trolley work to be done, but his Guy construction responsibilities were much greater than ours, so his absence was excused. We did however want to check on his progress and decided to visit him.

I expected to find him in his father's garden shed busy directing the labor efforts of Willis Gurney who would be manufacturing an inflammable dummy to compete with the Maudly-Creechoms offering, but he was nowhere in sight. Frustrated we walked down Mud Lane toward the High Street, and to our dismay we found Benito in the Maudly-Creechoms garden helping Oscar and Willis to stuff newspaper into an old brown flour sack that was to become the Maudly-Creechom Guy's torso.

"What's he doing helping them?" Crumb said angrily, ready to throw a small rock in their direction.

"Wait!" I urged him, "Let's see what's going on first."

Benito had stepped back from the sack stuffing and was now directing Willis to fill the arms of Maggot's old yellow shirt from a pile of tatty rags. Oscar was busy tearing and scrunching up sheets of old newspaper to be used as filling material.

"Hello lads!" Benito greeted us as if nothing was wrong. Crumb, hothead that he was, demanded an explanation, but before he could say anything Benito kept talking. "We've made a deal," he said quickly. "We're going to use our trolley and their Guy and share the winnings, so we're all in this together now."

This turn of events surprised me. Benito generally hated everything about the Maudly-Creechoms. He had protested bitterly when I had included Crumb because he did not want to share the spoils, yet here he was offering to share our profits with Horace and Maggot, Oscar and Willis and probably even Squeaky.

"Lets go and make some bows and arrows," Benito suggested enthusiastically, struck with inspiration. Now that he had been relieved of his Guy making responsibilities he sought new diversions, and a reenactment of ancient weaponry and human targets was just the type of entertainment he needed.

"Why are you making a deal with them," asked Crumb as we walked away from the industrious little group.

"Do you know any other way to get a Guy in two days?" asked Benito.

"No," replied Crumb, "but if you had started to build one last weekend like you said, we would already have one."

"Yes, but I couldn't find any old clothes to make one," said Benito.

"Your dad's got lots of old clothes," I said. I knew this having seen him wearing them on a daily basis.

"But he won't give them to me," argued Benito.

"Well I'm not happy about having to share the collection with the likes of them," Crumb jerked his head in the general direction of the Maudly-Creechom home.

"So what about the trolley?" I asked.

"We'll use it to take their Guy around the village," Benito said as if this was obvious.

"No," I said. "We worked hard on this. We risked our lives making the trip to the Tip. We were chased by cows, were nearly sucked into the swamp getting the wheels, slaved all morning making the trolley and destroyed Crumb's shirt painting it, and now they get to use it free."

"Look," said Benito, "we have no money and no Guy, what else can we do? And anyway Crumb's shirt looks better like that." I had to agree.

"It's not fair," said Crumb.

"It's better to have half the money than nothing," Benito reasoned.

As we walked back to my house, Crumb dared to suggest that Benito had planned this all along to avoid the effort of building the Guy, and when I considered that avoiding effort was something that Benito excelled at, I began to believe that there might be something to Crumb's argument.

A sudden sound caught our attention – it was Squeaky coming down the lane from his house, riding what appeared to be a new bike – a bright red shiny mount. Squeaky wasted no time in pointing out a brass plate on the crossbar that read Phantom Flyer. He felt that this name described the mysterious individual that he assumed himself to be.

After a few initial words of congratulations and inner feelings of jealousy and hatred, we listened intently as Squeaky told us that his new possession was the result of a rich uncle's untimely demise. This news was followed by his mother's long list of stringent conditions concerning safety related issues and ended with a convincing argument why he was to be the one and only pilot. Under no circumstances should Benito or I, or any of our family members be allowed to ride the new bike.

"What are you going to do with your old bike?" asked Crumb.

"I don't know," said Squeaky. "My Dad will probably sell it."

"It's not worth much," said Crumb.

"I don't know," said Squeaky.

"I do," replied Crumb.

"Let me ride your new bike," I asked, hoping to break down his resistance.

"No," said Squeaky.

"Well, then let me," said Benito.

"Definitely not," said Squeaky defiantly.

"Go and get your old one," interjected Crumb, "and we'll have a race."

"No," replied Squeaky, "there will be no racing and no riding except for me."

Squeaky said that he had to tell his Mum where he was, and that he would return shortly. We began walking into our back garden and I had a clear view of him as he sped off up the lane. Squeaky was now circling his driveway and shouting something to his mother. I did not hear her reply clearly, but she didn't sound happy. Trusting her son's friends was not high on her list of priorities.

"Is that the trolley we are taking the Guy on?" asked Squeaky as he reappeared on his bike. Crumb and I had left the trolley in front of rat barn to dry after we had painted it.

"We?" said Benito. He was outraged that Squeaky would include himself in our money-raising venture.

"Well, the Maudly-Creechoms said that we would all go round the village together, and collect money like you said." Squeaky was beginning to feel unsure that he understood the exact terms of the Rolonzio-Creechom peace accord.

"No!" Said Benito emphatically. "We..." he moved his finger in a rough triangle to include Crumb and myself, "...are going with the Maudly-Creechoms and Oscar and Willis Gurney. And then we", he made the triangular gesticulation again, "are splitting the money in half. Half for them and half for us."

"Yeh," said Crumb. "And were going to spend our share on fireworks." He then added in a suspiciously friendly tone, "Are you getting any fireworks this year?" Crumb wasn't that interested in Squeaky's firework procurement plans. He just wanted to give Squeaky a friendly pat on the back and casually leave four short green smudges down the back of Squeaky's duffle coat, a present from the still not dry glossy green trolley paint that remained on Crumb's fingers.

Benito felt very strongly that if Squeaky needed fireworks, his parents should provide them. After all they were almost as rich as the Maudly-Creechoms.

Benito and I knew that the more people we had on our mission, the less work we would have to do. Additional personnel would also allow us to knock on more doors and that meant more money. And with Squeaky along on the mission, his rich parents would surely donate generously to our cause.

"If...you really want to come..." Benito stuck his jaw out and rolled his eyes high up and to the left. He did this whenever he wanted people to believe he was thinking, "...you can, but you have to be on the Maudly-Creechoms team and share their money."

"OK" said Squeaky, nodding, but within seconds he realized that the Maudly-Creechoms might not want to share their take with him.

"What if they won't let me come with them?"

"That's your problem," said Benito in a tone that expressed the finality of the situation, and the end of the conversation.

"Can I be in your gang?" Squeaky asked, his tone almost plaintive.

"No," came Benito's instant reply.

"Why not?" inquired the rejected lad.

"Because we already have enough people in our gang." This part was true. Chucky Billings had recently been added to our ranks and along with Basher and Crumb, was usually included in our escapades. I hadn't seen Chucky today and wondered where he was. But we were going to add anyone else, it should be the Pilchard boys. Squeaky's money and breeding were inconsistent with our humble means and more suited for the Maudly-Creechoms and their ilk.

"Anyway," Benito continued, "you haven't passed the initiation test."

What was I hearing? Was Benito actually considering letting this stupid and unpopular boy in our gang?

"I'll take the test," said Squeaky. Then, with one of the delayed afterthoughts for which the slow-witted boy was famous, he added, "What do I have to do?"

At that point Crumb and I realized that Squeaky had stepped firmly with both feet right into the middle of Benito's trap. Benito sat down on Dad's saw bench, the combination of powerful electric motors and very sharp quickly moving parts providing the perfect opportunity for Benito to flirt with danger. He rubbed his chin again and began to recall other fictitious tests that pre-existing gang members had allegedly been subject to.

In this fabricated performance Benito spoke in great detail about the bravery trials survived by each of us. Crumb had successfully jumped off the roof of Benito's house, Basher had eaten thirty-seven of Mrs. Snaggins's large green cooking apples and Chucky had performed the ultimate feat of courage when he walked across a narrow pole that spanned the village stream next to the hand bridge, while the rest of us had tried to knock him off with catapults and marbles. Benito and I, being founding members of the club, were exempt from the tests.

Squeaky listened uneasily to Benito, then even more uneasily asked "W..what would I have to do?"

Benito went back to adopting his fake thinking pose. Crumb, unnoticed by all save me, swung open the door to Rat barn and entered into the darkness searching for some string.

"Do you think you dare go down the big hill on our new trolley?" inquired Benito.

Squeaky stared at the bright green cart, fully considering that it was an untested design and was not equipped with brakes. He did not like the idea of being the test pilot on this cart's maiden voyage. Only the sound of Crumb clamoring around in Rat barn disturbed his thoughtful silence.

"Is that Crumb in Rat barn?" asked Squeaky.

"Yes," I replied, "See how brave you have to be to join the gang?"

Squeaky looked at the two large black wooden doors, one of which was half open.

"Hey, Crumb, aren't you afraid of the rats in there?" Squeaky called out.

Crumb obviously harbored a deathly fear of the rats because there now came a sound as if a lot of things were falling at the same time, followed by a loud and extended scream from Crumb. We heard him running quickly through the dim interior toward the doors.

Crumb's fear and anger were instantly directed at me.

"I told you there was something moving around in there and you said it was just Scraps," Crumb shouted. "Why didn't you tell me there were rats in there? I could have been eaten alive to death!"

"Sorry, Crumb," I answered as innocently as I could, "I thought you knew about them."

Crumb marched angrily over to the saw bench carrying a roll of rough twine he had found in the dusty darkness.

Meanwhile, Squeaky was still hesitant to make up his mind about the dangerous downhill test run. Benito hastened his agreement by suggesting that if Squeaky did not like the trolley and hill idea, he could sleep in Rat barn for a night.

Squeaky, now eager to ride the trolley and thus avoid the terror of a nocturnal escapade in the rat-infested barn, carefully leaned his bike against one of the upright support beams of the overhanging roof. With a large stride he swung one leg over the trolley and quickly sat down on the wet paint that covered the legless dining room chair. He did not at first realize his mistake. It was only after his admiring hands nonchalantly brushed over the main plank to discover the shiny sticky paint covering it, that the full extent of his predicament dawned upon him. He let out a pitiful, groaning sound and began to tear up.

Through his laughter, Benito apologized profusely for "forgetting" that the paint was not yet dry, and Crumb finding the whole incident hilarious forgot his anger toward me, and made some comment about the green hand print on Squeaky's back being almost unnoticeable now. I suggested that Squeaky go and visit my mother who would surely know what to do about his soiled condition. Squeaky raised himself up from the sticky seat and walked toward our front door with bowlegs and hands held out at his sides. We watched him waddle all the way across the garden, and continued chuckling as we saw him enter my house. Then we heard Mum as she started yelling at him, saying that he "should know what we are like by now," and "not to trust us, especially that Relonzio boy."

While Squeaky was inside the house being tended to by my mother, we returned to studying Crumb's escapades. He had come up with the idea to do a reenactment of a scene from an episode of Robin Hood that he had seen on TV. The fact that this required a simulation of men on horseback did not deter Crumb. He found it a true challenge. Crumb was now sitting on the saw bench and rubbing the twine back and forth on the stationary circular saw blade to cut a piece of string to the desired length. He explained that these would be the reins of the horse, and then walking over to Squeaky's bike, tied one end of the string to the left handlebar. He sat on the bike and assumed an upright position to measure out the correct length for the reins and tied the other end to the right handlebar.

"There, " he said. "Come on, Trigger!" Leaning back to keep the reins taut and the handlebars straight, Crumb began to peddle.

His forward motion was very good despite the uneven ground, and his control of the steering suggested to us that he had tried this particular stunt at least once before. Crumb made a slow circle round the saw bench shouting, "Hi, Ho Silver!" and "Tally Ho." He then peddled hard and disappeared round the end of the overgrown hedge next to Rat barn. We lost sight of him temporarily but could still hear the bike wheels on the gravel driveway as he made a tight circle outside El Paso before heading back toward us.

"Whoa, Trigger," he cried out as he approached us. I knew that "Whoa" was horse language for slow down, but apparently Squeaky's new bike didn't. More importantly, Crumb's grip on the reins to keep the bike under control on the rough terrain prevented him from reaching the brakes. He had stopped peddling now but the momentum he had already achieved on the straight driveway coupled with the slight downward slope heading to the apple tree only increased his speed. Being unable to stop, Crumb now had an important decision to make. Risk damage to life and limb by running directly into the apple tree or risk a reprimand from my father if he swerved right into the planted area of the garden to soften his impact. This was not a difficult decision.

The bike ploughed directly into Dad's tobacco plantation. But being November the prized nicotine plants had been harvested leaving behind densely clustered holes in the ground resembling a minefield. Trigger's front wheel became trapped in a large crater and then both horse and rider performed a spectacular acrobatic display for us. Squeaky, having just emerged from inside the house, wearing a pair of Pete's old jeans and carrying his own soiled garments in a grocery bag, saw the whole shocking incident and cried out in dismay as he ran over towards his injured bicycle.

Seeing Crumb crash his beloved new bike proved too much for Squeaky and he howled with alarm as he recovered the Phantom flyer from the uneven dirt. The bike was muddy and the handlebars were twisted off center. Fortunately Crumb was not harmed as he was quite proficient at surviving such vehicular mayhem. We all cheered his riding ability. A tearful Squeaky pushed his twisted bicycle off in the direction of his angry mother.

Contentment spread over me now that we had resolved the Guy situation. We had the Guy, we had the trolley, and now it was time to discuss the proposed money-collecting route for our parade. Benito had begun drawing a rough map in the dirt. It was of the village and he made a mark like an X everywhere he thought it was worth stopping.

Mum stuck her head out of the window and asked if we had eaten any lunch, and was horrified by the answer. With that we were promptly all rounded up and chased into the kitchen. It was not uncommon for us to eat at whatever house we happened to be near, so when Mum offered to feed the rest of the gang everyone predictably said yes. For once I was glad that Basher was not here. It would have been a little risky feeding Basher because if Dad came home and there was no food left, there would be hell to pay.

"Has Chucky found his dog yet?" asked Mum.

"Spot?" I asked.

"Yes," replied Mum.

"I didn't know he had lost her," I said, concerned that the lovable hound was missing.

"Yes," said Mum. "He's been wandering up and down the lane all morning looking for her."

Crumb began to complement Mum on the lovely color of the newly painted kitchen walls when Dad made an unexpected entrance, limping in just as the first food was served up.

"What happened to your leg?" asked Mum. "Why are you limping?"

"Don't ever paint a roof with Joey Dobbins," Dad said.

"Why not?" asked Crumb, as if it was something he would consider.

"Because he doesn't know how to do it properly," grumbled Dad.

"Are you sure it was his fault?" asked Pete, who had come inside to investigate the smell of food, and was currently washing the motorcycle grease from his hands.

"Of course I am," answered Dad with that unique tone of irritation he reserved especially for my brother.

"Is he limping as well?" Pete asked with raised eyebrows.

"No." This answer clearly gave Dad no pleasure.

"So what happened?" asked my mother in an irritated voice.

"Joey started painting behind me," Dad started to explain, "where I couldn't see him, and that roof paint is slippery..."

"You stepped in the slippery paint and fell off Dickey Braithewait's roof," said Pete, both anticipating the circumstances and completing the story.

"Well, the idiot shouldn't do that," protested Dad, "Any fool knows that you don't paint behind someone. You have to be careful of wet paint."

"Yes, you do," added Pete.

"Even Squeaky knows that," added Crumb.

We all laughed, which annoyed Dad because he thought we were laughing at him.

The mashed potato and Yorkshire pudding went down well after the mornings adventures, and rounding the meal off with chocolate biscuits and a cup of tea, we all thanked Mum and got up to go back out side.

"Don't disappear," said Dad firmly.

"Why not?" I asked.

"I've got a job for you to do." Dad thought nothing of also enlisting Crumb to do his bidding. He had long since discovered that it was easier to get one of the other kids from the village to help him than it was to suffer the endless arguments he would get from Pete.

"What do we have to do?" I asked, hoping that it wouldn't take long.

"Well, just stay out of my way because I have some washing to do," said Mum.

The kitchen floor was made of thick square red quarry tile. I am not sure what was under the tile but it could not have been very much. Anything spilled on the floor would easily drain away. This was a distinct design advantage for those times when my mother would do the washing.

She approached everything with enthusiasm and urgency, and the laundry was no exception. It seemed to me, that during the frenzy that was wash-day, gallons of water would be spread around the kitchen. At the center of it in a large cloud of steam, Mum would be pulling soaking wet clothes from an antique water heating device she called "the copper," and feeding them into "the mangle" a double roller contraption connected to a crank handle that squeezed all the water out. The result was wet, but not dripping, flattened clothes that would then be carried outside and pegged onto a clothes line to dry in the good British frost. Mum had actually been without her treasured mangle for some time now, following an experiment conducted by Benito to see what would happen to a tennis ball if it were rolled through it. The tennis ball did not survive. Neither did the mangle. With a sound that was cross between a twang and a bang, the mangles top roller popped out of its housing and was never able to provide the necessary squeezing power again. Dad had been promising to fix it using a wood working clamp, and an old car suspension spring, but as yet no progress had been made.

We left the kitchen to escape the hazardous combination of boiling water, electricity and unreliable machines, and willingly followed Dad. We all walked up the garden path to El Paso, and Dad opened the front wooden doors. What small amount of free space that used to exist just inside was now taken up by Dad's latest "special project."

I was beginning to understand. When Dad had discovered the old battered clothes dryer in Rat barn last Saturday while searching for Rodger Pilchard's groundsheet, his eyes had lit up as he envisioned his latest creation. Coincidentally, last Saturday Mum had been washing some clothes and was outside hanging them on the line to dry, when she saw Dad wheeling the device over to El Paso, on his home made sack barrow.

"Oh! That's nice," Mum had said. "What is it?"

"It's some sort of clothes dryer," replied Dad," smiling with anticipation. "Can you believe that Whitey Snow's wife was going to throw it away because it doesn't work?"

"Can you fix it?" she asked, with doubt beginning to show on her face.

"Yes, I'm sure it can be fixed," said Dad optimistically. "It just needs a heat regulating valve. I can make one from the petrol pump off the Austin."

My mother did not have one hundred percent confidence in Dad's inventions but, looking at her wet hands, blue with cold from handling the washing, she seemed quite pleased to see Dad wheeling the battered steel appliance from the bowels of Rat barn.

"I don't want the washing to smell of petrol," warned Mum, having previous experience of Dad's less that perfect ingenious solutions.

"Why should it?" said Dad. "The washing's not going in here. This is to dry my tobacco leaves."

With Mum's hope and joy for dry bed sheets dashed upon the rocks of despair, she quickly turned and went back into the house.

Dad had positioned the tobacco dryer just inside the doors to El Paso, where it would remain during its repair. Now we gathered round it as Dad removed the flat steel lid.

"Now," he said, "I'm going to need two bricks to replace the missing wheels, and this will need to come off." He reached inside and making a contorted face, began to wrestle with a small piece of copper tubing.

"What are you going to do?" I asked.

"Well," he said, kneeling down and reaching his arm up inside, "I am going to need a part from a petrol pump."

I was dreading the words that I knew would follow.

"What I want you boys to do is make a path to the Austin." He said as if it was a simple task.

The Austin finally stopped working due to a mysterious problem that caused the engine to constantly cut out. Even Mr. Snaggins couldn't fix it so it must have been serious. The car would start once every fifteen or twenty times, and once it fired up, Dad had to depress the accelerator all the way to keep it running. The engine would scream at maximum revs for about fifteen seconds and then cut out again. When the day came to abandon it, we pushed it to the side of Rat barn, pointing directly into the great uncharted wilderness, and went through the repetitive starting attempts. When it reluctantly gave up the battle and started, Dad put it in gear and gave it maximum power to bulldoze his way through the bushes, brambles and usually impassible undergrowth. Dad "parked" it, where it finally died, and climbed out of the back window to safely exit the wilderness. The car had remained there ever since. The tracks left by its entry had long since grown over, reclaimed by the jungle's re-growth. Now it was to give up its petrol pump so that other beings from the mechanical world might live again.

Pete had performed one of his famous disappearing acts, leaving Benito, Crumb and I to solve the problem. We stood on the edge of the high fertile vegetation barrier. Tangled vines and thorn filled wood created an impenetrable obstruction. After a brief discussion on the location of the vehicle, which none of us could see, Crumb was ordered to climb on the roof of Rat barn and perform reconnaissance duties. He was able to see the rusty roof of the car and with a long stick provide us with a bearing on which to commence our explorations.

At first we tried taking massive strides and crushing the brambles with our feet, but it soon became obvious that this was not going to work. Not only could the high growth not be reached with our feet but the low branches, once crushed down would immediately spring back again, often scraping our legs with thorns. Next, we tried using sticks to beat a path to the old car, but this proved an equal waste of time.

Then Benito, searching behind Rat barn, found an old water barrel with the bottom rotted out. In a moment of supreme innovative genius, we tipped it over and crawled inside. We soon found that by continuing to crawl forward inside the open ended barrel, in a similar manner to the way Toady Moady's hamster crawled around inside his little wire wheel, we could move through the thorn bushes, stinging nettles and weeds with impunity. There was not room for all three of us in the barrel, so we formed a system with a navigator, who would sit on top of Rat barn and two pilots who would steer the barrel.

It was quite enjoyable and adventurous, but in the end we were not able to find a clear path through the trees and thick bushes to reach the car. In desperation we gave up and sat down by the saw bench, exhausted. Just as we did this, my father walked up and demanded a progress report.

"Have you done it yet?" asked Dad.

"No," I said.

"It's impossible," added Crumb.

"I think I was bitten by a scorpion," said Benito.

"Well, you boys are no help at all," Dad said and disappeared into Rat barn.

"What's he going to do now?" asked Benito.

"I don't know," I replied.

We didn't have to wait long for an answer. Dad emerged carrying a machine with a long handle that had a steel tank on one end and on the other a large round tube with oblong vents cut into it. On the tank was a red symbol of a flame and the words "DANGER" printed underneath.

"This is going to be good," I said. It wasn't often we were treated to a display like this.

If I had to guess at Dad's three favorite tools, I would say that number three and two were an equal pick between chainsaw and sledge hammer, but number one was without doubt his flame thrower. Purchased from Mrs. Army at the ex government shop in town, it had given him many years of faithful service. We all nudged each other and grinned widely at the prospect of seeing this machine in action.

Dad bent down over the device, released a latch and began to work a small hand pump vigorously. He kept one eye on a glass-fronted pressure gauge, and when the needle crept round into the section colored red, he began to twist a round steel knob. We all heard a hissing sound.

"Aren't you worried that you'll start a fire?" asked Benito.

"No," said Dad with an all-knowing air about him. "Everything's too damp to catch fire, but this should make a good path for us."

"Why didn't you use that before?" asked Crumb, but his question was lost as Dad touched his cigarette lighter to the end of the large steel tube and the hissing turned into a dull roar. Instantly, a blue flame about eighteen inches long jumped out from the front of the machine. Even though not pointed directly at us, the heat generated from the jet of fire was welcome.

"Where is it?" Dad shouted over the noise of his fire breathing companion and we all pointed in the direction of the Austin.

Dad slowly marched forward swinging the flame from side to side to clear a wide path. Whatever the blue cone of fire touched instantly burst into flames. Stinging nettles were incinerated and evergreen shrubs bearing dangerous thorns shriveled and were reduced to ash in the path where my father walked. I was quite proud of his prediction that he would not start a brushfire. The vegetation was, as he said much too wet to cause any problems, but the burning shrubbery crackled and gave off a thick pungent smoke, not unlike emissions from Pete's motorbike.

Onward he slowly walked, determined and deliberate, burning a pathway wide enough for us to follow. I was beginning to think that we must be almost at the car, but instead of finding the Austin, in pieces and rusted, Dad was tackling a large bramble bush, keeping the flame focused on the greenery. It was a large target and required an extra long dose of the flamethrower, before it gave up its guardianship of the aged automobile. It did eventually burn and reveal the car behind it, which had sustained considerable heat damage during the attack. With the vehicle revealed Dad turned the round steel knob again and the roaring stopped, leaving behind a silence that hung in the air like the acrid smoke from the charred plant life.

Dad carried the incendiary machine back to the barn and we followed, eager to see what piece of equipment he would unveil next. We were disappointed to find that it was only a screwdriver. Walking back toward the Austin I was amazed to see smoke still emanating from the burnt remains of the bramble bush. As we drew nearer, I could see that it was in fact the Austin that was burning, not the bush. The seats were ablaze and the interior was filled with orange flames. Crumb even suggested that we roast some potatoes in the flames, but no one else was hungry. Undeterred, Crumb went to ask Mum for a potato to roast. The only thing that Dad did not have in Rat barn was a fire extinguisher, but he demonstrated effective improvisation by making Benito and I fill a couple of buckets of water from the rain barrel and throw them through the car's shattered back window to douse the flames.

The derelict vehicle was no longer burning but it was still hot enough to provide some comfort against the cold temperature, so we stood warming our hands on the glowing metal as we waited for it to cool. Dad did not share our patience and retreated to the comfort of the kitchen while he waited for the car to cool down. It had taken about an hour before the car had cooled enough for Dad to remove the required tobacco drying machine repair component.

Dad was angry at having burned the Austin, since he had planned on it being a source of spare parts for many long years to come, but what was done was done. The fuel pump was in a difficult spot that required Dad to lean over the mudguard by the car's right front wheel and reach deep inside the engine compartment. He skimmed his knuckles twice on the engine block, and after losing his temper almost accidentally stuck the screwdriver through his wrist, but after about ten minutes he emerged victorious, bloody, and smiling as he triumphantly held a small brass fitting high in the air.

We returned to the drying device, and saw that while Benito, Crumb and I had been attempting to clear a jungle path the safe way, Dad had already begun the modification process. Several large tobacco leaves had been loosely packed in a rusty steel milk crate, which had been bent to fit perfectly inside the clothes dryer. A second crate was loaded and ready to be placed on top, to fill the machine up.

Dad was grappling around underneath again and explained,

"Now, all I have to do is tighten this bolt, and connect the fuel pipe to the paraffin tank and we're ready to go."

"How long will the first load take?" I asked. Now that I had been a part of the modification team, I felt a certain interest in seeing the results of our efforts.

"Oh, I would think no more than a couple of days," said Dad, not really knowing.

"Now, while the machine is in operation," he said cheerfully, "El Paso will probably smell beautiful as the tobacco slowly cures while it dries."

I thought it more likely that El Paso, and most probably the tobacco, would smell of paraffin.

CHAPTER 13
AN ARCHERY LESSON

A bow and arrow are one of the easiest weapons to make, second only to the spear in simplicity. But it took two of us to use the axe effectively – one to provide balance and support by holding the end of the axe handle, and the other to guide the heavy sharp head down on the carefully chosen branch. Within minutes we had the bows cut and using the saw bench, had rubbed the stick against the blade and made a deep narrow notch in either end to secure the twine. Crumb and Benito had been the first to select their bows, and I had been left with an inferior specimen. The arrows were more difficult. Ordinarily there would have been a plentiful supply, but the Pilchard boys had recently been on a raiding party for cricket stumps, which they had tried unsuccessfully to sell going from door to door in the village. Even so we were able to find enough worthy projectiles. Benito and I sat securely on the axe handle as it lay across the saw bench and Crumb dragged the wood across the shiny blade until he was satisfied with the sharp point. With our weapons finished, we set off for Snobbit's field. As we walked we discussed among ourselves what roles we would play. We could all agree that our opponents would have to play the Sheriff of Nottingham and his wicked army and that we would be the brave and noble folk heroes.

We found Horace and Maggot, along with Oscar and Willis Gurney, gathered round a water trough for cows but now being utilized for target practice. Three arrows had their rubber suction cups stuck to the smooth steel sides of the oversized drinking vessel but most of the wooden missiles lay on the grass nearby.

"Are you going to use that thing?" Willis was staring at my frail bow as he and his brother chuckled at my expense. But I felt that we would have no trouble beating the Sheriff and his men, especially considering Crumb's excellent aim and Benito's ability to cheat.

"OK. Willis, you can be the Sheriff of Nottingham," Benito said, immediately taking control of the situation.

"I want to be Maid Marion," Maggot wined.

"You can't." said Benito abruptly without even looking at her. "Maid Marion is one of Robin Hood's men. You can be the Sheriff's wife."

"That's not fair" Maggot complained as she turned her back on us, at which point Crumb added injury to insult by shooting her in the back.

"Aaaaaaaaaw," grumbled the girl. Not really hurt, as the damage that could be inflicted by the homemade weapon was very minimal.

There was no more time for discussion. Benito yelled, "Take cover!" and ran quickly to a safe spot behind the water trough. This completely took the Sheriff by surprise and we, from the only safe cover in the field, began launching arrows at our enemies.

Having no time to prepare for the attack our assailants could do little but run. Once safely out of range of our arrows they bravely hurled insults at us about our poor aim and lack of archery skills. I was the primary target of their verbal abuse, since I possessed an inferior weapon that would barely hurl a projectile three quarters of the distance of Benito and Crumb's equipment.

I realized my bow was an inappropriate weapon for this battle, and that I must do something to even up the odds so I stood up and announced to everyone that I was going home and would be returning soon.

"Watch out for the arrow," I heard Willis shout. Immediately I felt one of his rubber tipped arrows bounce off my back.

"Very funny," I snapped.

Several months earlier Dad had made his weekly pilgrimage to Bollingtons and returned home with a pair of Russian boots, some old picture frames and a professional archery set. It contained a bow that stood about my height, and three arrows with feathered shafts and sharp pointed conical steel tips. There was also a large straw target marked with concentric rings of diminishing size.

Dad's original intent in buying the outfit was unknown. He joked about poaching some of the sheep in a nearby field, and although I knew he was partial to mutton, I don't think he liked it enough to resort to murder and rustling, but you never knew with Dad. At first he practiced every day but quickly became frustrated by his inability to hit the red spot on the target. In fact, many of his carefully aimed arrows missed the target completely and ended up disappearing into the hedgerow beyond. He lost two arrows and now was down to one.

Luckily Dad was something of an expert on wood and was soon able to determine that the problem was with the bow. Apparently the shaft of the bow had been cut from a tree with a 'twisted grain' causing it to be highly inaccurate. Nobody in the lane understood the explanation, but Dad said that was because the neighbors lacked the expertise of woodworking that he himself had achieved over the years. Mum said that Dad should sell the archery set since he had now given up on the idea of becoming a world-class archer, and the bow now leaned in the corner of the hall.

I reached the house and grabbed the bow, along with the one remaining arrow, and ran back to Snobbit's field. I understood that the weapon was defective but that was fine because I did not plan on shooting it. I just wanted to show off with it.

Passing Mrs. Snobbit's house I noticed that she had taken up a good lookout position leaning on her white painted wooden fence.

"Be careful with that," she advised, lowering her binoculars for a second.

"Don't worry," I replied, "I'm only going to show it to them."

Having now managed to engage me in conversation, she seemed intent on detaining me. "Did you hear that the doctor had to visit Mister McKenzie this afternoon?" she inquired.

"No." I said, "Why?"

"Well he left the pub early last night" she continued, "and when he woke up this afternoon he couldn't remember what happened but his trousers were ripped and he had bite marks on his legs."

"Were they bites like vampires?" I asked.

"No," she replied, "more like dog bites."

I thought for a moment and concluded that old Grizley must have left the pub unusually early to get home before the ghosts came out, but found himself the unfortunate victim of a werewolf attack. I told Mrs. Snobbit as much and added that I hoped that the doctor didn't have to shoot him with a silver bullet.

All play stopped when I returned carrying the bow, and everyone ran over for a closer inspection. Oscar ran his fingers down the carved wood and admitted that it was a stunning design. Benito admired the tautness of the tightly woven string and Crumb marveled at the craftsmanship and construction. Willis wanted to feel the weight and was amazed at the weapon's lightness. It was truly a thing of beauty, desired by all. And it was mine!

"Let's see how well it shoots," said Benito enthusiastically.

I had not actually planned shooting the bow, but giddy with my new social standing and feeling the need to give something back to my adoring fans, I reluctantly agreed. Each contestant selected his or her best arrow and we all stood in line some considerable distance from the cow trough. I positioned myself at the end of the line to shoot last, thinking that this would create the most dramatic effect. We took turns firing arrows at the tank and I watched patiently as one by one a selection of rubber tipped arrows and roughly cut sharpened sticks fell short of the target. At last it was my turn to perform.

I raised the bow with outstretched arm, and resting the metal tipped arrow lightly over my thumb, I drew back. I had shot the bow several times in our backyard and knew how hard it was to pull back the string. I wrestled with the deadly device as I slowly stretched the wood into a firing position. My right arm trembled from wrist to shoulder with the strain as I tried to line the arrow up with the center of the tank.

Then Willis did something very, very stupid.

"Hold on a minute," he said, and ran into my field of vision to collect his spent arrows. Then I did something even more stupid.

I knew that I couldn't hold the stretched string much longer, and I also knew from my father that the bow was hopelessly inaccurate, so I didn't think there would be any chance of hitting Willis if I released the arrow. I remembered his insults regarding my previous bow, and clearly recalled his sneer. A little harmless scare would do him good,

"Hey Willis, watch out for the arrow!"

Maggot looked from the taut bowstring to my facial expression and anticipating my next move she began to scream. With a twang of the chord and a whoosh of air, the arrow arched high into the sky, where a slight breeze guided it away from the trough and directly toward Willis, who hearing my friendly warning about imminent danger, now stood paralyzed with fear as the arrow came closer. Willis's eyes were wide with panic, like those of a rabbit at night caught in the headlights of Roger Pilchard's oncoming car.

Chucky Billings used to say that when you are about to die, your entire past flashes before your eyes. I had seen the reckless and irresponsible way that Chucky climbed trees and believed that he was probably speaking from experience about impending death.

Oddly enough Willis may have been reliving his past, but I was far more concerned with my own future. As a result of my harmless prank, the boy would be killed. And of course my life would be ruined. My father would beat me to within an inch of my life, after which I would be disowned by my parents and friends. I would be told to leave the house forever and, stroking Scraps for the last time, would walk off down the lane alone and tearful while nosey neighbors peeked from behind lace curtains, whispering cautionary tales to their children. About half way down the lane I would have to confront Willis's parents who, dressed in black and gathered round the lifeless body of their son, would be wringing their hands, and weeping. At the bottom of the lane while bidding farewell to a village from which I would be forever banished, Constable Smith would ride up on his black bicycle and slap some handcuffs on me. After a long and miserable life of solitude and torment I would die alone in a rat-infested cold damp jail cell.

The arrow started to descend in a long slow curve and I held my breath and watched in horror as the steel tip of the arrow approached Willis. All I could hear was Maggot's screaming, which was instantly replaced by Willis bellowing in pain. This was quickly followed by the sounds of running feet. Everyone was bolting toward Willis, who was lying on the ground face down, howling. Dashing to the scene I found Willis on the grass.

Willis's wound was not anywhere as bad as I had imagined. The sharpened metal had pierced the skin of his lower leg, but the weight of the wooden shaft had then pulled the arrow out and it lay on the ground next to Willis. There was a little blood on the arrow tip and a little more on Willis's trousers. Benito, who had picked up the arrow to inspect it, now wiped the remaining blood on Willis's jeans next to the small round hole created by the assault.

I immediately fell on my knees beside Willis and pleaded with him not to tell his mother. But I realized that his mother would find out because Mrs. Snobbit had observed the whole tragic incident.

With the help of Oscar and Maggot, Willis struggled to his feet and made a whining sound as he rested his weight on the afflicted leg. I sensed that this was more for effect than because of genuine pain.

"Come on, Willis, you big baby," jeered Crumb. "Graham Smith almost lost a finger yesterday at school and he didn't complain like you."

"You be quiet," said Maggot in one of her rare confrontational outbursts.

"Owww," cried Willis as he tried a few tentative limping steps.

Willis delicately probed his war wound with his finger, and Maggot glared at me.

"That was a silly thing to do," she shouted. Benito came to my rescue.

"Wait a minute," he said, "It was just as much Willis's fault, because he got in the way." I hadn't looked at it this way, but there was some truth to the argument.

"Well, what if he can't walk now?" continued the hysterical girl.

"He IS walking now," I said.

"It hurts a lot though," winced Willis.

"Well, we're not going round the village doing the penny for the Guy with you now," said Maggot.

I instantaneously forgot that one of my comrades was mortally wounded and once again slipped into Guy-less despair.

"We don't care," said Benito. "We'll make our own."

"You don't have enough time," said Oscar.

"But I've got lots of brothers and sisters," said Benito.

"You're going to burn one of them?" asked Maggot, obviously thinking Benito capable of such a thing.

It was a long walk home and our normal walking speed was reduced by Willis's wound. By the time we had reached our house the smell of tobacco coming from El Paso was overwhelming, and for a moment I had a vision of thousands of people crammed into the old stone building smoking pipes.

Willis was beginning to walk normally again and only started limping when someone chose to remind him of his battle wounds. Although he had agreed not to relate the painful misfortune to his mother, it was obvious that the whole unpleasant incident had left considerable ill will between our two rival groups. The devastating collapse of our new Guy Fawkes joint venture had occurred just hours after its commencement, and I could think of no easy way to heal the mental, physical and contractual wounds.

I walked through the front door and into hall. For once I could hear no commotion in the kitchen.

I opened the door slowly. Pete and Mum sat at the table across from each other in stony silence. A box of six-inch nails was scattered over the table, and Dad stood at the sink staring out of the window. His hand had been bandaged up, and for a moment I thought that the first-aid dressing must surely be in some way connected to the nails. As odd as this situation was, the most striking thing about the scene were the kitchen walls.

All over Mum's recently painted surfaces, red streaks had appeared and were dripping down the walls in thin trickles. I crossed the room to the sink where the effect seemed most pronounced and ran my extended finger down the wall. I held it up in front of Dad's nose, in case he was not aware of the catastrophe. He took a slow deep breath, rolled his eyes and turned away.

I once heard Mario Rolonzio talking about a horror film he saw called *The Walls That Dripped Blood*. I imagined that it contained a scene somewhat similar to this. No one spoke. We gazed around failing to find an area that did not look too bad. Mum wore an embarrassed frown but seemed unable to give voice to her feelings. Pete would have normally loved a situation like this to enrage Dad. But even he was silent.

"What happened to the walls?" I asked.

"What are you doing with my bow and arrows," replied Dad.

"Arrow," interjected Pete. "Remember you lost two in the hedge."

I had been so puzzled by the uncharacteristic silence in the house that I had forgotten to replace the weapon in the hall, and was still carrying it.

"What happened to your hand, Dad?" I could not see Dad from my position next to the coat rack, but I could clearly see Pete wincing at my question. This expression suggested that I should not quiz my father about whatever unfortunate incident had befallen him.

Dad continued to look out of the kitchen window dreaming of escape, and watching the lane, saw Willis as he limped by.

"What in heaven's name has happened to that boy now?" he said, and then slowly turned from the sink to look at me as he realized I had been in possession of his bow.

"Did you hurt your hand?" I asked in a desperate effort to distract him, but the veins in his neck were already beginning to swell, and I thought I saw slight traces of steam escaping from his ears.

"Did you shoot that boy?" Dad asked firmly.

"He sort of got in the way," I said.

"He got in the way?" shouted Dad, "What were you doing with the bow?"

"Well, I just wanted to show it to them," I stammered.

"You had no business taking it," he continued, "let alone shooting someone with it."

"I didn't think you'd mind," I suggested, trying to convince Dad that he was really a reasonable man. I thought that if I could get him to believe this he wouldn't resort to violence. But it looked as if his fall from the roof that morning, combined with the impending workload of repainting the kitchen, had placed him in a rather foul mood.

"You didn't think I would mind?" he repeated. "What in God's name made you think I wouldn't mind?"

I just shrugged and silently slumped into the chair.

"I've had a devil of a hard day at work," he bellowed. "I've fallen off a roof, burned my favorite scrap car, smashed my knuckles, and almost speared myself with a screwdriver. Then I burned my arm trying to save the tobacco crop when my new drying machine caught fire, and I come home to find that someone has crashed someone else's bike, your mother has destroyed the kitchen walls and you have stolen my bow and almost killed the neighbor's kid with it!"

Dad stopped and took a breath. He was making some faces at no one, and kept clenching his fists. He was a desperate man, who had been pushed far enough today and I wanted nothing more than to be out of his way. As it was I got my wish. "You go straight to bed now," Dad ordered. "No supper and no television!" As an afterthought he added an extra ration of punishment.

"And don't think you're going to go out with your dead beat friends on Friday. You'll be coming to the talent show with us."

I lay on my bed in silence and reflected on my condition. I had survived the wrath of my father and was currently paying the price for my misdeeds. I could well understand that Dad had experienced a day that was by no means perfect, but I had problems of my own that were not at all simple to solve. Foremost on my list was, of course, the Maudly-Creechom's retraction of our Guy deal. This latest development had left us once again in a position where the collection of firework funds seemed unlikely. Benito's gradual change of character from friendly and easygoing playmate to something much darker and ominous also made me unhappy. Could it be that this was only the effect of the pressure he brought upon himself because of his inability to provide a Guy Fawkes, or was it as Crumb had suggested, that Benito had plotted and schemed to minimize his own share of the work? The incident with Willis's leg was regrettable, but in the end I knew that a real arrow scar would be the envy of all who saw it.

And now Spot was lost. In terms of real tragedy this was probably the worst problem of all. It would break my heart if anything happened to Scraps, and I only saw her about once a week. Spot was Chucky's permanent companion. I didn't think he could survive without her.

I sank deeper into despondency, trying to grasp how everything could change so quickly. This morning life was simple and full of hope, now my world had come unraveled and no longer made any sense.

"Did you see Dad's shirt," said my brother, who had appeared at my bedside.

"What happened?" I asked.

"His tobacco dryer caught fire," Pete replied. laughing.

"Did you see it?"

He nodded, unable to disguise his amusement.

"Dad started the machine and was standing watching it, when all of a sudden flames started coming from underneath," said Pete.

"The area that he fixed?" I asked.

"Yep, he tried to put the fire out but his shirt caught light, and while he ran to the water barrel by Rat barn to save his shirt, all the tobacco inside caught fire. It was great."

"I think I smelled it when I was coming home," I said. "What happened with the kitchen walls?"

"Oh that was even better," said my brother trying to suppress his giggling as he told me.

It seems that last week, when Mum had decided to paint, she conducted a thorough search of the numerous storage facilities around the property for paint, but turned up nothing that was appropriate for her needs. Dad's award winning collection of old paint contained no soft pastels or warm tints.

So Mum being ever resourceful took one of the old cans of white ceiling paint and added a few drops of red food coloring. This created a nice shade of pink that Mum liked. Within a couple of hours, the walls had been painted with broad even brush strokes, the furniture was put back in place and the clean-up process was complete. The results were impressive. Mum was truly satisfied with a job well done. And we thought that was the end of it.

But today Mum had decided to do some washing, which along with a constantly boiling tea kettle had produced clouds of steam in the room. The windows soon fogged up and condensation clung to every surface in the room. Apparently, professional paint manufacturers use a more reliable technique to tint their products. In the case of Mum's homemade creation, the food coloring had leached out of the paint, and caused the red streaks that marred the surface of the walls.

"Did the nails all over the table have anything to do with the bandage on his hand?" I asked.

"No," said Pete. "That was another thing that made him angry. The bandage was from the burn he got when the tobacco dryer caught fire."

"Then what were the nails all about?" I inquired.

"Remember when Dad sent away for those two hundred and fifty coat hangers from the *Exchange and Mart?*"

"Yes," I replied.

"Well they came in the post today and that's them laying on the kitchen table," Pete said.

The sound of one of my parents banging on the ceiling with a broom handle was intended to let us know that my punishment was not designed to include conversation and laughter with Pete. Given my father's delicate disposition, we thought it best to heed the warning and Pete left me in silence.

CHAPTER 14

DAD AND I TRY SPACEFLIGHT

Yesterday's very enjoyable and productive day away from school was over. It was now time to return to Mrs. Diggsmore's Torture Chamber. With my mind still immersed in hazy half sleep, and my body wrapped in bed sheets that were far more warm and comfortable than that which awaited me on the long frozen walk to school, I reflected on the previous day.

We had learned many important things that were far more useful than anything we could be taught in school. What was the value of knowing your seven times table when you can learn that a good bike manufacturer should always make the brakes accessible to the rider, even if the rider, under some spell of foolishness, is using rope to steer! Surely it was more important to be able to recognize wet paint than to find Australia on a map. And where was the need to spell "avoidance" if you couldn't do it when an arrow was heading straight for you.

It didn't take me long to decide that school was not really of any value to me. I just didn't know how to convince my mother of this. Debating the issue with her was pointless; she would never be able to understand, being too old to remember what a senseless waste of time it was. It's a pity because I am sure she would have loved to have us home all day. It was time to dig deep into my bag of trickery and fake an illness.

I visualized my body from my feet, all the way up to my hair as I looked for a good ailment. Anything from the waist down was out of the question since I had never been able to perfect a phony limp. Stomach pains were also a questionable choice because I didn't want any self-imposed illness to prevent me from eating. I had tried a bad back before but my mother was convinced that I was too young to have one, and anyway, Mum's solution to most aches and pains was to keep on with your daily schedule and simply "work it off." Problems with sight and hearing were also not a good idea, as Mum had become an expert at detecting trickery of this nature. My mother would reveal alleged audible problems as fiction by quietly mumbling something like, "Would anyone like some chocolate?" A slight variation of this test in the form of, "Isn't that a bar of chocolate on the table?" would similarly expose any claimed vision deficiencies. It would be a sore throat then. I lay in bed imagining the rough soreness of an inflamed throat and tried to hypnotize myself into believing that I actually had one. I was unable to practice the harsh and strained voice that went along with the malady, but thought that I would be able to summon up a fairly convincing act when the time came.

Pete and I had already been called twice and were already in the "ultimatum" stage as I heard my mother's exasperated steps climbing the stairs again. Mum entered the room and scowled at us.

"For the last time, GET UP!" She began tugging the covers from Pete's bed.

"OK Mum," said Pete. "I'll help you make breakfast."

There was something wrong here. Either Pete was guilty of a very serious crime or he was intending to ask mom for petrol money.

"You, too!" Mum kicked one corner of my bed to make sure that I was conscious, but I thought it better to just lay there. I imitated a little groan for effect as I heard the rustle of blankets being thrown off Pete's bed.

"Come on," he said, with an eagerness that caught me off guard, "We don't want to be late for schoooooaaaaaargh!"

I peeked out from the covers to find Pete lying on the floorboards beside his bed. He was clutching his lower leg with both hands as he rolled around on his back. His face was twisted with pain, and it looked as if tears were about to form in the corners of his deceitful eyes.

"What's the matter?" asked my mother suspiciously.

"It's my leg," moaned Pete.

"What's wrong with it?" Persisted Mum.

"I don't know," groaned Pete, and for good measure added, "Aaaaaaaaaaaawwwww."

"Come on, stand up and walk," commanded my mother like some biblical healer. Pete rose to his feet and executed two incredibly realistic limping steps.

"You, too," Her prompting was directed at me now. "I…thin..k, I… uuh … sore, th..roat."

"Well, get up and see how you feel after a cup of tea." That was Mum's answer to everything. Had she been a doctor tea would have been the only medicine that she prescribed. If you had the flu, it would be two cups of Earl Gray three times a day. Complaints of an upset stomach would be dealt with by administering three cups of Ceylon, to be taken with meals. For a broken leg it would be four cups of Darjeeling before going to bed.

I dressed without much interest, and wandered down stairs where Pete was making a failed attempt to get his shoe on. I watched him wince with theatrical pain and realized then that my well thought out plan to forge a medical ailment had failed. Mum had believed in Pete's agonizing performance and considered my complaints a copycat phenomenon. I had been beaten by my older brother, falling victim to both his skill and timing.

Shortly after breakfast Pete disappeared into the living room, limping as he went, and occupied Dad's chair by the fire. I considered that

Pete was an expert limper. He had fallen off his motorbike so often, and spent so much time with injuries to at least one of his legs that he had studied and perfected the art of emulating it. It had now become a prize winning performance. With a groan he lowered himself delicately into the throne, and heaved a sigh of relief. He risked a cheeky grin at me even though Mum was in the room and could have seen him, but that was the kind of risk taker that Pete was.

He leafed through back issues of *Motorcycle News* while he rested his affected appendage on a square velvet cushion that had been placed on a wooden chest to bring it up to the most comfortable height.

Meanwhile I layered on additional clothing and waited for the determined knock on the door that would signal Chucky and Squeaky's arrived. It came too soon and together we collected Benito for the walk to school.

The walk was strange without Spot, whose whereabouts was still unknown. Chucky was silent and uninterested in anything we had to say. He shuffled on beside us with his eyes constantly searching the surroundings for signs of his beloved Spot. Although our hike to school was generally a depressing experience we frequently found occasion for joviality, but this morning nobody wanted to laugh or joke, for fear of somehow disturbing Chucky in his sorrow.

By the time we reached the High Street Squeaky had already started. He offered each of us one of his liquorices allsorts to establish good faith.

"If you let me in the gang, I can help you build a Guy." he pleaded.

"We don't need your help," said Benito, spitting out the words as clouds of condensation spilled from his mouth in the frigid morning air. In my opinion this was not so. Since the Maudly-Creechoms had rescinded the deal made yesterday morning, and we would no longer be able to join them in their cash gathering undertaking, we were once again in need of a Guy, and I didn't see how Benito was going to make one in time. This meant that we needed as much help as we could possibly get. I thought about injecting this reasoning into the conversation but Benito already had some hostility toward me because somehow he felt that I was at fault for the arrow in the leg incident, and he saw that as the pivotal reason for the broken agreement.

"My Mum has a dressmaking dummy," offered Squeaky.

"Your Mum is a dressmaking dummy," offered Benito, but Squeaky being too stupid to get the joke continued without taking offense.

"No, I mean we could use it for the Guy, I'm sure she would let us."

"We should use you," said Benito. I was beginning to think that Benito's anger was the result of being reminded that he was primarily responsible for the difficult task ahead.

I joined the conversation in an effort to bring some sanity to it. I had seen the object of Squeaky's proposal and it was definitely not suitable for a Guy.

"No, Squeaky, your Mum's dress making thing has no head and no arms, and instead of legs it has a steel rod like the base of my Granny's birdcage. I don't even think it would burn."

Squeaky went quiet, not having thought the tailoring mannequin idea through to its fiery end.

As we reached the church, Crumb joined us. There was no need to inquire about Spot, but he did ask Benito how he was going to solve the Guy problem. It was clear that this was on everyone's mind. Benito had already been wound up quite well by Squeaky's incessant probing, and now snapped at Crumb.

"Just don't you worry about it, I'll make us a Guy." He turned to Squeaky.

"How long do you think it will take you to make a Guy out of that dressmaking dummy?"

"Well....." hesitated Squeaky. He was now less sure that the plan was a good idea,

"I don't think we should use it if we're going to burn it afterwards, or my Mum will be really mad."

"I thought you wanted to be in the gang," Benito snapped back.

Just as the conversation was getting interesting we had arrived at the big iron school gates, and we were once again late, something Benito also blamed me for. The responsibility that Benito carried was clearly taking its toll. Benito was never what you would call an attentive pupil, but at least most of the time he could be counted on to take an active roll annoying other classmates and being generally disruptive. Today was different – he spent most of the morning staring out of the window.

By lunchtime the reason for Benito's withdrawal was made clear to me as he reached a decision and approached Squeaky with an offer. Crumb and I watched in disbelief as Benito told Squeaky that he was prepared to let him join the gang if as his initiation test he procured his mother's dress-making mannequin and decorated it in the fashion of Guy Fawkes. Realizing that there was very little likelihood of this happening if the whole plan was to culminate in the effigy being burned, Benito said that the dummy would be returned to Squeaky's mother upon completion of the money collection. Squeaky was thrilled and felt sure that his mother would permit him to borrow the wooden statue temporarily, but he said that we must all swear that no harm would come to it. We each raised three fingers.

"Scout's honor," we said in unison.

Never having been in the Boy Scouts, we were not at all sure the salute was accurate, and certainly not legally binding, but it seemed to satisfy Squeaky.

Our newest gang member considered himself lucky that this came at a time when he could easily satisfy our need for an initiation trial. Benito was much more sociable now that the pressure to produce a Guy had been transferred to Squeaky, and Crumb and I were content that in the hands of Squeaky, and almost certainly his dressmaking mother, the Guy would be clad in an authentic period costume, probably complete with leather thigh boots, sword and a traditional hat, even if it was composed of a mismatched selection of unorthodox materials and colors. A short argument broke out about who would keep the sword, but this was solved when Benito laid claim to it.

About half an hour before we were due to go home, Mrs. Diggsmore was discussing something about ancient Greece. There was a story about a group called Jason and his Argonauts, although I think she meant Astronauts, and half way through it whatever work the plumber had done yesterday, came undone. While Mrs. Diggsmore droned on about a one-eyed giant called cycleclips, a large puddle of water had begun to form in the boy's bathroom and slowly spread to the corridor outside. Nobody noticed it until the water had advanced into the classroom pooling on the floorboards in front of the blackboard. Several of the more delinquent members of the class were immediately blamed for the disaster, and I was unfairly included in this round up, probably because I was one of the first to laugh when I saw it. It wasn't until Mrs. Diggsmore traced the source of the flood to the pipes under the sink, still bearing the recent marks of the plumber's wrench that we were pardoned.

Mrs. Diggsmore said that it was a terrible shame that this had happened and sent us all home about twenty minutes early. Chucky Billings remarked that it was a terrible shame that it did not happen at nine in the morning so that we could have spent the day looking for Spot. Mrs. Diggsmore angrily set off to pay a little visit to the plumber. I set off home with a spring in my step. Tonight was Thursday, and Dad had promised to take us to the fun fair.

I was, of course, as thrilled as Mum was surprised that Pete's leg had made such a complete recovery from his excruciating morning agony. The miraculous healing had occurred a little before two in the afternoon, coincidentally this was the point where Mum would not think it worth him going to school for the rest of the day. The upturn in his medical condition was signaled by Pete suggesting that a little ride on his motorcycle might do him good, what with the fresh air and the exercise. At this moment Mum understood that Pete's earlier complaint was not entirely genuine, and I am sure she suffered the resultant irritation that my brother had put one over on her. This led to Pete being told that there would be no motorbike riding today.

By the time I got home, Pete had retired to Dad's chair with a frown, a cup of tea, a warm fire and a stack of comics.

"Mrs. Diggsmore missed you at school today and wants you to write a story about the invention of South America." I said.

"I won't have time to do that," Pete said. "We're going to the fair tonight."

"Dad might not take you because of your bad leg," I jeered.

"No, it's fine now. Look." He sprung up from the chair and jumped up and down a few times to demonstrate.

"I thought it would be," I said and gave him a disgusted look.

During the car trip, Pete once again began perfecting his art of irritating Dad. I had a bag of sweets and Pete was trying to eat them as noisily as he could, knowing that this would have the desired effect on Dad. When Dad's eyes appeared more frequently in the rear-view mirror, Pete took up a position in the center of the back seat to deliberately block Dad's view out of the back window. Dad had to instruct Pete to move several times before he shifted just enough to easily bob back into the mirror's view in a split second. Threats of violence from Dad followed, and Pete was told to sit as close to his door as possible. He did this, but he also opened the window causing all of my discarded sweet wrappings to blow and swirl around the car.

The fairground workers had arrived in a variety of vehicles that looked in no better repair that the contraptions that my father drove. They set up the fairground outside a nearby town and parked their trucks and vans in a circle to form what would become the outside boundary of the fair. They had erected several large mechanical rides that my mother didn't think looked safe and a number of smaller kiosks that Dad said contained air rifles with bent barrels, yellow plastic ducks that were somehow able to avoid capture and some sort of super tough balloons that could not be burst with a dart. Each of the wooden stalls was brightly painted and adorned with stuffed animals. Loud pop music filled the air, and in the gaps between the songs, noisy electrical generators labored on the trucks as they fed power through thick rubber cables that lay on the grass between the rides.

A gaunt wrinkled man with a mass of oily hair and more tattoos than teeth was collecting money at the gate. Dad handed him some loose change and he jerked his head to one side, meaning that we could enter. Once inside, I marveled at the assortment of thrill rides and diversions, the brightly colored lights and the delicious aroma of greasy food. My attention was immediately drawn to the very center of the group of attractions where there was a high round wooden building with pictures on the walls of spacemen floating effortlessly through the cosmos. Red and yellow light bulbs were evenly spaced round the top and similarly colored writing on the side informed me that this amazing creation was an "Astro-Flight." I always fancied that I had a pretty good chance of being England's first man in space, being a passenger in Dad' car had prepared me for dangerous and turbulent transportation and I even possessed my own parachute if an en emergency exit was required.

"Are there really astronauts inside there?" I asked the man in the leather jacket standing by a table containing a cash box and a roll of tickets. This man still had most of his own teeth, but they failed to hold back the smell of cheap alcohol so reminiscent of the scent in Granny's house.

"No," grunted the man, "but this is where they train." I noticed that his grubby nicotine-stained fingers were never far from the cashbox.

"How much is it?" I asked.

"Sixpence for one, a shilling for two," he replied, scratching his unshaven jaw.

I knew then that I had to experience this ride and hurried off to convince my father of my need for sixpence.

I found my parents standing near one of the wooden booths containing a row of milking pails, tilted over and pointing to the group at the front of the booth. A sign above the wooden stall informed the gamblers that a ball in a bucket would win a large stuffed animal. A line of people tried to throw cricket balls into the buckets, each having three chances, but to the dismay of the fairgoers the balls were just bouncing right out as soon as they hit the springy bottom of the buckets. As I approached my family, I saw that Dad was leaning over Pete dispensing another large slice of anger. In one hand Dad was holding a stick of candy floss, and he had asked Mum to momentarily take charge of his toffee apple so as to leave one hand free, which he was using to wag his finger back and forth at Pete.

I looked for anybody with a visible cricket ball bruise but could find no one nursing such an injury. As I got closer I could hear Dad say,

"...So next time, PAY, before you try the side shows!"

"But Dad, the balls were just sitting there in a basket. I thought they were free," said Pete, attempting to defend himself. "I wouldn't have taken the prize anyway, even after I won."

"Can I have sixpence so I can be an astronaut?" I asked, hopping up and down with impatience.

"Oh Dad, don't let him go on that thing," pleaded my mother.

"But I want to be an astronaut, and train on the Astro-Flight," I begged.

"No," said Mum, "it's too dangerous."

"I'm going to give each of you a shilling," said Dad patiently. "That's enough for four of the three-penny sideshows, or two of the big rides."

Mum frowned at him.

I heard the jingle and felt the weight as Dad deposited twelve large worn coppers in the palm of my hand. My brother received a similar gift and immediately ran off to the air-rifle range. I joined him to see if it was something worth spending my money on. Pete picked up one of the six weapons on the counter and looked down the barrel toward some paper targets that were moving on wires back and forth against the rear of the booth. As he did so, I reminded him of Dad's warning.

"Remember that Dad said the barrels were all bent on these so that no one can hit the target." I said it a little too loud and two people who were considering trying their luck at the game, put down the guns and walked away to find something with better odds. They headed over toward the buckets and cricket balls. The scruffy old man who was collecting the money and dispensing the air-gun pellets also heard my comments and after making a rather angry face at me, which involved him squinting his one good eye and barring his rotten teeth, he made a public announcement to the effect that all the weapons were recently serviced and verified to be accurate by one of the country's leading firearms experts.

"How many do I have to hit?" asked Pete.

"Two out of five. Two out of five," the man repeated to make quite sure that Pete understood the terms of the deal. He had obviously run up against Pete's kind before.

"What do I win?" asked Pete.

"One of those stuffed toys up there," replied the man, pointing to a line of fury gorillas hanging from the front roof edge of the stall.

"OK," said Pete as he handed over three of his large copper coins, and received five shots in return.

I watched as Pete squeezed of each of the five shots, and one after the other each missed the target. Pete was beginning to believe that Dad's bent barrel theory may be correct. The shots appeared to be going high and left, but Pete now thought that he had a system and, quickly invested in another five of the small hour-glass shaped lead bullets.

"Watch this," he said to me, the ugly stall owner, and anyone else who would listen. "I'm going to fire low and right and I bet I hit every one."

He tried his plan with the next four shots and again hit nothing. So, with the remaining shot Pete tried to shoot the stall owner in the behind as he reached to get a soft toy for one rare lucky winner, but a length of chain at the front of the gun barrel, probably put there for that very reason, prevented him from doing so.

We caught up with Mum and Dad standing by the open window of a red caravan serving fish and chips and cold drinks.

"Spent all your money yet?" asked Dad, washing down a mouthful of chips with some lemonade.

"Can we have some food?" said Pete.

"Of course you can," said Dad. "The fish and chips cost nine pence and the drink is sixpence."

Pete looked from his remaining coins to the tasty fried potatoes and mumbled something about a mean father.

"Oh, just get it for them," said Mum with exasperation.

Dad wiped his greasy hand on his trousers before putting it in his pocket.

"Fish, chips and a drink twice, please mate," Dad said to the mobile chef, then a small burp escaped his lips and he placed his free hand flat across his beltline and grimaced. "Make that just chips and a drink each," he said, revising the order.

"Is there something wrong with the fish, dear?" was my mother's concerned question.

"Tastes a bit off," replied Dad.

Pete now had only sixpence remaining from the shilling that Dad had given each of us. He was torn between a ride on the Flying Dutchman, which was a large fake boat that swung back and forth on long chains or another trip to the shooting gallery. Pete had become convinced that the gun on the far end of the booth was more accurate than the others, and also had a longer barrel chain in case he was wrong about the accuracy.

I knew exactly what I wanted to spend my money on. A shilling was exactly what I needed for two rides on the Astro-Flight, but Mum still seemed very opposed to the idea.

"Why don't you go on the big swinging boat with me, Dad?" suggested Pete. "It'll be just like being back at sea. They might even let you be the captain."

There were some additional rumblings in Dad's stomach, as the fish settled in, and Dad declined Pete's invitation.

Suddenly, the sound of a motorcycle being started brought Pete out of his daydream.

"What's that?" he asked.

"That's the wall of death!" Dad replied.

We had both heard of the wall of death but other than in a few pictures, had never seen one.

"Oh, let's go," Pete implored.

"All right," said my father, "we'll all go and see it."

At the far end of the fairground was a drum like building with a staircase going around and up the outside. Dad negotiated a family rate with the man in the gray overalls guarding the bottom of the stairs, and to our amazement paid for everyone. Dad handed over the money and we ascended the stairs. The top of the round building was open to the sky and we claimed our place on a circular walkway around the edge of the wall and looked down inside. When enough people had gathered round the top of the wall, a motorcycle, stripped down in the fashion that Pete was partial to, entered through a door, which was quickly closed, and began to ride in circles on the dirt floor. The sound of the engine drowned out the distant pop music and the smell of petrol fumes replaced the fragrance of fried fish. With a loud rev of the engine the bike went up a short ramp and began riding around the wall parallel with the ground.

The physics of this did not really surprise me. I had seen my father demonstrate a similar principle in the back garden with a bucket of water on a rope. He had swung the bucket quickly round and round his head on a short length of rope, without spilling any of the contents. I tried to demonstrate this to Benito a few days later, but met with only limited success. Mum complained about me soaking her tablecloth, which had almost dried on the clothes line, and Dad was annoyed that he had to retrieve the bucket from the apple tree.

The attraction lasted several noisy, thrill filled minutes, and upon its completion, Pete ran off to the rifle range again while I continued my request for Astro-Flight riding permission.

"Noooow, can I go on the Astro-Flight?" I asked again tirelessly.

"OK," said Dad. "Just be careful."

"Oh, are you sure about this?" said Mum, filled with maternal concern.

"Well," Dad hesitated. He appeared to be having second thoughts about his agreement.

"Aw, come on, Pete got to go on the wall of death." I said, stamping my feet impatiently.

Mum considered the safety issues involved.

"Well, all right then," She said finally, "but Dad will go with you."

Dad responded by rubbing his stomach again.

"I don't know, that fish is not sitting at all well with me," he said.

I ran to Mum and hugged her, thanking her profusely for her generosity and supreme understanding.

"Oh, go on," she said to my father. "It doesn't look like it will bother your stomach."

I added to the logic of my mother's argument by pointing to the picture on the outside of the ride showing smiling astronauts floating pleasantly in space. Dad finally relented.

We climbed a flight of steps, which extended all the way to the roof, but about a third of the way up we were directed through a small curved door in the side of the wall and found ourselves in a room, not unlike the inside of the wall of death. The round room was painted a bright red and white checkerboard pattern, and completely without windows. There were outlines of human forms painted on the wall so we took our position and waited for something to happen.

Looking around I could see that, like the wall of death, the top of the room was open to the sky creating a viewing area. A woman in a blue hat leaned over the edge and waved to a man in a green sweater, who had just entered through the curved door. He waved back. I wished I had known this before so that Mum and Pete could have watched us.

I could see now that the alternately painted wall sections were in fact different panels that had been assembled together to make a complete structure, and for the first time I considered just how this weightlessness might be achieved. Another rider entered the room and we were all told to space out evenly. This instruction, along with the multiple floor sections made me feel a little uneasy. I looked at Dad who was rubbing his stomach again and breathing out through clenched teeth. What would happen after they closed the door? What if I didn't like it and wanted to leave? Another person came in and took his place in the room. Could it be that this was a rocket and we would be going on a space trip? No, that wasn't it, because the top was open for spectators. Maybe we were going out through the roof.

I started to panic now. What if the floor, which was clearly capable of moving, worked like a giant catapult and hurled us into space. What about space suits? How would we breathe? How would we land?

"No more riders," the man outside shouted and the door began to close. In a moment it would be too late.

With a terror filled sprint, I dodged out of the closing door and back onto the wooden staircase outside.

"Same price upstairs," said the man attending to the door, and he pointed up the steps to the viewing gallery. I reasoned that this would be a safe location to view the ride, and then decide if I wanted to participate or not on a subsequent trip. I followed his direction and found a place against the rail on the top of the wall.

I looked down and saw my father. He was watching the door from which I had just exited in surprised disbelief, and we could both hear bolts being drawn across sealing him inside, possibly forever. He looked puzzled, and then as he instinctively looked up, perhaps as part of a prayer, he saw me, and his expression changed from hope and despair to anger. Our eyes locked. Dad began to mouth a swear word at me, then his face went from anger back to puzzled again as the machine gave out a groaning sound and the room began to slowly turn.

Dad jumped a little with shock and then anxiously began to scrutinize all the gaps where the red and white sections joined, just as I had done immediately before leaving. He was looking round nervously now, realizing that escape was impossible. The turning motion of the room began to increase in speed and I saw my father take a deep breath and hold it with puffed out cheeks and closed eyes. The loud whirring sound of the motor driving the spinning room began to increase in pitch as the speed of the rotation got faster.

"Are you all right Dad?" I yelled, but there was no answer.

Dad was motionless now, stuck and unable to move, his loose clothing beginning to spread out flat against the curved wooden surface of the red wall. The room spun faster and faster, and Dad's face was beginning to distort as his cheeks were pulled back in an artificial grin which I was sure in no way betrayed his real emotion. Just when I thought it could get no worse, the floor began to drop away.

The only part of Dad's body that moved were his feet, so I suspected that he was at least still conscious. The toes of his boots flexed downwards slightly to feel out a floor that no longer existed, and one of his eyes opened to confirm what his feet had told him, but his brain refused to believe. Now he released his held breath in a long and drawn out agonizing moan. I was relieved by this sound as it indicated to me that Dad had not passed out. From my stationary vantage point I could see him as he spun around, stuck to the wall, unable to move or reach the floor. I got a better view of him on the far side of the wall, than when he was directly beneath me, but the screams were much louder when he was on my side. Faster and faster the room spun and my father's cheeks were now trying to imitate his clothing and flatten themselves out against the wall. His eyes, like his mouth were wide open as his frightful yelling became a constant blaring howl that because of my motionless perspective seemed to grow louder and softer each time he passed below me.

I turned around and looked through a wire fence out over the fair to quickly try and locate my brother before the show finished. He and Mum were walking slowly over toward the Astro-Flight.

"Pete!" I yelled loudly because I felt sure that he would want to see this, but over the sounds of Dad's screams Pete couldn't hear me.

The machine soon began to slow down and Dad stopped hollering. I waited until it had almost stopped and then hurried down the steps. Having watched Dad on his training mission I decided that I wouldn't ride the Astro-Flight today. I reached the curved door at the same time Mum and Pete arrived at the bottom of the ladder. Dad was the first one out, but rather than take the time to give us all a thrilling account of weightlessness, he brushed by us, snarled at me, and ran staggering and dizzy in a snake like path to a group of portable toilets. There was a line of people waiting to use them but Dad pushed his way to the front of the line and entered one of the mobile stink boxes, just as someone vacated it with a similar urgency.

"Is your Dad all right?" Mum asked with obvious concern. "Yes," I answered. "He looked as if he enjoyed it. It's probably just the bad fish acting up."

"What was it like?" she inquired as Pete came closer and showed considerable interest in my response.

"Don't know," I shrugged, and explained what had happened, where upon Pete started laughing that evil laugh that he did so well.

Pete was in a good mood, probably having something to do with the small stuffed black and white cow he was carrying. I later learned that Pete had returned to the rifle range again and through careful shooting and persistence had hit the target once. He needed two shots for a win, but the man running the stall rewarded his perseverance and gave him a prize anyway. A short argument followed, because Pete thought he should have received a larger version of the stuffed toy, but in the end he took the gift with a smile, and decided that he would try and sell it to either Mrs. Snobbit or Chucky Billings's mother.

Dad burst forth from the portable toilet holding his nose and wiping his mouth. He strode directly over to me.

"Never..." he seemed lost for words.

"Never...," he tried again, but this time was interrupted by Pete.

"Will you go on it again, Dad, so that me and Mum can see what you look like in there?"

Dad was so overcome by the thrill of the ride that he could not even find the words to answer Pete. He had to walk away and spend some time alone. Mum tried to suppress a smile.

During the ride home, it was obvious that something was bothering Dad, because he refused to speak to anyone, even my mother. She finally said, "Are you all right dear?"

"I think that fish is still bothering him a bit," Pete said innocently.

CHAPTER 15

SQUEAKY JOINS THE GANG

"She said no."

"What do you mean she said no?" Benito shouted at Squeaky. We had been standing in the cold playground, underneath the overhang by the doorway to escape the drizzling rain.

"She said we couldn't borrow it." Squeaky was very apologetic but I suspected he was more concerned with being unable to join the gang than he was about his mother refusing to loan us the dressmaker's dummy.

"What are we going to do now?" I asked to no one in particular. This Guy Fawkes business had been a problem from the start. Crumb and I had upheld our part of the deal and provided very suitable transportation, but Benito, in my opinion had not taken his duties seriously. His laziness had prevented him from actually making one, even though he had a huge family to help. Then his bargain with the Maudly-Creechoms had gone sour, and finally he was being double crossed by Squeaky who had promised to make a Guy from one his mother's prized possessions.

"Well, you'll just have to steal it then." Benito offered what in his mind was the ultimate solution to the problem, despite the fact that it involved a certain amount of dishonesty.

"I can't do that," said Squeaky. "It's in the living room with a half-made dress hanging on it. She'll notice."

The ringing of the school bell summoned us indoors, temporarily ending the conversation. Benito looked at each of us.

"All right then," he said, and turned to me.

"Get the apple," he ordered. These words struck fear into the hearts of every gang initiate.

To roll your own cigarettes, as my father did, you need only rolling papers and tobacco, and of course, someone you could scrounge a light from. But there was one more indispensable item that was a part of Dad's smoking equipment. In his tobacco tin, which was faded and worn at the edges, my father kept a piece of apple. About once a week Dad would walk out into the garden with his pocketknife and standing beneath the apple tree, would select a suitable piece of fruit to place in the tin. I didn't really understand the selection process, but Dad said that ripeness and taste were a critical part of the choice. During the winter months, when we lacked a ready supply of the fruit, Dad would usually settle for one of the apples that sat in a crate out side the door of the post office.

One day I asked for an explanation for this and was told that over time, the tobacco in the tin would deteriorate and lose its freshness. It would start with a nice dark spongy consistency and over time would lose its moisture content and dry up, spoiling not only the appearance but also the taste.

The apple would be placed in the tin with the tobacco, and gradually surrender its moisture and taste to the worsening weed, and in return, receive everything that the tobacco did not want. By the end of the week, the tobacco would remain fresh and the piece of apple would become, dried up, brown and nicotine-flavored. The only reason I knew that it was nicotine-flavored is that Joey Cave once dared Chucky Billings's younger brother, Matthew, to eat a piece of it. We all knew Matthew was young and that day he proved that he was also very foolish. Not knowing what to expect, and eager to impress the older boy, he put a piece of the pungent substance it in his mouth and began to chew.

His jaw moved twice and then stopped in the open position as his brain caught up with his taste buds. His eyes opened wide to fill with tears and his skin turned a pale shade of green that perfectly complemented the pieces of brown apple now visible lying on his extended tongue. Beads of sweat instantly appeared on his forehead and upper lip, and goose bumps emerged on his arms and neck. He began to tremble and breath in and out very rapidly. Then after two or three seconds of this spectacle, his chin thrust forward and his shoulders raised as he made a horrible choking noise before falling on his knees to become violently sick.

This incident, although only witnessed by a few had become folklore among the children of the village, and was used jokingly as a threatened punishment or ultimate dare. Squeaky now realized that this was to be his initiation test to join the gang, and was clearly concerned about it all morning. Even before we had our morning milk, Mrs. Diggsmore had already asked three times if Squeaky was all right, seeing this normally healthy and outgoing boy, as he sat pale and silent in his chair. Although it is true that Benito possessed an evil component to his personality that by the grace of god I lacked, rarely had I seen him behave in such a vengeful and vindictive manner.

By lunchtime, Squeaky had whittled himself into a panic and as the morning classes ended, he went over to Benito.

"I..I can't eat the apple." he said, his voice filled with fear.

"Do you want to be in the gang or not?" said Benito ruthlessly.

"Yes, but…" Squeaky shuffled his feet tensely and fidgeted with the collar of his shirt.

"But what?" Benito interrupted.

"Well, there's that story about Chucky's brother, and he got very ill indeed."

"Were you there?" asked Benito.

"Er…no?" Squeaky responded.

"Well, I was," Benito replied coldly.

"And it wasn't as bad as everyone says. Matthew was back at school in less than two weeks and the scars from the operation had healed by the end of the summer."

Now I was lost. The conversation had just fallen through a hole. I thought Benito was trying to convince Squeaky to eat the apple, but his latest comments seemed designed to dissuade him.

"I can't," said Squeaky firmly.

"Well, you have to if you want to be in the gang." Benito seemed without compromise, and didn't even look at Squeaky. Instead his attention was focused on a minor scuffle that had just broken out in the playground.

"I'll do anything else," said Squeaky in a very honest and committed tone.

Benito's head quickly spun round to look at Squeaky. "Anything?" Benito asked, raising his eyebrows.

And now it was clear to me. There never was a plan to have Squeaky ingest the foul fruit; it was just a dreadful suggestion to make the next option seem acceptable. I had once again watched the master play with his prey, teasing it, cornering it, and outwitting it until the trap was sprung.

"All right." Benito said slowly smiling.

After lunch, Mrs. Diggsmore announced that since there were only a few weeks remaining before Christmas, we would be practicing the school Christmas play every Friday afternoon from now on. This was Friday, and we would be having our first rehearsal.

The inmates of the school were called upon several times through the school year to perform various public functions for the entertainment of Great Biddington's bored villagers. At least twice a year there was a jumble sale held in the church rooms or the village hall. All the children of Great Biddington would be responsible for going door to door with trolleys, or cardboard boxes and beg the occupants of the visited houses to donate anything they did not want. This might include old clothes, electrical appliances, books and household items. Needless to say, the pickings were slim to none ay my house since Dad was never willing to part with any of his treasure.

Manning a stall at a Jumble sale was a highly prized job, and I have seen fragile communities torn apart and old friends pitted against one another in the race to play shopkeeper. Anyone fortunate enough to occupy one of these prestigious positions would have a chance to look over the goods before the anxious public seethed in to squabble over the bargains, but more importantly they would have the opportunity to snap up any desired items before they officially went on sale. Mum always volunteered early to get a job "helping" at the sale and applied all available social and political pressure to secure the position. Once, Dad was able to purchase a lawnmower, which my mother had lowered the price on before carefully hiding it under a picnic table. But alas, it never worked reliably and was donated back to the jumble sale the following year.

But it was the annual school plays that drew the biggest crowds, and made the most money. Once again we were called upon to act, dance and sing for the benefit of paying customers, and we suspected, Mrs. Diggsmore's private holiday fund.

Two years ago we had staged our version of the "Wizard of Oz." It was a modest production in two acts with tea and biscuits being served to the audience at half time. We exercised a degree of artistic license where necessary to avoid the costly special effects like tornadoes and flying monkeys, but all in all it was a very impressive first half. It was the last play that I was allowed to act in, and I played a daisy, complete with a short-legged green tunic and little hat made of yellow flower petals. Benito was my twin and it was our punishment for the events that had occurred the previous year.

Big Gina played an unlikely Dorothy, and Benito and I lobbied hard to get Chucky's dog Spot hired to play the part of Toto, after being assured by Chucky that she would be fine if we kept her on a short leash. Because of his build, Basher was assigned the role of the Cowardly Lion, and also given the task of holding Spot's lead. Mrs. Crippin being partially skilled on the piano was rounded up to provide musical accompaniment, which went quite well except for Gina's solo of "Somewhere Over The Rainbow," which in my mind was spoiled by Spot's off key howling.

Crumb was the Scarecrow, dressed in his Dad's old gardening clothes, with handfuls of straw stuffed inside to complete the appearance, but there must have been the scent of some backyard creature adhering to his outfit because Spot got quite excited and pinned him up against the side of the piano, refusing to release his left trouser leg. Chucky was

eventually able to restrain the hound, but Crumb was too shaken to continue with his role. As it happened he didn't need to, because as some of the younger children served up the half time tea and biscuits, the show became disrupted beyond recovery. Benito and I were standing in a line with the other daisies and shoving each other, trying to create a domino effect along the line of green clad flowers. When without warning......
CRASH!

Spot, who was accustomed to sharing her master's food at home, had broken free from the grip of the Cowardly Lion, and in a relentless pursuit of a chocolate cream wafer, had succeeded in upended the entire tray and now had her nose in a tin of biscuits on the floor.

This disrupted the show and unnerved the audience to such an extent that several of the paying guests, who were not at all keen on dogs, particularly one of Chucky's, went home. The second half of the show was aborted.

There were a number of church elders in the village who had not liked the decision to perform "The Wizard of Oz," feeling that the whole idea of wizards was far too satanic for our community. At the time they had made their feelings quite clear that what the village needed was a good representation of our Christian values in the form of a nativity play. After the episode with Chuckey's dog, whom they began calling the "hound of hell," they regrouped and once again presented their God fearing opinions. They had a surprising amount of support from others who had seen the play, many feeling that the biscuit shortage caused by the hound of hell was the last straw.

As a result, last year we were forced to enact the story of baby Jesus, although this was no more successful than the previous year's effort.

It should have been clear to all that the play was going to have problems. Vicar Hobbins was brought in as a technical consultant because many felt that he was old enough to personally remember the events of the nativity firsthand. Despite this holy guidance, inevitable conflicts followed.

The first disputes were caused by the casting sessions. Basher, Crumb and Chucky were ironically cast as The Three Wise Men. Brian Pilchard was Joseph, and Benito's eldest sister Antonella was to play the part of

Mary. Almost immediately artistic differences grew into arguments, and sprang up in the pubs and shops and places of worship, dividing the village and setting family members against each other. Many blamed Chucky for the fiasco that occurred the previous year, since it was his dog that had caused it, and they did not want him to participate in this production. In the end Mrs. Diggsmore, who was the producer and director, resented being told how to do her job and out of spite, cast Benito in Chucky's place. Then a small group of religious troublemakers raised objections about the choice of Brian Pilchard as Joseph, on the basis that they had never seen his parents in church, but Mrs. Diggsmore stood her ground on this one.

Just as the village was finally in agreement about the assigned actors, someone started a rumor that Spot was going to appear as a special guest star, playing one of the sheep. It took several days to completely dispel this falsity.

Another potential problem emerged when we tried to design the set. We put a large cardboard star covered in tin foil on top of the maypole and arranged the desks to form the outline of a stable. A drawer from the pencil cupboard was lined with straw and a plastic doll was placed in it to become the baby Jesus. Crippin once again provided music on the upright piano, and all the leftover children who didn't make the actor's grade were told to gather behind the piano out of view as back up singers. Some, including me, were given musical instruments to play. I had a triangle, but traded Graham for his drum. I also had the job of being the lighting expert.

The presentation started off well, but just as everyone expected it wasn't long before calamity struck. I was flashing the stage lights on and off to simulate a thunderstorm, and must have hit the wrong switch because I plunged the room into complete darkness. Joseph, stumbling around in blindness, stood on the back of Mary's dress causing her to bang into the stable wall which, in turn, crushed Ahab The Wise Man's finger. We recovered quite well, but several lines were forgotten as a result of the disturbance. The play continued, without incident until the part where an angel appears, or in this case, it was Big Gina wearing a white bed sheet and some cardboard wings. I sat quietly behind the piano cramped up and squeezed together with several other classmates. It was not very comfortable but I was relieved to take a break from singing, musicianship and lighting control.

As I listened to Gabriel mumble on in the background, I saw Sarah Crabtree open her mouth slightly and her nose twitch noticeably. A sneeze of biblical proportions was clearly brewing, and I raised my hymn book in front of my face for protection. Peering around the edge of my sacred sneeze shield, I could see that several others had noticed the impending and potentially very disruptive sneeze. We all looked at each other not knowing quite what to do. Mrs. Diggsmore had been adamant about us remaining perfectly quiet during the performance.

Gabriel was about to finish her speech, which I knew from rehearsals would be followed by a short peaceful, thoughtful silence that would descend upon the school like a blessing from God, giving the assembled crowd time to marvel at the reality of the stage show. But Sarah's involuntary body spasm was about to destroy the show at the most critical and poignant part. We were about half a second away from the sneeze, and on the very edge of catastrophe, when Celia Marsden reached over and pinched Sarah's nose.

It seemed to me that Celia had a good idea, but apparently neither of us understood the physics of sneezing. Just prior to a sneeze there is a tremendous buildup of pressure, and during a sneeze that pressure is discharged rapidly though the nose with tremendous force. Thus when you get to within half a second or so of the pressure equalization process, nothing in the universe can stop it. This is something Celia learned too late.

Upon feeling Celia's thumb and forefinger clamp firmly around her nose, Sarah opened her eyes. She had just a moment to be startled, before there was a sound like the mixture of a balloon popping, and several horses snorting at the same time. Her eyes popped out and her mouth opened wide but with the sides turned down in a painful grimace. Most of the sneeze material was expelled through Sarah's mouth with incredible power, but I think at least some escaped through her eyes and ears. Sarah began to cry fiercely, frightened that she had suffered some permanent damage. She stood up and looked over the piano at the rows of audience members, who recoiled in horror. This only made Sarah cry more and sent Crippin shuffling off for the first aid kit.

Another year had gone by in which we failed to complete a play.

This year it would be different, as "The Great Biddington Primary School Theatrical Company" attempted "Oliver Twist." Mrs. Diggsmore was going to rehearse every week and learn from her previous mistakes. We spent the afternoon reading different parts of the play out loud as Mrs. Diggsmore selected what she felt were suitable actors to play the various parts. I was pleased to be judged unsuitable for any role whatsoever. Benito was a shoe in for the Artful Dodger.

At the end of the day Mrs. Diggsmore sat us all down and tried to give us an historical perspective on the Guy Fawkes story, but finding it hard to capture our interest she resorted to reminding us not to forget the bonfire celebration on Sunday, adding that the Maudly-Creechoms Guy had been selected to occupy the incendiary pinnacle of the fire. She also added a few words of encouragement for us to attend the talent show and dance tonight at the village hall. Her theatrical flair caused her to be more interested in this than the fireworks, but we guessed that she would probably grow out of it.

The end of the school week was especially sweet because it was Friday, although the joy of the weekend was overshadowed by our lack of a Guy Fawkes. We had begun walking home and were about fifty feet into our journey when Squeaky came trotting up to us. I was beginning to dislike all these cat and mouse games with Squeaky, and considered the Guy problem much more serious. Why was Benito wasting so much time on this nonsense?

"Well, did you decide what I have to do?" Squeaky asked, relieved that he did not have to eat the tobacco apple.

"Yes, "said Benito. "You have to climb over the Maudly-Creechom's fence and borrow their Guy for us."

"I can't do that," Squeaky mouthed the words in shock. he had not expected a test of this magnitude.

"Why not?" asked Benito with a perfectly reasonable tone, as if he had just asked for a piece of chewing gum.

"Because it's stealing," replied Squeaky, but this argument probably wasn't going to cut any ice with Benito. Dishonesty was not only his personal creed, but it was also a guiding principle of Benito's entire family.

"No," he replied slowly, as if explaining it to a very small child, "it's borrowing."

"They didn't say you could use it," reasoned Squeaky.

"How do you know?" countered Benito.

"Because they are angry at you about shooting Willis's leg." This part was true, and I listened with interest to hear how Benito would explain it away.

"Oh that?" scoffed Benito, "We're all friends again now, haven't you seen Maggot riding Crumb's bike around the village, and Basher's been taking Morris for walks."

"Are you sure?" asked Squeaky slowly and suspiciously.

"Listen," Benito took a deep breath and began, "they won't mind. I guarantee that if they were here now, they would be delivering it to us themselves, but they're away for the weekend, so we have to go and get it."

"Well…" said Squeaky, beginning to come around to Benito's way of thinking. But Benito gave him no chance for rebuttal.

"You know, it's really not a very difficult job to gain membership in the best gang in Great Biddington. 'Course, if you would rather eat the apple?…."

"No," snapped Squeaky. "I'm not eating the apple, but I'm not very happy about stealing the Guy either."

"It's not stealing," repeated Benito. "We had agreed that we were going to do it together anyway. It's just that they can't be here for it."

"Yes, but then afterwards they said that the deal was off, remember, after Willis got shot."

"Look," Benito continued, "when they said the deal was off, they meant that we couldn't go round the village together. They don't mind us going on our own."

"I still say we should ask them," protested Squeaky.

"How can we? They've already left and won't be back until Saturday night." Benito had tried to adopt the vocal tones that my father used when talking to Pete, but it was not very well done.

"Why don't we go on Sunday after they get back? We wouldn't have to go together?" Squeaky's question was a good one, but neither he nor I could have predicted Benito's answer.

"Because I have to go to Sunday school."

"But you don't go anymore." said Squeaky, believing that he had found a flaw in Benito's argument, but the more cunning boy had a response prepared.

"I had stopped going," he said, "but I decided to start going again because I think it will help me be a better person."

"Alright," Squeaky finally agreed, his voice filled with trepidation. "When do I have to go?"

"Tonight," instructed Benito.

"Tonight?" Squeaky, the soon-to-be Guy kidnaper said in a loud voice. "Why tonight?"

"Because we have to take it round the village tomorrow," explained Benito, and then for extra credibility added, "so that the trolley is free for the Maudly-Creechoms on Sunday."

"Well, it will have to be Saturday afternoon, because I'm having my hair cut with my Dad in the morning." There was nothing wrong with Squeaky's hair, but knowing his mother, I believed what he was saying.

"Yes," agreed Benito," we will all be busy in the morning too. It has to be the afternoon."

"OK, where shall we meet tonight?" asked Squeaky.

"We?" replied Benito. "There is no we, just you. I have to help my Dad clean the shed."

"At night?" asked Squeaky.

"Yes." Said Benito. "At night."

Squeaky turned to me. I knew what was coming.

"Will you help me?"

"No," I said, "I have to go to the talent show with Mum and Dad."
This was unfortunately true.

I walked away.

Upon arriving home I found the house in the usual turmoil. My parents were very happy to be going to the talent show and dance and, much to my disappointment , I had been instructed to accompany them. Dad, who had arrived home early in preparation for the evening's festivities, had already changed into the suit that he was issued when he left the Navy fifteen years ago. He was now sitting and staring intently at the radio, which delivered the marine shipping forecast without emotion. As Dad continued to track Rodger Pilchard's progress, he was dismayed to discover that the area where the Pilchard family had made camp was suffering some of the worst weather in the last decade. Dad made some comment about "poor Rodger," and then wondered about his wayward son Pete's whereabouts.

Understanding dawned on Dad's face at the sound of Pete's motorbike in the backyard.

"He's going to have to hurry to get ready for the dance tonight."

"Oh, he's been here since school finished," said Mum. We all then realized that the engine sound we heard was probably Pete leaving to escape the village hall merriment. I was then instructed to clean myself up in readiness for tea. I brushed my hair in a fashion that I knew would annoy my parents and donned a pair of jeans and a different sweater.

"You're not wearing those jeans to the dance," said Dad.

"Why not?" I asked, honestly not understanding his complaint.

"Because they are working clothes. Put a nice pair of trousers on."
He then continued to mumble to himself, as was his habit, "...dance in jeans...make me ashamed..."

"Yes," my mother agreed, "how about your brown ones?" She had begun to serve the tea, so I was told to 'eat it while it's hot' and change afterwards.

The meal took longer than expected, because halfway through, when my father stood and went to the mirror to fix a large Windsor knot in his only tie, Scraps got involved in his steak and kidney pie. By the time the crafty cat was spotted by us, she had been able to get her entire nose under the piecrust of Dad's principle menu item and Mum had to prepare another dish for Dad, while simultaneously getting herself ready for the celebrations. Dad wolfed down the food, grabbed the car keys and his tobacco tin and ran out of the house.

"Change your trousers and catch up with us," he called over his shoulder to me. "And tell you brother to come as well."

I knew that Pete had no intention of attending the dance, but I could use the excuse of looking for him as a reason to be late. The evening's entertainment would consist of a short talent show, probably very short because no one in our village had much talent, followed by the Guy Fawkes dance. I had little interest in either phase of the gathering, and would use whatever means I could to avoid making an appearance there. As it turned out I failed to "catch up" with my parents and took a slow walk to the village hall.

It was dark and eerily quiet as I passed the Maudly-Creechom's house. I looked for signs of a shadowy figure sneaking through the blackness of night with a floppy fake body over his shoulder, but I could see nothing.

On my leisurely stroll to the village hall I ran into Benito and Basher, lurking on the bridge. Basher still had his fishing rod and had not been home yet.

"Where's Squeaky?" I asked.

"He should be stealing the Guy," said Benito.

"Borrowing the Guy," I corrected.

"Yeh, that's right." Benito said with a nod.

Tonight was actually perfect for the crime – dark, moonless, and almost the entire village was at the talent show.

"What's he going to do with it afterwards?" I asked.

"I told him to put it in your barn," said Benito, automatically involving me in his crime by making me guilty of receiving stolen property.

"You know," I said thoughtfully, as I leaned comfortably on the wooden rails of the bridge," it's not going to be any fun having him along tomorrow."

"He's not coming tomorrow," said Benito in a matter of fact tone.

"Well, I bet he shows up after lunch, to come with us," I said.

"That's why we're going in the morning." replied Benito with a sly smile.

I had delayed my arrival at the talent show as long as I thought I could without risking a potential whack from one or both of my parents, and so I pressed onward. When I arrived, the talent show was already in progress. I was somewhat pleased to find that I had already missed Chalky White's attempts at juggling and Mrs. Leecham's dog tricks. Toby Lawson was currently in the middle of a poem about the French countryside. Luckily it was in English so the audience could follow along with the story. If the show's organizers had decided to save the best for last, I'm glad that I missed the beginning.

I looked around for my Dad and spotted him in the third row near the front, with my mother on the inside and Mr. and Mrs. Stuart on the outside. I made a hissing sound, and whispered the word Dad loudly through cupped hands. This clearly annoyed several members of the audience who frowned at me and several more people made a "Shhh." sound that I found quite rude.

Mr. Lawson continued to deliver his lines with great feeling and passion as Dad tapped his chair, pointed to the storeroom and then to the spot next to Mrs. Stuart. I crept out on tiptoes to get a chair from the next room. Reentering the room with the heavy chair was difficult, and I accidentally banged it into the doorframe. The legs of the chair dragging on the floorboards added to the cacophony of unwanted sounds, and more members of the assembly were giving me dirty looks. Fortunately the noise of my chair handling finished to perfectly coincide with the end of the poem. Everyone clapped but most turned to look at me. Despite my apologetic demeanor everyone was still irritated by my actions. Then Dad looked over, touched his trousers and pointed at mine, reminding me that I had forgotten to change. He then shook his fist at me.

Fred Pollard was introduced next and came on stage. He sat on a barstool, put his guitar across his lap, closed his eyes and took a deep breath as he began to strum. I didn't enjoy the tune very much but had to admire his playing ability. Dad sat intently watching with a clenched jaw, the way he did whenever he was concentrating. I knew that Dad harbored a secret ambition to play the guitar and was clearly studying Fred's technique.

The local butcher, who was doing double duty as the master of ceremonies, announced that we would now be blessed with a song from Mrs. Stuart's daughter, Belinda, who was planning to attend music school next year. I was seated next to the star's mother, and sensed her back stiffen with obvious pride as Belinda took to the stage.

She wore a flowing green evening gown, in the style typified in the dreadful old films that my parents enjoyed so much. She was carrying a frilly blue umbrella folded, with a black curved handle that lay across the palm of her white-gloved hand. Surely she was overdressed for an occasion such as this since all she was doing was singing. I looked over at my father to see if he had any answers. Dad was just sitting there staring at the singer and frowning.

A few piano chords played with an impressive harmonious flurry and Belinda opened the umbrella. What on earth was the point of this I wondered? Dad was just looking down and shaking his head. Mum hit him with her elbow and I felt the need to giggle but repressed it. Then Belinda began to sing, and I was quickly able to deduce that her taking lessons would be a total waste of money.

It wasn't just the high notes, it was every note that she had trouble with. I looked over at Dad again, who was still looking down, but now clearly chuckling at the scene before us. I glanced at Mrs. Stuart, who was staring proudly at the stage. I found this even funnier and began to laugh silently to myself. Although I thought that I was concealing my mirth very well, I was aware that my shoulders began moving rhythmically up and down. I heard someone in the row directly across from me emit a little smirking noise, and clamped my mouth closed, but I wasn't sure that I could hold it in.

I risked another glance at Dad, knowing that if I saw him laughing as well, I would not be able to contain myself. Our gaze met, just as Belinda finished the verse on an unreachable high note. Dad looked at me and rolled his eyes, and I erupted.

The sound was not unlike Sarah Crabtree sneezing behind the piano, but this quickly became a roar, which I tried to disguise with a cough which really didn't fool anyone. This inappropriate outburst broke a lot of the tension in the room and about twenty people now joined me in full, unbridled laughter.

Mrs. Stuart looked at me with a mixture of hatred and disgust, and then without changing her expression, looked at my father, who was by now looking at me, but pointing toward the door. Dad's earlier prediction about me embarrassing him was apparently very accurate, so again I followed his direction and left.

Benito and Basher had been outside watching through a window as the performance unfolded, and when I found them they were laughing as hard as everyone else.

"Well done," said Basher.

"It was my Dad who started it," I said in defense of myself.

"Is there any news from Squeaky?" I asked.

Nobody had heard or seen anything from him, which left us all worried and doubtful that he had completed his mission.

When the talent show was over, people started clearing the chairs off what was to become the dance floor as the butcher carried a record player and a stack of ten or fifteen records onto the stage.

For about half an hour we watched and laughed as villagers tried to dance their own versions of the waltz and the foxtrot. Belinda Stuart, having recovered from the mass ridicule she received began dispensing instruction on performing the tango, although the puzzled looks on the faces of her disciples suggested that she was no more adept at this than singing. There was Fizzy pop and brown ale to drink and once the traditional dances began to wane, the butcher came up onto the stage.

"Alright, everyone," he announced, "We're going to liven things up a bit now, and play some of the young people's music."

"Oh good," my father yelled out. His confidence bolstered by several glasses of brown ale.

"It's a bit modern and it's a bit fast, but I think everyone will enjoy it," continued the butcher.

"What is it?" Dad interrupted again.

"It's called "the Twist" and its all the rage," said the butcher.

My father sprang to his feet.

"I know how to do that one; come on everybody, I'll show you."

Now it was my turn to be embarrassed as Dad lined everyone up on the dance floor and one by one was adjusting the position of their legs or bending their arms slightly.

"Now, all you have to do," Dad announced, "Is to pretend that with your right foot you're putting out a cigarette."

Everyone began to mimic Dad's instructions, their right feet simultaneously swiveling.

"And while you're doing that, put your hands by your sides and move them back and forth as if you are drying your backside with a hand towel."

I could watch no more. I had a Guy to find.

CHAPTER 16

WILHELM'S PARADE

"Ahh," I thought. "Saturday." I awoke with an energy and love for life that was noticeably absent on school days. Today promised to be extremely busy. I had to check up on our Guy, assemble the troops for our begging march through Great Biddington, collect the money that we so rightly deserved, and with it, buy our fireworks. Tomorrow was the big village bonfire, and we could not consider attending without fireworks. There was going to be an official display of fireworks, but we knew from experience that there was nothing like having your own.

The weather was sunny but cold. I dressed quickly in some warm clothes and ran out of the bedroom throwing a shoe at my still comatose brother. Rushing downstairs I took my place at the breakfast table. Weekends were always hectic for my mother as it meant feeding everyone at the same time.

"Where's Pete?" she asked.

"He's still asleep," I said, and suggested that she prepare the ice water.

"No," she said sympathetically, "let's let him sleep a bit more." Mum knew that the longer my brother was kept apart from my father the more peace we would all have.

"He should get up with the rest of us," grumbled Dad.

"Did you have too much brown ale last night?" I asked. Unlike Pete I did not deliberately say things to annoy my father, but that was often the unintended result.

"No, I didn't," he said in a gruff irritated tone.

"Morning," Pete greeted everyone as he entered the kitchen.

Dad remained silent.

"What's the matter with you?" Pete asked Dad, sensing his annoyance.

"There's nothing the matter with me," replied Dad as he finished his tea and picked up his tobacco tin, "Damned if a man can't sit and have a quiet cup of tea without everyone bothering him." He opened the kitchen door and walked into the hall on his way outside for a smoke and his traditional early morning weather check.

Pete fired a loud parting shot.

"What he wants is another ride on the Astro-Flight," Pete said with a chuckle.

Dad responded by slamming the door.

"Damn it!" We all heard my father yell and ran outside to investigate.

In his haste to get away from his infuriating son, Dad had tripped over something. It was the tarpaulin that we all believed was in Scotland with Rodger Pilchard and family. Instead, it lay in a crumpled, soaking wet heap, piled up in front of our door.

"What the devil..." said Dad picking himself up and staring at the canvas mass. He had suffered no physical damage during the fall, but was dusting himself off and rubbing various body parts for effect. Dad was now trying to grasp the peculiar nature of this very odd situation.

In the first place everyone expected that Rodger would return it by hand, and tell exciting tales of his trip to Scotland. Or at least he would wave or just open the front door and hand one of us the neatly folded canvas. How did it even get here? The Pilchards were supposed to be in Scotland for another week.

Dad looked at the sheet again and then up toward Rodger's house where his car could clearly be seen in the driveway. He shook his head a few times, then gathered up the canvas and handed it to me.

"Fold that up and put it away," he said. Then he went inside for another round of breakfast.

I dropped the sheet and ran up the garden path to El Paso, and peered in through the dusty window. I scanned the gloomy interior but failed to find what I was looking for. I unlatched the barn door and went inside. There was no Guy. My heart sank – tomorrow was Sunday, bonfire night, and we simply had no more time and no more options.

I wondered if Squeaky had mistaken Benito's instructions and put the Guy in Rat barn. For a moment I had a picture of Squeaky lying unconscious face down in the dirt next to the Guy, his motionless corpse being nibbled on by a pack of wild rats.

I ambled miserably back into the kitchen. An argument was in progress about whether animals should be allowed to attend village talent shows, and upon my arrival the emphasis shifted slightly toward whether I should be allowed to attend village talent shows. This abrupt change in subject matter gave me an indication of the reason for Dad's foul disposition.

Breakfast ended with my brother and Dad failing to reach an agreement on exactly what the correct volume for a motorcycle exhaust system should be and Pete thanked Mum for the breakfast and stormed out. I followed him in order to escape Dad's harsh criticism of my behavior last night.

"What do you want?" he asked.

"I might need some help to search rat barn," I replied.

"No," he said automatically. "What's Dad mad at you for?"

"I don't know," I replied. "I think it's because I wore my jeans last night."

Pete was in no mood to help me, being anxious to start up his motorcycle and ride off through the cold still morning air.

He was mumbling something about Dad having forgotten what it was like to be young as he swung open the door to the old toilet where the bike was stabled.

"Damn!" he yelled as he jumped back in surprise.

I was also shaken for a moment before a slow smile crept over my face. Sitting astride the bike was the Maudly-Creechom's Guy.

"What the hell is this doing here?" Pete said. He grabbed the belt of Guy's trousers and the front of its shirt, and dragged the straw filled dummy off the bike. He held it above his head in a pose reminiscent of one of Granny's wrestling heroes and then looked at me.

"Did you do this?" he demanded.

"Squeaky." I replied.

Pete threw the intruder several feet onto the grass outside, then starting his bike, he took off down the driveway, almost running over Benito, who was jogging toward us.

"Did he get it?"

"Yes." I nodded, and Benito ran over to look at the dormant figure lying next to El Paso's half open doors.

We bent down to examine it in detail. The upper body was made from an old yellow work shirt, which we doubted had belonged to Mr. Maudly-Creechom, as he only seemed to possess starched white ones that he wore with a suit. This had probably been donated by their gardener, as had the trousers, which had been attached to the shirt by some of Maggot's inaccurate and messy needlework.

I poked one of the legs and asked, "Are these filled with straw?"

"No," Benito replied. "The body is made from an old flour sack filled with straw but the legs and arms are filled with crunched up newspapers."

It was well formed. The feet and hands were made of old socks and gloves, similarly stuffed and fixed in place with more of Maggot's substandard sewing skills.

The head was a very impressive affair, and had been added since we last saw the Guy. It had been painstakingly created from a mixture of flour and water paste and ripped up newsprint to form the hard shell of the head. Judging from the shape it had probably been modeled over a balloon. It had been carefully painted with flesh colored paint, and hair and beard had been added using some of Squeaky's Mum's black wool. All in all, we had to admire the hard work the Maudly-Creechoms must have invested in this effigy. Together we dragged Mr. Fawkes over to the front of rat barn and seated him on the trolley. He looked very comfortable there and we became quite enthusiastic about the money that would surely soon be rolling in.

We left him there, under the shade of the ramshackle wooden canopy so that the sun wouldn't be in his eyes and walked over to the house. Crumb and Basher had not yet arrived, and we had to keep a close watch for Squeaky, so after we had our tea, we walked outside to take our place sitting on the stone wall overlooking the road. Crumb soon appeared riding a bike.

In recent weeks he had been able to scrounge three broken bikes, and using the good parts from each, plus the handlebars that he found at the Tip, he had been able to construct some fairly reliable transportation.

"Did he get it?" asked Crumb as his front wheel skidded across the dew soaked grass.

"Yep!" I said. Crumb threw the bike on the ground.

"Let's see it then," he said removing goggle-eye from his head and threw it on the grass next to the bike.

Benito suddenly leaped into action and scrambled behind the wall.

"Quick, here he comes. Hide."

We jumped behind the wall with Benito and crouched down. Soon we heard the sound of a car pass.

"That was him." Benito said. "He's off to get a haircut. Come on."

Crumb quickly agreed with our earlier observation that it was nice of the Maudly-Creechoms to build it for us.

"Let's call him William," said Crumb. Clearly the recent altercation between Crumb and William resulting in physical combat had left Crumb with some mental scars that had not yet fully healed.

We all agreed that William was as good a name as any and it appeared to provide Crumb with the necessary therapy, knowing that his aggressor would soon be burned.

The first thing we needed to do was disguise William so that he wouldn't be recognized as someone else's property. There was every chance that when the Maudly-Creechoms returned tomorrow, they would take William, or whatever they called him, round the village, mimicking our route. The last thing we wanted was someone to tell them that we had used the same Guy. Under Benito's direction Crumb grabbed the loop of string that had been attached to the front axle of the trolley and we all marched over to El Paso where we knew we would find some new clothing for William.

Basher was, of course, nowhere to be seen. His usual style was to remain absent so as not to deprive the rest of us of the joy of hard work, but he would always show up at the last minute to take some credit for the project and to offer his congratulations on a job well done. He was good that way.

Benito was already prowling around in the barn, ducking under the few unburned bunches of tobacco leaves that still hung from the roof, and occasionally knocking stuff over. There was more room in there now that Dad's scorched drying machine had been removed and stood outside waiting for its date with destiny at the Tip. Benito emerged carrying Dad's full-length German army coat, and hit it against the wall a few times so that the clouds of dust that had been resident in the material mingled with the cold air.

"This'll be a good start," he said, and we all wrestled with William's limp form to try on the coat for size. It was a little big, but as Crumb pointed out, that was better than being too small. We buttoned up the front as high as we could to disguise the yellow gardening shirt, and stood back to admire our work. The sleeves hung down past the end of William gloved hands, which was good, but some of the lower part of the dummy's legs remained visible. Crumb and I joined Benito in the barn to see what other materials we could find to complete the camouflage of our stolen prize.

We all thought that the head was going to be difficult to cover until Crumb emerged.

"Ah-Ha!" he said triumphantly.

"This will cover the face all right," Crumb said, holding up the black rubber gas mask, which my father had been keeping in case of another attack by the Germans.

"And it will go well with the coat," I added.

We carefully placed the mask, making sure to tuck the entire black wooly beard inside. It covered William from forehead to chin. We decided not to clean the glass in the twin round eye windows, as we all agreed that the dust would prevent any possible recognition of the eyes.

I found a pair of Dad's old rubber Wellington boots that looked to be about William's size and we all thought they would cover the legs pretty well. We spent the next few minutes stuffing the newspaper filled appendages into them, and when finished, we tied the boots in place on the axle board with string that not only secured the Guy in place on the green cart, but also made him look as if he was actuality steering with his feet.

We congratulated each other on the hard work done so far, and Benito said that we should change William's name to Wilhelm which was the German version of William and much more in keeping with our Guy's coat and wartime gas mask. We then went back into El Paso to look for a hat. Despite our continued searching there were no coats with hoods that could be removed or wigs that could cover Wilhelm's flowing black locks. We all soon began to get depressed at our inability to find suitable headgear in a barn that seemed to contain everything else.

"Hey, it looks really good," Basher's voice was unmistakable as he walked up the gravel driveway.

After we had all thanked him for all his timely arrival and hard work, he began inspecting Wilhelm.

"I think you should cover the hair," he said casually.

"Well Basher, we thought we'd leave that bit for you to do." Benito said, in a masterful display of sarcasm.

"OK," replied Basher, "be like that then," and he walked off.

"I think you've have upset him," I said.

"Serves the lazy sod right," opined Crumb. We went back inside the barn, but no sooner had we started to scrounge around again, than we heard Basher's voice, jubilant and full of satisfaction.

"How's that?" he asked.

Once again we emerged into the light to find Basher, but this time he was standing proudly next to the trolley pointing at Wilhelm, whose head and hair had been completely covered by goggle-eye.

We all had to admit that it looked very good.

"I don't know what you lot would do without me," Basher said with a sigh.

There were only a couple of reasons why the children of the village would collect money from door to door. One of these was the "penny for the Guy" endeavor, in which we were currently engaged. The other was for sponsorship in some event or other, usually walking or running. Back in the spring we had a sponsored walk to raise money for church roof repairs and it was the duty of every child to get as many sponsors as possible to donate a certain amount of money for each lap around the village. A lap consisted of a circuit from the school to the butcher's shop, after that a sharp left, right along to the church with the leaking roof, another right to the pub, and diagonally across the playing field back to the school. The total trip was about half a mile. I got three sponsors: Mum, Dad and Granny. I completed three laps before losing interest, and was ultimately responsible for sixpence worth of lead on the church roof.

Although I was by no means an expert at collecting sponsorship money I was well aware of the preferred method. The richest people in Great Biddington should always be visited first, and their names and pledges written on your sponsor sheet. The theory was that as you went begging at the less wealthy households, they would see the pledge of the wealthy and be encouraged to donate more than they could afford to avoid the embarrassment of appearing cheap. It was time consuming and inefficient where distance was concerned, but produced the greatest sponsorship yield.

When using the Guy to collect the fireworks money, the approach was just the opposite. It was important that every contributor saw how little money we had, and thus be encouraged to take pity on us. To aid us in this plan, Crumb had fashioned a string handle onto a jam jar as a collection device that would display the contents.

We set off on our mission and started with Mrs. Snaggins. I knocked on the door and Crumb stood beside me holding up the empty jar. Mrs. Snaggins finally opened the door.

"Penny for the Guy," we all shouted, and Crumb shook the empty jar back and forth.

Penny for the Guy may have been the traditional greeting for this event but nobody expected to get just a penny. Perhaps at the dawn of civilization when this ritual began, a penny was an acceptable amount, but in these modern times we expected at least three or four. Mrs. Snaggins gave us three, we thanked her and moved on to the next house.

Mrs. Granger was next.

"Penny for the Guy!" we all cried.

"My, what a lovely Guy," she said, then a puzzled expression flooded her face and she asked. Why is he dressed like a German?"

"That was the only coat we could find," replied Basher, as if he was actually part of the team that dressed Wilhelm.

"Why is he wearing a gas mask?" Mrs. Granger inquired.

"It's holding his head on," Benito lied easily.

"Oh," she said, and gave us fourpence.

We skipped Benito's house, and obviously the Gurney and Maudly-Creechom residences, and moved on to Mr. Pinknee. He lived alone and didn't come out much. He opened the door a few inches and demanded to know what we wanted.

"Penny for the Guy!" we told him.

"Are you going to burn those boots?" he asked in a grumpy tone.

"No," I said, "they belong to my Dad. Why?"

"I'll give you a shilling for them," Pinknee said.

As tempting as this was, I was not ready to incur my father's wrath for selling his best boots and so declined.

Mr. Pinknee reluctantly gave us twopence, and that's exactly how much gratitude Benito gave him in return.

After a few more houses we were at the corner where Mud Lane meets the High Street. We were outside Grizzly McKenzie's house, but no one dare go inside so we rounded the corner and walked over the bridge to where there would be a more densely populated area of four stone homes all clustered together. It was a little bit tricky getting Wilhelm's trolley through the unusually narrow gates, but once we had mastered the technique the next three houses were relatively easy.

"Penny for the Guy!" we all cried outside Mrs. Blinkton's house.

"My, what a lovely Guy," she said as she dropped four coppers into the jam jar. Then she leaned over to inspect Wilhelm more carefully.

"Hello again Benito. Why is he wearing a gas mask?"

This had been the most common question and we stuck with the party line about it being necessary to hold the Guy's head on.

"Penny for the Guy!" we begged at Mr. Harboro's house.

"Hello, lads," he greeted us, "Back so soon, Benito?"

Crumb shook the jar in Mr. Harding's face, but we didn't receive any reward until we had answered all the usual questions about Germans and gas masks.

"Very good job lads," Harding finally said and deposited a shiny silver sixpenny piece into the jar. As soon as we had moved on Benito reached in the jar and removed the sixpence and about half the coppers. The appearance of affluence, could severely limit our take.

While the other three squabbled about how much we had collected so far, I remembered that Mrs. Blinkton had clearly said "Hello again Benito." I attributed this to the possibility that Benito had seen her in the village earlier. Now Mr. Harding had just said, "Back so soon?" Could it be that Benito had simply run an errand for his mother that involved Mr. Harding? I thought it unlikely.

When our journey reached the Red Lion pub, I crossed the road to determine if there was a large enough crowd inside to make it worth hauling Wilhelm over. As it was, the pub was quiet, the only inhabitants being Billy Tadcome and two strangers, all locked into a heated discussion about football. I crossed the road again to rendezvous with my colleagues at Betty Adlar's house. By the time I had rejoined the gang a struggle was in progress. Like several people before him, Betty Adler's husband had wanted Wilhelm's boots. He had already managed to remove one of them from the artificially stuffed leg, and Crumb was trying to reclaim it while Benito attempted to negotiate a price. This dispute caused us to leave on bad terms, and, more importantly, without a donation from Betty.

And so it continued, house after house as we chanted our battle cry of "Penny for the Guy," and were in turn rewarded with loose change. By the time we had made it halfway around our carefully chosen route, we had emptied the jar three times in order too maintain our image of poverty. We were on our way back down the hill now, heading for Mrs. Davis's house.

"Penny for the Guy!"

Mrs. Davis must have received word that we were doing the rounds, because she already had her purse open as she opened the door.

"Hello, lads," she greeted us. She nodded at Wilhelm and gave him a thumbs-up sign as she deposited two three penny pieces in the jar. We thanked her quickly and turned to leave. Time was beginning to become our enemy now, as we had to finish before Squeaky returned. Mrs. Davis almost had the door closed when as an afterthought she opened it again and asked,

"Did you do it yet, Benito?"

"Errr, no," he mumbled sounding embarrassed.

We all hurried on and began the long stretch of road that led down the hill towards the bridge. As we walked I could contain my curiosity no longer.

"What did she mean by, "did you do it yet?"

"I don't know," replied Benito innocently. "You know how old people are."

"Yes," I said. I knew how young people were too.

"She must have thought I was ill or something," said Benito nonchalantly.

"Hmmm," I mused. "How about when Mr. Harding said 'back so soon?' to you?"

Benito looked at me and realized that I was not going to believe his lies. He went very quiet.

We had reached the bridge now and Crumb began complaining that it was Basher's turn to pull Wilhelm around.

"Why would you being ill make him say 'did you do it yet'?" I persisted.

Benito became very uncomfortable, which drew the attention of Basher and Crumb.

"Well?" I asked. Benito looked at all three of us and sighed with resignation.

"My sister was doing a sponsored swim," he said.

"Where?" asked Basher.

"In the indoor pool in town. It's for the Catholic Church," he answered.

"So what?" I asked.

"And so last week I went round collecting sponsors," Benito mumbled.

"But you can't swim," protested Crumb.

"And you're not a real Catholic either," added Basher.

We had all stopped walking now and stood to one side off the High Street on the bank of the stream.

"I wasn't going to join in. I was just collecting sponsors," explained Benito.

"For your sister?" I asked.

"No, for me," he replied.

"But you weren't going to swim," I said.

"No," he replied, "just get the money."

"And you weren't going to tell us." stated Basher.

"Yeh, I would have told you…but," protested Benito as he tried unsuccessfully to think of an explanation that would convince everyone that this was a group affair. We looked at Benito, convinced that he had engineered a money making scam that he alone would benefit from.

"And you were going to keep the money yourself," yelled Crumb as he kicked Wilhelm's trolley in anger.

As a result of Crumb's furious outburst, the trolley along with its unwilling occupant rolled forward. We all realized what was about to happen but were unable to stop the trolley from descending down the bumpy bank into the stream. Luckily, it was very shallow. Unluckily the green wagon tipped over as it hit a large slick boulder in the gravel streambed. We all raced down the incline to the impact site. The trolley was lying on its side in about six inches of water just out of reach.

"What did you do that for, idiot?" said Basher.

"Why weren't you holding it? You had just agreed to," countered Crumb.

"I wasn't holding the string; you never gave it to me," complained Basher.

"Stop arguing," said Benito. "Let's just get it out."

"You should get it out," said Crumb. "You're the swimmer."

"Look, just everybody shut up," I said. "I have a plan." I went on to direct the operation. "Basher, sit as close to the water's edge as you can. You two," I pointed at Benito and Crumb who were still glaring at each other, "grab Basher and don't let him move."

Everyone complied with the order and I continued, "OK, grab my hand."

Basher grabbed my hand and I leaned over as far as possible. If anything went wrong at this point, I would be as wet as Wilhelm. I was able to reach the rim of one of the back wheels with my thumb and forefinger but that's all I needed. I pulled and tugged and eventually got a better grip on it. I was finally able to drag the trolley over to the bank. I had remained dry but Dad's coat was wet on the side that got submerged so I supposed that a good part of Wilhelm's torso and left arm were also soaked. His left leg was also wet.

"It's a good thing we didn't sell his boots," said Crumb, with relief.

"And lucky he was wearing Goggle eye," added Basher.

This literally put a damper on the operation. During the walk home questions were raised about whether the wet Guy would dry out by morning, and if not, would the Maudly-Creechoms know that he had been borrowed. Another subject for debate was whether or not Wilhelm would burn if still damp, since this could also cause problems tomorrow night.

But the overriding topic was Benito's dishonesty. He fervently denied that he had any intention of cheating us, be we weren't so sure about that. In the end he agreed to tear up the sponsorship form and avoid any bad blood between gang members. As I watched him tear the paper, I was pleased that a little honesty had prevailed in his otherwise deceitful cranium, but I doubted he would have shared the money. That day another sliver of mistrust was driven between Benito and the rest of the gang, and I was no longer sure that our former bond of brotherhood could ever be re-established.

When we were almost home, tired, but a good deal richer, and pulling a slightly soggy Wilhelm along on the trolley, Squeaky drove by with his father. I could clearly see him through the window of the car, sporting his new haircut which, in my opinion, looked as ridiculous as his father's. He wore a vacant and puzzled expression when he saw Wilhelm, which no doubt strained his limited intellect.

It was noon before we got back to my house. Arriving at El Paso we reclaimed the coat, boots and gas mask and put them on the wall hooks where they belonged. Goggle-eye was also removed from the dummy's black wooly head and hung on a large rusty nail in Pete's motorcycle toilet. Wilhelm was separated from the trolley and leaned against the barn door in hopes that the sun would dry him out. Then we all sat around and waited for Squeaky's inevitable arrival.

"Well, are we ready to go?" asked Squeaky, but there was doubt in his voice.

"Ready?" quizzed Benito. "We got tired of waiting for you, and had to leave."

"We said that we were going in the afternoon," complained Squeaky.

"No," corrected Benito. "You said that you had to get your hair cut in the afternoon. We waited around most of the morning and when you didn't show up we went on our own."

"Aaaaw," wined Squeaky. "No, I said my haircut was in the morning not the afternoon."

"Well, it sounded like afternoon to me, didn't it, lads?" Benito turned to us and we all nodded in agreement.

Benito was quick with a solution. "Squeaky, you could go with the Maudly-Creechoms tomorrow, and give us some of the money you get."

"Why? What for," complained Squeaky.

"Because," Benito explained, "you made us late for our rounds so we couldn't get all the money we needed, and it's your fault."

"That's not fair!" Squeaky was now sulking.

"All right," offered Benito, "We'll go with the Maudly-Creechoms, and maybe we'll not charge you for our lost time. Especially as you went and got the Guy and are going to take it back."

"I'm not going to take it back," protested Squeaky.

"Fine," replied Benito in a carefully thought out response. "We'll just tell the Maudly-Creechoms that you took their Guy and loaned it to us."

"Why would I do that?" Squeaky whined.

"Because you were trying to impress us to get in our gang I suppose."

Squeaky had been backed into a corner now. He had been tricked into borrowing the Guy, would now be tricked into returning it, and would not receive any of the collected money for his efforts. Benito was now about to play his trump card.

"I would take it now if I were you. They'll be home in about half an hour."

"No," Squeaky argued. "They're coming back late tonight."

"Not according to Mrs. Snobbit," said Benito calmly, while he pretended to remove some grime from his fingernail. "She said they had changed their plans and were coming home early."

Squeaky knew better than to question the quality of Mrs. Snobbit's information. He got a panicked look on his face. He also didn't think to question weather Benito was actually telling the truth about Mrs. Snobbit.

"Oh no," Squeaky said, and picked up the Guy. He climbed back on his bike and threw the straw filled dummy over the crossbar, thinking that it was the easiest way of carting it.

"It's wet," he said.

"Really?" said Crumb with a puzzled expression. "I wonder how that happened."

Squeaky cycled off down the road towards the Maudly-Creechom's house. In this well calculated move by Benito, several people would spot Squeaky on his return trip, either from their windows overlooking the road, their gardens, or as they drove by in cars. This would create multiple witnesses that could testify to seeing Squeaky with the Guy. Additionally, we had all been seen at the talent show last night, and so had alibis as watertight as Wilhelm's Wellington boots.

After a light lunch of cheese on toast, once again provided by my mother we began to plan the fireworks purchase in detail. Mum, of course had seen our shenanigans with Wilhelm and asked where we got him. I explained about Squeaky's generosity, and Mum commented that he didn't inherit it from his mother.

Walking up the hill to the center of the village we divided up the collection money. Everyone was happy with the amount, and it promised to provide us with a good selection of explosives.

Fireworks came in four basic designs. Rockets designed for aerial explosions, hand held variations like sparklers, motionless cones in various sizes that did little more than fizz and look pretty, and last of all bombs designed to make loud noises. While girls gravitated toward the sparklers and pretty fizzy things, we tended more toward the "bangers" that produced explosions and loud noises.

We went to the post office first where we found a large flat tray between the birthday cards and the ice cream refrigerator, containing a fine selection of miscellaneous fireworks. There were two different types of bangers, the larger ones were colored red and had the word "Boomer" printed on them. The smaller ones were orange and green.

At the village grocery store there was more of a selection, but the prices were higher. So we all returned to the post office.

Benito and I decided that we would purchase the boomers exclusively, quality was the important thing. Crumb planned to get a combination of Boomers, bangers and some jumping jacks, which would provide multiple smaller explosions, one every second or two. With the leftover coppers we bought two boxes of matches and filled our pockets with our newly purchased munitions.

No sooner had we stepped outside, then Benito extracted a boomer from his jacket pocket. I did likewise and began to study the explosive device. There was some small printed instructions that basically said, don't set it off near people, do not use it indoors and after lighting the blue paper fuse, get away from it fast. These were the three golden rules of fireworks. We knew very well the dangers of handling fireworks, but usually chose to ignore them, forever finding new and interesting variations for detonation. Benito had stepped into the alleyway next to the post office and was standing by a group of three galvanized steel dustbins. I heard the fizz as the fuse to his first boomer was ignited and looked around just in time to see him drop it into the empty dustbin, replace the lid and run past me. I gave chase with Crumb following. Basher, who was not particularly athletic, brought up the rear at a much slower pace. There was a terrific boom followed by the crash of steel dustbins. The explosion had lifted the top of the metal can several inches, and it seemed to hang motionless in the air for a moment before falling back and failing to re-locate itself on top of the bin. Instead it fell on the floor and rolled out into the street after us. The procession was completed by Mr. Collins from the post office who was either chasing after us or the dustbin lid.

We ran down Church Street, and climbed over the fence to Farmer Wilmot's field. This would be the location for the village bonfire tomorrow night and preparations were already underway. At the bottom of the pasture, a row of beer bottles had been half buried in the soft soil to become the rocket launching area, and an old gatepost had been stuck in the ground nearby to serve as a Catherine wheel staging area. A pile of burnable material had been donated by various village folk and was now heaped up by the gate, ready to become part of the bonfire. Grizzly McKenzie's old armchair had been scrounged by Wilf Tadcome and would soon assume it's proud position on top of the fire as the final resting place for Wilhelm Maudly-Creechom.

This would have normally been a place that we would hang around for hours, but our desire to blow things up was too great so we hurried on down to the bank of the stream, here we knew we would find suitably muddy conditions for our experimental demolition.

"OK, watch this," said Crumb, removing a boomer from the brown paper bag containing his supply of combustible delights. Leaning over, he placed the firework deep in the mud so that only the fuse was visible, and rushed to light it before it got damp. The rest of us stood on the bank and watched the fuse as it glowed bright orange and fizzed. Then it appeared to go out.

"Oh no," said Crumb, stepping back toward the partially buried bomb. He reached for a match to relight the dormant device.

"You should never try and relight a firework," preached Basher with an air of expertise.

Boom! The firework exploded in a shower of mud leaving a soccer ball sized hole in the wet soft ground.

"And that's why," added Benito.

"Let's walk along to the road, "said Basher, and we all started following the bank toward the road bridge. Crumb washed the mud off his face and clothes as best he could and then scrambled up the bank to follow us.

Basher wanted to try one of his smaller bangers in the mud of the streambed, and Crumb being more experienced at this maneuver offered to do the dangerous part. It made sense really, because if this undertaking resulted in another messy misfortune, Crumb was already dirty.

Bang! This time everyone was able to avoid the blast and flying mud. The consequential crater was disappointingly small, and Basher regretted not purchasing at least a couple of Boomers.

"I've got an idea," I said, and asked Crumb for the paper bag that contained his fireworks. Crumb transferred the fireworks to the same pocket as his matches and offered me the brown paper bag.

"While you're down there, fill it with some of that mud." I pointed to an area where the wet dirt looked firm and not too wet.

"It's going to soak the bag," said Crumb. "It might split."

"Try not to let it rip," said Benito, having already caught on to my plan.

Crumb returned carrying the bag of mud in both his hands.

"Stand it on top of the corner post," I directed, pointing at the red brick column at one end of the bridge railing. Crumb placed the bag of mud squarely in the middle and I pushed a boomer into the mud. Now all we had to do was wait. If we were lucky, before long a white car would come by.

We waited patiently for an appropriate vehicle to drive by. Our plan was to hide behind the bridges brick pillars and when a suitable vehicle was spotted, three of us would scurry under the bridge to hide, and the remaining member would carefully time the lighting of the fuse, and then sneak beneath the concrete bridge to join the rest in hiding. The urgency that we felt to light the fuse made the minutes seem like hours. Several vehicles crossed the bridge but they were mostly noisy farm equipment that would neither hear the bang nor notice the extra dirt. Eventually our waiting paid off and we were very, very lucky.

"Who is it?" Benito asked Crumb, our designated lookout. Basher and I were standing next to Benito in the well-shaded area under the bridge on a narrow cement ledge.

"It's Squeaky, on his new bike," Crumb declared, laughing with malevolent glee.

Secrecy was no longer important, and we emerged from our place of concealment to gather around the brick column.

"Did you take the Guy back?" asked Benito sternly as Squeaky rode into hearing range.

"Yes," replied Squeaky. "I left him sitting under the tree."

"Was it the right tree?" Basher inquired.

"I think so," replied Squeaky. "What's that?" He had noticed the bag of mud that was starting to soak the paper, and I was afraid that if we left it much longer the boomer would be damp and useless.

"Oh, it's just a firework," said Benito. I was amazed at his honesty. I expected that we would be treated to some story about it being a birthday cake waiting for the candle to be lit.

"What kind of firework?" asked Squeaky, moving a little closer to the bag.

"It's a roman candle," said Benito. "A lovely sparkling thing with lots of different colored sparks."

"Why is it in that bag?" Squeaky was becoming suspicious as Benito lit the fuse.

"That bag looks wet," Squeaky said.

The fuse was fizzing now and I prayed that the boomer wasn't too damp to go off.

"Are you sure that's a roman —"

Boom!

Squeaky and his bike were instantly covered in blotches of mud. Crumb was the first to lead us in a laugh as Squeaky began yelling. In the space of just a few hours Squeaky had been lied to, tricked, blackmailed, and now mud bombed. He had reached the breaking point and turned his bike around to leave.

"You lot are horrible liars," he screamed over his shoulder. "I never want to be in your horrible gang. Not ever. I hate all of you!"

He continued calling to us hysterically and he, his bike, and a fair portion of the mud bomb cycled home.

Having seen the destructive power of the boomers, Basher was regretting that his original purchase did not include any, and he was now anxious to acquire some. So Benito and I each traded him one boomer for two jumping jacks. Basher was keen to set them off there and then, but we all advised him to wait until tomorrow; We needed to be making our way home. Basher and Crumb went off in one direction and Benito and I in the other.

The sight of Taddy Bascome delivering the evening papers alerted us to just how much time had passed. Taddy was heading directly for us on his bike with a large canvas bag full of newspapers slung over his shoulder. Benito and I stopped to talk with him, and he seemed genuinely interested in seeing a firework demonstration.

"Watch this," Benito said as he grasped the handlebars of the bike and twisted both the plastic handle grips to find the loosest one. Having determined that it was the left, he removed it, and taking a boomer from his pocket, he lit the fuse and with a flick of his wrist threw the ignited boomer into the chrome handlebars. He then quickly and strenuously replaced the handle grip, and leaned the bike over to the right. There was what seemed like an unusually long period of silence, and then with a metallic sounding, very loud pop, the white plastic grip was launched into the sky, shot gracefully through the air, and over a hedge to disappear into a weedy area overgrown with stinging nettles.

"Ah well, that's gone," sighed Benito.

Taddy was still reeling in shock at the loss of his handle grip, as Benito lit one of the Jumping Jacks. Before Taddy had a chance to make sure that Benito's next trick would not result in damage to his personal property, the lit firework with its promise of multiple explosions was dropped unseen into the canvas bag which still hung over Taddy's shoulder.

Taddy was still for a moment. He could see from our faces that something was very wrong but wasn't sure what it was, until the explosions started. Crack! Crack! With a look of horror, Taddy started jumping around like a cat that had inadvertently strolled onto a hot cooking surface. Crack! Crack! Crack! He continued with his primitive dance as he struggled to get the paper bag off his shoulder. Crack! Crack! He wrestled the bag free and inverted it to remove the jumping jack. Crack! The firework cracked its final crack as it fell to the floor along with several newly scorched newspapers. Taddy stamped out the still glowing edges of the Evening Post, and stuffing them back in his bag, jumped on his bike and rode off. The insults that he was yelling at us during his retreat were not unlike the ones that Squeaky had used half an hour before.

"Must be in a hurry?" I said. "He didn't even say goodbye."

"Who cares?" said Benito. "I'm not wasting any more of my fireworks for his amusement. Let him buy his own."

As we passed the Maudly-Creechoms house we looked in for signs of life, but they hadn't returned yet.

"Do you think Squeaky put Wilhelm back in the right place?" I asked, fearing discovery.

"I don't know." Benito sounded unconcerned, but the fear that we would be discovered was weighing quite heavily on my mind.

CHAPTER 17

SUNDAY 5ᵀᴴ NOVEMBER

LOST AND FOUND

Today was Sunday – the big day. It was a day that promised to be adventurous and exciting. We would spend most of the day setting off more fireworks, but keeping some in reserve for the evening's big bonfire and supper. I gulped down my breakfast, grabbed the remainder of my explosives from their secret hiding place under my dresser and headed out the door. Next stop Benito's house.

Halfway to Benito's house, I met him on his way to meet me. A firework had been discharged inside the house beneath his father's favorite chair, and judging by the speed with which Benito was putting distance between himself and a very angry Mr. Rolonzio, I deduced that his father was probably in the chair at the time. During his hasty exit, Benito had pilfered an empty olive oil bottle from the kitchen rubbish and explained that his intent was to place a lit boomer inside and put the bottle in the cow-drinking trough in Mr. Snobbit's meadow. His goal was to emulate a depth charge effect that he had recently witnessed in a submarine film on television, in which one of Hitler's U-boats was sent to a watery grave.

Mrs. Snobbit was outside in her garden spying on the world.

"And where are you boys going so early?" she asked, suspiciously eyeing Benito and I. "Oh, just for a walk," I answered.

"You know," she said, wagging her finger, "Mr. Pilchard is not very happy with you."

"How can he be mad at me?" I asked. "I haven't done anything."

It was true. I had not seen the Pilchard boys for over a week.

"Well, it's about his holiday," Mrs. Snobbit explained.

"What about it?" asked Benito, showing interest now that it looked as if I might be in trouble.

"Well, as you know, he packed all his things inside the boat and put it on the roof of his car."

"Yes, I know, we gave him the canvas sheet to cover it with." I tried to help her move the story along. Mrs. Snobbit had a tendency to make a short story as long as possible and I didn't have the time to waste listening to it. I had a submarine to blow up.

"Well, do you know," she continued, "that he had some dreadful weather on the trip, storms and so much rain."

"Yes," I said. "I know."

"And then he thought he was having problems with the car," she said.

I hadn't heard this bit before, and wondered if the car was the reason he returned a week early from his trip.

"What kind of problems?" asked Benito, he enjoyed any story that involved problems, hardship and catastrophe.

"Well, I'm really not sure," continued the old lady. "Something to do with the steering because he said that he couldn't keep the car in a straight line – it kept swerving back and forth."

"That doesn't sound very good," said Benito, encouraging Mrs. Snobbit to keep going.

"And then," the story continued," he got as far as Birmingham and the brakes began failing." She paused to make mental note of a distant figure walking a dog at the other end of the field.

"Now I wonder who that is?" she said, distracted. "He was down there last Thursday, I think. With the same dog."

"What about the brakes, Mrs. Snobbit. What about the brakes?" I asked.

"Oh, yes," she went on. "Well, you can imagine how dangerous it must have been."

"So is that why he turned around and came back?" I asked.

"No. Well, you know how determined Mr. Pilchard can be. He carried on going north to Scotland. He wanted to camp outside Birmingham but the weather was so terrible that he and the whole family had to go to a hotel."

I was sure there was a point to this story, but so far I was unable to see it.

"Well, he reached Scotland with all that terrible rain, then had to go on the car ferry across to the island where he was going to camp. It's only a small ferry you know, just for two or three cars."

"Yes," I said, following along with her tale.

"Well, the ferry was rolling so badly that it almost tipped over and sank. The captain of the ferry said he had never seen such a bad crossing, and thought that the car ferry may have taken on some water."

"Did the boat sink?" I asked, thinking I had predicted the end of the story.

"No,' said Mrs. Snobbit, "but everyone says it was a miracle that it didn't."

"Did the Pilchard's car fall off?" Benito asked hopefully, thinking he had predicted the end of the story.

"No," came the answer, "They reached the other side and crossed over a very high hill. Anyway you can imagine those narrow mountain roads and the bad brakes he had and the steering being so difficult, but when he got the other side it had stopped raining and got quite sunny."

"That was nice," I said, Benito looked disappointed.

"Yes," continued Mrs. Snobbit, "but when they got to the camp site and climbed up on top of the car to remove the sheet they found that the boat was full of water."

"Well, yes, I expect that it would be. It wasn't tied down very tightly," I said.

"But that wasn't it," she persisted. "It seems that there was a tiny hole in the sheet and all the rain collected in the canvas sheet and poured through into the boat, just like a funnel."

I was starting to see the problem.

"The tent and food and bedding were soaked, and there was so much water in the boat that, well, you can see why he thought the steering and the breaks were going bad. And no wonder the ferry almost tipped over.

"How is that my fault?" I inquired, trying to remain polite.

"Well," she answered, "Mr. Pilchard thinks that either your father lent him a waterproof sheet with a hole in it, or that you made the hole."

"Why would I do that?"

"Well, perhaps it was an accident or something – you might have put the sheet down on something sharp."

All at once I remembered the spilled nails on the floor of rat barn, and how they fell out of the sheet when Mario was fixing his bike's flat tire. I thought it better not to mention this.

"Anyway," continued Mrs. Snobbit, "Mr. Pilchard is angry at your whole family now because he doesn't actually know who made the hole."

"Didn't he check it before he used it?" I asked.

"I don't think he could have," she replied.

"Well," I said with righteous indignation, "I hope he's learned his lesson now." We quickly walked away before Mrs. Snobbit became offended by Benito's laughter.

At the bottom of the Mud Lane, Brian and Ryan Pilchard were huddled together next to the storm drain, studying something. At their feet was a small backpack and on top of it were Mrs. Pilchard's clothes line, two flashlights, and some kneepads that Mr. Pilchard had purchased when he was going to start a gardening business. The object of the brothers scrutiny was the same paper they had been examining the day before they went on holiday, the day their Dad tried to run me over.

"My Dad's really mad at you," said Brian, as Benito and I came up to them.

I shrugged and asked, "What are you doing?"

Brian showed me the paper. It was a carefully drawn map of our end of Great Biddington.

For some time now the Pilchard boys had been obsessed with mapping the underground drainage tunnels that were built to handle the Mud Lane's floodwaters. They had explored several of them and today they were going to complete their survey. The starting point was just below us in the wide concrete lined trench filled with five of six inches of dirty water. A circular concrete pipe that opened into the trench halfway up the wall ran horizontally into the earth.

"So you're actually going to crawl down that pipe just to see where it goes?" asked Benito.

"Exactly," replied Ryan.

"You're mad," I said, without needing to put much thought into it.

"Want to come?" invited the older of the Pilchard boys. "We've already charted it up to that manhole cover over there."

"It's a crazy idea." I repeated as the two brothers began to put on their equipment.

Ryan struggled into the straps of the small backpack, while Brian put his head and one arm through the coiled up clothes line, in the fashion of a mountaineer.

"What's the rope for?" I asked.

"You never know," replied Brian, "It's always best to be prepared."

As I watched the two prepare for their excavation I became strangely intrigued. It might actually be fun to explore the drainage pipe a short distance with the adventurous brothers.

"OK," I said, "I'll go with you."

"You're mad," said Benito, and leaned on the black railings fondling one of his remaining boomers.

Getting into the pipe was not easy. The Pilchard brothers had managed to pull away the safety grating that covered the round hole and we squeezed ourselves through and swung down to squat in the small opening. By the time I was crouched in the round opening the boys had already started to crawl forward, so I hurried to catch them. The first few feet were still illuminated from the natural light reflecting of the water in the trench, and caused eerie rippling patterns of light on the curving walls.

On we crawled, hand over hand. My knees were beginning to hurt and I now felt foolish laughing at Brian's kneepads. It began to get darker, and the pipe was curving slightly obscuring the tiny disk of light behind us. The air was damp and the concrete walls felt cold on my hands and knees. The brothers were beginning to distance themselves from me, and their voices were fading. My part of the tunnel was getting darker and quieter.

"When you get up here you can see the manhole cover in the High Street," shouted Brian. I could barely hear his voice echoing in the dank, clammy darkness, and the first hint of nervousness touched me.

I was starting to lose confidence in this mission, since I was falling behind and had no map. What if I were to get lost? By the time a search party had found and resuscitated me, I would certainly have missed the fireworks. What if there were sudden flash floods? I had heard of this happening.

I had to get out. There was no room to turn around which meant that my retreat must be accomplished by crawling in reverse. My mind was working overtime to fight down the flash flood panic.

My backward retreat continued, shuffling along occasionally feeling the walls with my hands, when suddenly I noticed that the tunnel was wider than it should be. Testing the internal shape with my fingertips and by extending my legs to feel the way in the darkness, I concluded that I was at a junction. Another tunnel had joined this one at a very sharp angle. Is it possible that I could have crawled right past the juncture in the dark without knowing it? My fear of being hopelessly lost returned, and I felt the terror rise in me. I had to make a choice and go left or right – a wrong turn might mean certain death. If I was lucky, death might come quickly in the form of a faltered step, then a sudden downward vertical drop into a bottomless abyss. But it was far more likely that my tragic demise would be by slow starvation after I had crawled around for weeks, blind and hopeless, finally surrendering to loneliness and exhaustion. My dry and brittle bones would be discovered on some future Pilchard quest, and the village would erect a marble monument as a reminder to foolish children everywhere. On top of the monument would be a bronze statue of me, and below a brass plate that read. 'In memory of a courageous boy, who will be missed by everyone except Squeaky and the Maudly-Creechoms." The vision shook me to my senses. This was not how I wanted to be remembered. Was my legacy to be that of someone who brought sadness and anger, dark deeds and mischievous mayhem, leaving those lives that I touched with disappointment, regret and broken bicycles. I had to live. I had to live so that I could put right the wrongs I had done. I would survive. I would get out and make amends for my wrongdoings. Summoning my remaining resolve I chose to go to my right, and continued on, gripped with fear and hope.

I was sweating and had trouble breathing, but I was determined to survive. Gradually the tunnel started to get lighter. I was within fifteen feet of the opening, and pretty sure I would survive a sudden wall of water heading my way or an unexpected tunnel colapse, but one more image haunted me.

I remembered the look in Benito's eyes as he fondled the boomer. He would surely be hovering around the mouth of the tunnel, listening intently for approaching explorers, holding a boomer in one hand and a match in the other. A boomer thrown into this confined space would leave me deaf for weeks and deprive me of the joy of hearing my remaining fireworks exploded.

My feet at last sensed the edge of the pipe and I scrambled up the wall, sweating despite the chill in the air.

"Don't even think about throwing a boomer..."

But Benito was gone.

I sat down next to the railing to get my breath back and waited for my hands to stop shaking. I had not become lost, had avoided drowning, missed a perilous plunge into the depths of the earth and not been deafened by Benito. I started to feel more relaxed. Was it unreasonable to expect that Benito would direct his mischief toward me. I was his best friend and oldest gang member, but he had certainly been acting strange lately. There was an "edge" to him, particularly where Squeaky was concerned. Benito had been under a lot of pressure to provide a Guy, and he had taken this out on Squeaky, who had done everything we asked. He had shown genuine courage in kidnapping Wilhelm and even some backbone when he stood up to us on the bridge. The more I thought about it the more I started to respect him. It was true that nobody liked his mother, and having money separated him from us, but that wasn't his fault.

The Maudly-Creechoms were another case. They had always been our traditional enemy, and they were a little strange sometimes, but rich people were like that. They had been prepared to join forces with us until the unfortunate incident with the bow and arrow and Willis Gurney's leg. Which was, to be honest, completely my fault.

My close call with death in the tunnel had caused me to reexamine some of my core values and question my beliefs and behavior, and I now began to feel much better about my life, and the people in it.

On the way home I saw the Maudly-Creechoms and the Gurney boys outside on the neatly trimmed front lawn. They did not appear to suspect that this would not be Wilhelm's first outing.

"Are you taking Wilhelm round the village?" I asked.

"Who?" asked Maggot.

"The Guy, I mean the Guy," I replied, attempting to recover.

"We want to but we don't have a trolley or anything," complained Willis. "If you lend us your trolley, you can have a share of the collection."

"How much?" I asked.

"A quarter of it." said Horace.

In my current state of mind, thrilled to be alive, and full of joy for the world, I would have probably loaned it to them for free, but it was not only my trolley and I had the other gang members to consider.

"OK," I agreed. "You can borrow the trolley if you want. It's standing next to the barn. We can work out the rent later."

Oscar thought that my agreement came too quickly. His suspicions were raised. "Is this a trick?" he asked.

"No," I said. "It's not. Good luck with your collecting."

"Thanks," I heard someone say with a puzzled tone as I walked away. It felt good.

At Sunday lunch the frustrations from the preceding days that had befallen my father, were now tempered by the excitement of this evening's bonfire and fireworks. We sat and ate while the radio delivered musical entertainment in the form of 'World Wide Family Favorites,' Dad's second favorite program after the weather forecast. It was a relief that we managed to get through the whole meal without Pete and Dad coming to blows, even when Pete expressed some very personal and unpopular views about world events.

I lounged around the house for a while perusing out of date comics, and later went outside to watch Pete perform yet another modification to his motorcycle, this time it was the passenger seat that fell victim to the hammer and hacksaw. I tried unsuccessfully to wish away the afternoon, and make the night come quickly so that the burning of the Guy and the glorious fireworks display could commence.

I wandered outside aimlessly to see if there was anything going on in the lane. Everything was quiet, no sign of Benito or Squeaky and I thought perhaps they had already gone to Farmer Wilmot's field and the site of the bonfire to hinder the progress of people trying to work.

From the top of Mud Lane, the sounds of Chucky calling for Spot reached my ears. She had been missing now since Wednesday. In the last five days Chucky had all but dropped out of sight. Since Spot's disappearance he had spent his days wandering the roads and nearby fields calling for his lost dog. Chucky was despondent and inconsolable.

Any attempts to locate the dog by anyone other than Chucky would be futile. She would only respond to his voice. Feeling helpless in this matter and realizing that there was nothing I could do, I set off to Wilmot's field.

As I crossed the bridge where only yesterday we were detonating mud bombs, Mr. Pilchard tried to run me down again. Like me, he was on his way to the bonfire. Having been tasked with buying the fireworks this year, he was now delivering them, and I suppose he felt that since he was doing the village a favor by organizing the fireworks, he might as well do them another one and rid the world of the boy who spoiled his holiday. I wasn't even sure why he blamed me for his soaked equipment and wrecked vacation – it was, after all, my Dad's property that had proved defective.

Opposite the pub I met the Maudly-Creechoms and the Gurneys, who had been joined by Squeaky in their "penny for the Guy quest." This was usually fun so I did not understand why they all looked so miserable.

"You used our Guy," said Horace.

"What?" I asked, trying to buy some thinking time.

"We just went to see Betty Adlar," Willis explained, "and her husband said we were cheating because this was the same Guy as yesterday."

"Why would he think that?" I asked, still not confessing to the crime.

"Because," continued Horace, "he said that yesterday he took off one of the Guy's boots and the socks and trousers were the same as this one. It was you, wasn't it? How did you get our Guy?"

I looked at the group as they eyed me accusingly. Squeaky, who was responsible for transporting the stolen property, looked at me with a pleading expression.

"I cannot tell a lie" I said, "Benito is responsible."

"Mr. Adlar's said that you were there too," Oscar joined in.

"I was," I said, "but I regret it now. You know what? Keep all the money. You don't have to pay for the trolley rental."

I was concerned that Benito, Basher and Crumb would not appreciate my act of generosity, but then I thought, after all that had happened, who cares? If the other gang members object to me lending the trolley out, that's just too bad. It was my paint on the trolley, my string that pulled it, and Wilhelm was dressed almost entirely in my family's clothes.

Squeaky looked at me with gratitude and I nodded to him as I walked away. He had been through enough lately.

Wilmot's field was filled with activity. The excitement in Great Biddington had been building all day. Volunteer workers had been continuing to throw additional rubbish onto the bonfire. Through the thick tree limbs stacked, and held in place with smaller brushwood, I could see a mattress, and some broken furniture, as well as numerous torn cardboard boxes donated by the post office and general store. The finishing touches were being made to the bonfire and Old Grizzly McKenzie's chair had already been placed on top to await the Guy, who I knew was on his way up the hill at this very moment.

Several tree trunks had been pulled into a large semi-circle by Wilmot's tractor to provide temporary seating. I found a comfortable section on one of them and sat down. It wasn't long before Benito walked in through the open gate and headed over to me.

"Got any fireworks left?" he asked.

"Yes," I said, "a few boomers I think." I put my hand in my pocket to verify the quantity.

"Let's set them off," he said.

"No." My answer surprised him.

"Why not?" Benito asked. "Are you waiting till dark?"

"No," I said. "I'm going to give them to Squeaky and the Maudly-Creechoms when I see them."

"What for?" Benito was astonished.

"Because they worked hard to build a Guy, and we took it." I said, "No, wait, we didn't even take it ourselves. We got Squeaky to do it for us."

"Yeh, but – " Benito started.

"But, nothing." Benito was about to try one of his slick speeches that made everything sound reasonable, but it wasn't going to work this time.

"What we did was wrong and I'm going to put it right. I've already loaned them the trolley. Free."

"What happened to you?" he asked, looking at me as if I had lost my mind.

"I want to have a nice statue when I die," I said, not really expecting him to understand.

It would soon be dusk and people were starting to arrive. Mr. Billings has built a mobile stove from an old oil drum and Mrs. Blinkton was baking some potatoes. Crippin was standing by ready to help serve them. Mr. Rogers from the pub was pushing a wheelbarrow across the field containing a steel beer barrel, and his wife walked behind him with some carrier bags.

Team Maudly-Creechom showed up with the Guy, and several men who had started to gather round Mr. Rodgers wheelbarrow helped to hoist Wilhelm up into the ancient and tatty Grizzly McKenzie armchair. The Maudly-Creechoms and Squeaky sat down on another tree trunk as far away as they could. Oscar and Willis stood round them anxiously holding unlit sparklers.

The Grangers and Mr. and Mrs. Snaggins had arrived together and must have been comparing notes on the walk to the field, because as they entered, they saw Benito and I and began pointing at us.

"What do you mean by a nice statue?" asked Benito.

"I mean I just want to be remembered for good things not bad ones." I drew his attention to the Granger and Snaggins families, and asked him what he thought the topic of their conversation was.

"I don't really care," he answered.

"That's the problem," I said, and walked over to where the Maudly-Creechoms were sitting. "Here," I said, holding out the remainder of my fireworks.

"Don't touch them." said Maggot. "It's a trick."

"It's not a trick," I said. "What we did was wrong, and I'm sorry and I hope this helps make it right."

"It's not really your fault," said Squeaky. "Benito is the one that causes all the problems."

"Yes, I know," I said, "but we had a deal to go round the village together, and if I hadn't shot Willis, the deal would still be on and Benito wouldn't have had to borrow your Guy."

I realized as I was saying the words that our actions can have far reaching effects. It is true that Benito had been mean to Squeaky but would he have done so if he had not been forced to acquire a Guy at any cost?

"It's OK," said Oscar. "We collected a lot of money, and Mr. Maudly-Creechoms got all these fireworks for us." he opened a brown paper bag and showed me a collection of sparklers, Catherine wheels and roman candles. No Boomers.

"Very nice," I said.

I turned round to see Vicar Hobbins sitting next to Benito. This was a shock. In the first place, Benito was Catholic and as such, had nothing to do with the vicar, who was Church of England. In the second place,

Benito, during the last week had proved himself to be one of the greatest sinners in the village – guilty of lying, extortion, fraud, blackmail, cheating, greed, stealing and blasphemy. He had broken almost all of the ten commandments, and the few that he missed were covered by Crumb, Squeaky and me, with our bike crashing, Guy kidnapping and subsequent attempted murder by drowning.

It was getting dark now and I saw that Basher and Crumb had arrived and were walking over toward Benito, but changed direction when they saw the vicar. They walked over to me, the Gurneys and the Maudly-Creecholms.

"What's wrong with Benito?" Crumb asked.

"What do you mean?" I said.

"Is he in trouble with the vicar?" Basher asked.

"I think he's in trouble with the vicar's boss." I replied.

"I hope he gets into trouble for that fake swim team sponsorship," said Crumb.

Willis Gurney added. "We gave him some money for that."

Allen Tidwell, the butcher, had joined the gathering and was placing a large tray of sausages on the picnic table set up by Fred Pollard, who had not brought his guitar this time. Three-fingered Gordon, the butcher's assistant, had arrived and was walking over to the same table with a case of pork pies. He saw me and immediately scanned the vicinity for my cat Scraps before leaving the pies unattended.

Chucky Billings arrived with his parents and managed a subdued greeting. His parents went over to the small group lined up at the beer barrel and Chucky sat alone, occasionally dabbing his reddened eyes.

There was an uncomfortable moment when Dad and Mum arrived at the same time as a number of the people who had sat next to them at the talent show. I could tell that Dad wanted to get as far away from them as possible, and he walked towards the still unlit bonfire. As he rounded the large wooden mound he found the area already occupied by Mrs. Stuart and her daughter Belinda, so he was forced to stand near Rodger Pilchard and the two men soon settled into a staring contest. Dad had insisted on wearing his German Army coat, even though he couldn't understand why it was wet. Wet clothes alone should have given him something in common with Rodger Pilchard.

Mum had settled into conversation with Mrs. Stuart, they were laughing so clearly the Stuarts blamed my father alone for shameful events at the talent show.

Villagers were now pouring into the field taking their places awaiting the grand fire-lighting ceremony. Squeaky's parents appeared and immediately attached themselves to the Maudly-Creechoms, much to the Maudly-Creechom's dismay. And Mrs. Snobbit was hobbling from group to group on her bad leg trying to piece together the events of the kidnapped Guy and Benito's phony swim team sponsorship.

Grizzly McKenzie soon began to fight with Wilf Tadcome about rightful ownership of the arm chair, and as if their bickering was a sign of what was to come, the entire Rolonzio family entered the field.

Benito had now shaken off the vicar, who had moved on to a heated argument with Mrs. Diggsmore about this year's nativity play. They were standing by the Gurneys' parents, who every so often would turn and scowl at me. I sensed that Willis had informed her of the arrow in the leg incident, but did not blame him.

Crumb and Basher warmed up to the new group and were glad that I had been able to negotiate a peace treaty. We looked at Benito. He was sitting all alone now, and obviously sensed the disapproval from his former playmates and rival gang members alike. He was once the proud chief of a group to be reckoned with. Now he was reduced to a deposed leader, abandoned by his friends and family.

News of the attempt to pass the same Guy off twice had spread round the field, and most people simply blamed "the kids." Everyone who was present at the talent show gave me the evil eye, and Mrs. Blinkton, Mr. Harding and the Smiths were spreading their own version of Benito's phony sponsored swim.

Benito walked over to the row of bottles in the dirt where he stood alone in the encroaching darkness. Looking toward us, he slowly walked over.

"Sorry about taking your Guy" Benito said to the group, and asked, "Do you want to see some fireworks?"

"OK," said Horace.

I sensed that our previous rivals were forgiving Benito far too easily, and that he should be made to suffer more, but maybe they were just better at forgiving than I was. In that moment I understood that it doesn't matter if you are sorry for your thoughtless and hurtful actions, the effects will continue on, out of your control. The fact that the rift between two childhood gangs had been healed, and the harmless pranks they committed forgotten about, didn't stop the rest of the community from blaming us.

But I was pleased to see a change of heart in Benito. He was much more like the Benito that we used to know. I was unsure if my revelation had somehow affected him, whether the Vicar's wisdom had improved his outlook or if the combined aggression from most of the village and his previous friends had caused him to reform. In any event, we were all grateful for the change. It wasn't long before the small talk subsided and we all agreed that we couldn't wait any longer for the proper demonstration. We began setting off our own remaining fireworks. Soon after the first boomer exploded, the silence was interrupted by the village butcher.

"I would like to welcome everyone to the annual bonfire night and fireworks display," Allen Tidwell's booming voice rang out from his improvised stage on the top of a picnic table.

"This display is hosted by the combined efforts and financial contributions from the church, the chapel, the mother's union, the two pubs, and Farmer Wilmot. Let's thank them all very much."

Everyone clapped, and a few of the people who had been camped out round the beer barrow cheered loudly with great enthusiasm.

"OK," said the butcher, "Let's light up."

The sun had dipped below the horizon that was the edge of our world. The crimson stained sky it left behind had disappeared, leaving the inky darkness behind to steal our vision. Chalky White huddled at the base of the giant bonfire, cupping the match as it fought for life against the slight breeze that had cleared the skies of cloud whips.

The small twigs of wood caught fire first, and then with a crackling sound the flames raced on to new fuel, and the spreading glow cast a warm orange light. People drew closer, extending their open palms toward the heat. The fire was burning well now, with the heat driving the chill from their bodies, it seemed that the chill from their emotions was also being expelled. Or maybe it was the beer or the warm food, or maybe the darkness herding us all inward towards the firelight made us feel closer. Whatever the reason, everyone seemed a little happier once the fire got started.

The foul aroma of homegrown paraffin flavored tobacco emanating from Dad's pipe was thankfully disguised, as it mingled with the bonfires wood smoke. Dad looked over at Rodger Pilchard.

"Nice fire." Dad said as showers of tiny orange-red embers drifted upwards into the darkness.

Rodger nodded.

"I could have used one of these on holiday." He said with a chuckle.

"Yes," replied Dad. "Though it's a shame to see all this good wood going to waste."

The two men laughed as things returned to normal.

Some of the older boys in the village who were lighting cigarettes instead of fireworks, sipped on beer as they joked. Grizzly McKenzie and Wilf Tadcome finally agreed that perhaps the old armchair did look better on a fire. Taddy Bascome, the paperboy joined us and Benito gave him two jumping jacks as a reminder and an apology for the burned newspapers.

Final proof that the village had healed came when Billy Tadcome, momentarily discarded his communist ways to discus football with Mr. Maudly-Creechom, and when my brother arrived without motorbike, he even helped Mrs. Wiggins, the hairdresser find a good seat on one of the logs. Mrs. Leecham, the garden seat's first victim, was overcome with forgiveness and shared a toast with Dad as she laughed about how hard it was to remove the creosote from her clothing.

Allan Tidwell poked at it with a long stick and the fire readjusted itself, settling in for a long hot burn. Some people were heating potatoes in the ashes around the base, as small orange and blue flames danced over Wilhelm's shirt. Others just stood and watched, finding the shifting shades and flickering flames hypnotizing. Soon the sausages would be ready and…Crash!

Like several others standing near the sausage table, waiting to be first, I turned to look at the source of the noise.

Spot had upended the entire tray and had her nose in a pile of sausages that lay in a heap on the ground.

"Spot!" At the sound of Chucky's cries, Spot bounded over and met him as he was running toward her. He fell to his knees, she jumped up putting her front paws on his chest, and wagged her bushy tail. This did a better job than the fire of warming everyone's heart.

Pete found the soiled sausage fiasco hilarious. He thought it particularly humorous because sausages were one of my father's favorite foods. But instead of antagonizing Dad about the loss of his preferred menu item, he exhibited true compassion and tried to console Dad by pointing to a half-burned coffee table in the fire, and saying what a lovely saw bench it could be converted into. Dad began moving toward the flames.

I looked up at the night sky and marveled at the wonder of it all. I heard Allen Tidwell announce the start of the fireworks display.

There was a whoosh, followed by a bang and I saw the shower of orange sparks cascading down against the coal black November sky.

One after another, the rockets burst into the sky as we all looked up, lost the moment.

10373674R00161

Made in the USA
Charleston, SC
29 November 2011